THE PEDAGOGICAL IMAGINATION

The PEDAGOGICAL IMAGINATION

The Republican Legacy in Twenty-First-Century French Literature and Film

LEON SACHS

UNIVERSITY OF NEBRASKA PRESS | LINCOLN AND LONDON

Library of Congress Cataloging-in-Publication Data
Sachs, Leon, 1967–
The pedagogical imagination: the republican legacy in twenty-first-century French literature and film / Leon Sachs.   pages   cm
Summary: "Study of French education and republicanism as represented in twenty-first century French literature and film" —Provided by publisher.
Includes bibliographical references and index.
ISBN 978-0-8032-4505-1 (hardback: alk. paper)—
ISBN 978-0-8032-5511-1 (pdf)—ISBN 978-0-8032-5512-8 (epub)
ISBN 978-0-8032-5513-5 (mobi)
1. French literature—21st century—History and criticism.
2. Education in literature. 3. Education in motion pictures.
4. Republicanism in literature. 5. Motion pictures—
France—History—21st century. I. Title.
PQ317.S25 2014
840.9'0092—dc23   2013043102

Set in Garamond Premier by Renni Johnson.
Designed by N. Putens.

Contents

Illustrations

Acknowledgments

Many individuals have generously given of their time in reading and commenting on parts of this project at various stages of its development. I owe a debt of thanks to the following for sharing their insights and expertise: Ora Avni, Kim Benston, Stefan Bird-Pollan, Anna Bosch, Gil Chaitin, Jeffory Clymer, Isabelle Dellanoy, Andrea Goulet, Peter Kalliney, Ed Lee, Bettina Lerner, Suzanne Pucci, Marion Rust, Alan Singerman, Patricia Tilburg, and Michael Trask. My work has also benefited from conversations with a number of scholars more knowledgeable than I about the history and current state of French schooling, namely Myriam Boyer, Martine Jey, Pierre Kahn, and Hélène Merlin-Kajman.

I am especially indebted to M. Martin Guiney, both because his own work on literary education in France has been a constant touchstone for my own inquiry and because his penetrating criticism of my manuscript has helped me to better define and frame my own contribution to this growing field among Anglophone students of French culture.

I would also like to thank Patrick Bray and the French Department at the University of Illinois at Urbana-Champaign and Bruno Chaouat and the French Department at the University of Minnesota for having invited me to present my work in their departments.

I am grateful to Gaston and Mary-Elizabeth d'Harcourt, who repeatedly and warmly hosted me in Paris, where much of the research for this project was conducted.

Needless to say, I owe a debt of gratitude to those who read my manuscript for the University of Nebraska Press; their detailed and judicious comments provided indispensable guidance for improving the project. I am also grateful, of course, to Kristen Elias Rowley and Kyle Simonsen at the press for their able, cheerful, and steady stewardship through the publishing process. I am equally indebted to Jane Curran for her masterful editing of the manuscript.

At the University of Kentucky, I have greatly benefited from many conversations with Richard Angelo, who not only read and commented on my work but also invited me to present my ideas in his department's colloquium in the College of Education. Ted Fiedler, in my own department, meticulously read the entire manuscript and offered invaluable editorial advice at a crucial moment in the revision process. I also owe a debt to the University of Kentucky's College of Arts and Sciences for providing me with a release from teaching duties in order to progress in my writing.

There are no superlatives strong enough to convey the extent of my debt to my friend and colleague Jeff Peters, who not only tirelessly read and commented on many drafts of the entire manuscript but also maintained unflagging faith in the project even when I had my doubts. A remarkably creative thinker whose enthusiasm for the exchange of ideas and intellectual discovery is contagious, he persisted in challenging me to deepen and extend my arguments in ways that I could never have done on my own. My debt to him is immense.

It is always difficult to articulate one's debt to members of one's own family, for their greatest assistance comes in intangible and very personal forms. I must nevertheless make explicit my gratitude to my mother and to my father for so readily and instinctually offering the kind of indispensable support that only family can provide. I owe a particular debt to my father, an accomplished wordsmith who, despite bemusement with the discourse of literary studies (beginning with words like *discourse*), has helped enliven my prose throughout.

The most essential thanks is reserved for the person with whom I share everything. Pearl James, the best reader I know, has sweated every page, phrase, and word of this book along with me (while simultaneously writing her own to boot). More importantly, however, she and my daughter Chloe have reminded me every day, unwittingly and simply by being who they are, that there are things even more — much more — important. That reminder deserves my greatest thanks of all.

Introduction

Reading the Republican Legacy

Alphonse Daudet's short story "La dernière classe" (The Last Class), published in 1872, takes place in a rural schoolroom in Alsace shortly after France's defeat by Prussia in 1870–71. Beyond the classroom walls, in the distance, one hears the military exercises of the Prussian troops, a reminder that the annexed provinces of Alsace-Lorraine have fallen to Bismarck. The story describes the schoolchildren's last French class. Thereafter, they will be required to study German. The narrator, a mediocre student named Franz, arrives late to class to discover a curious scene. Adults from the village occupy the empty seats, and the teacher, Monsieur Hamel, dressed in his Sunday best, conducts the lesson with unusual ceremony. Amid the exercises on grammar, reading, writing, and spelling, Monsieur Hamel pauses to celebrate the richness, beauty, and clarity of the French language. He also admonishes his pupils and fellow citizens for their past neglect of their studies. The teacher stresses, in particular, the urgent need to preserve and defend the French language. The nation's survival, he explains, depends on it: studying French, learning to read and write the language, is tantamount to fighting for France. As this, the last French class draws to a close, Monsieur Hamel begins to offer some parting words. Overcome with sadness, however, he cannot speak. Instead, he turns to the blackboard and painstakingly writes in capital letters: VIVE LA FRANCE! He then, with a wave of the hand, dismisses the class.

Daudet's story is as relevant today as it was at the end of the nineteenth century. Though the threats to France's security have changed, the crucial connection between education and national welfare continues to dominate politics, public debate, and even literary and cinematic production. Modern communication technologies spawning pidgin languages (of email and SMS), cultural globalization typified by the boundless American entertainment industry, and the growing impact of beliefs and practices of immigrant communities from former colonies have generated an anxiety about the survival of both the national language and republican values. Daudet's Prussian troops have been replaced by text messaging, Hollywood movies, and the *hijab* (or headscarf) worn by some Muslim schoolgirls.[1] Just as Daudet did in 1872, France's leaders, intellectuals, and educators today invoke the school as a bulwark against these potential threats to French culture and identity. And just as Monsieur Hamel's lesson suggests, the French language and literature class — the place where one learns to read and write — still constitutes the epicenter of the struggle.

The Pedagogical Imagination examines present-day versions of Daudet's story. It studies some of the most popular and critically acclaimed works of recent literature and film treating problems of education in France: François Bégaudeau's *Entre les murs* (2006), Erik Orsenna's *La grammaire est une chanson douce* (2001), Abdellatif Kechiche's *L'esquive* (2004) and, a less obvious, more subtle example, Agnès Varda's *Les glaneurs et la glaneuse* (2000). All of these works are concerned in one way or another with what many refer to as the school crisis in France. Though typically defined in terms of academic underachievement, school violence, and student disregard for republican values, the school crisis that concerns us here is more closely related to the issues that concern Daudet: questions of language learning, reading and writing instruction, and literary studies. The works studied in these pages place the very act of reading — how we read and how we *should* read — at the center of their reflections on republican schooling and French education.

They do not merely depict scenes of learning, however. The works of Bégaudeau, Orsenna, Kechiche, and Varda engage with the question of education through experiments with form. They represent the educational milieu — teachers, students, classrooms — but they also use formal devices such as *mise en abyme*, the play of text and image, fragmented narratives, and curious interpolations of realia to stimulate the reader's or viewer's active engagement with the material. They promote, quite simply, an act of critical reading that in and of itself, I argue, reproduces basic pedagogical principles of modern education, principles that have been especially consequential in, and central to, the French republican tradition. To put it another way, *The Pedagogical Imagination* argues that a particular conception of modern progressive pedagogy manifests itself in techniques of form and in the kinds of reading activities to which such techniques give rise. I argue that critical reading is an enactment of republican pedagogy; indeed, that the critical reader *is* a republican reader.

Over the course of the book I clarify and nuance this central claim and explore some of its broader implications for literary and cultural studies more generally. Suffice it to say for the moment that, by republican pedagogy, I am referring to a conception of teaching and learning devoted to cultivating the student's skills of independent, empirical observation leading ultimately to intellectual autonomy. To be sure, this pedagogy is not unique to France; it has deep roots in the Western tradition of scientific inquiry. But it enjoyed an exceptional pride of place in France under the regime of the Third Republic established in 1870; it became a vehicle for the spread of republican ideology inherited from the Enlightenment, the Revolution, and the first republicans of 1792 who championed education reform as a sine qua non of building a democratic, egalitarian society.

To say that the critical reader is a republican reader is, in some sense, obvious. Of course any reader who enlists his or her skills of textual analysis to interpret a work of literature or film is using skills of scrutiny deemed indispensable for citizens in a democratic society. What is less obvious, however, is how specific pedagogical doctrines believed to cultivate these skills manifest themselves in artistic form, or, more precisely, in the reader/viewer's engagement with questions of form. We can begin to get a sense of how this occurs by returning to Daudet's story. Our reading of it remains incomplete. It is not enough to summarize its themes. If it is to serve as an exemplum for the larger study to follow, we must attend to its form.

There is more in Monsieur Hamel's VIVE LA FRANCE than the obvious expression of patriotic devotion. His patriotic cry takes a vivid, graphic form. What matters here, to use a familiar formula, is not only *what* the words say but also *how* they are said . . . or, in this case, not said, but written. The mode of delivery means everything. When the teacher switches from speaking to writing, the students are no longer listeners; they become readers. His change in mode of address demonstrates — and compels his students to perform — the very connection he has previously established between language study and the nation. After all, in order for the students to understand Monsieur Hamel's cri de coeur, which appears to them only in graphic form, they must decipher the marks on the blackboard. Patriotic communion occurs here through the act of writing and reading. The students assimilate the patriotic message through an act of decoding that is itself an enactment of service to the nation. In other words, what is patriotic in this scene is not only the content or message of the words on the blackboard but also the medium of communication, the fact that the words are written, not spoken, and that they oblige the students to read. Thus, with the inscription of VIVE LA FRANCE, reading becomes a doubly patriotic act.

Monsieur Hamel's students are not the only readers of these words. They are also addressed to Daudet's reader. As if to remind us of this, the teacher's switch from speaking to writing is accompanied by a typographical change on the page. Set off from the surrounding text in a separate, freestanding paragraph and a distinct typeface, the three words — apart from what they signify — call attention to themselves *as* written words. Of course, from the reader's perspective, all of the words on the printed page are written. But these three words are written differently; they identify themselves as being written within the fictional space as well. The same graphic image presents itself, simultaneously, to the fictional characters and the real-life reader. Reading the same words at the same time as the schoolchildren, Daudet's reader simulates participation in the lesson. He has become in some sense a student. The typographical maneuver creates the momentary illusion that the reader and the fictional students occupy the same space of instruction. An imaginary space has come into being that conflates the boundaries of two otherwise distinct domains: the fictional classroom and the actual reading experience in the present. As a result of the particular layout of words on the page, the classroom, one could say, has been opened up or extended to include the space of the reader.

Though certainly a hymn to the nation in a moment of despair, Daudet's story is also a literary monument to France's new Republic, its third since 1792.[2] This is not an obvious point. The author himself was only a moderate supporter of the republican cause, Monsieur Hamel's teaching practices show no trace of the progressive doctrines that would dominate republican educational debates in the decades to come, and his patriotic tribute reveals no explicit political or ideological alignment. He writes "Long Live France," and not, as an ardent republican would, "Long Live the Republic." Nevertheless, the story plainly illustrates the close connection between popular education and national cohesion that, still to this day, has been a central tenet of republican ideology since the Revolution. While other regimes certainly made significant contributions to national education, it is the Third Republic that treated the topic with unprecedented urgency and invested the resources necessary to produce lasting, widespread change at all levels of schooling.

Part of the story's republicanism, however, lies also in its form, in the teacher's graphic message, its eye-catching presentation, and the reader's attention to it. The three words, we have seen, draw attention to the medium of the text itself as opposed to the message alone, to the linguistic vehicle as opposed to the story being told, to the act of perceiving the graphic marks on the page as opposed to the events narrated.[3] This attention to modality — to the medium of communication — changes the reader's role and engages his participation in the story. The reader who pauses to reflect on this effect of form is no longer a passive observer of the narrated events. He has become an active participant in the story, awakened to the fact that he enacts the very lesson about reading the story imparts. In sum, what we see here is a technique of form that draws attention to the concrete nature of the text, which, in turn, highlights the reader's task of observing, analyzing, and drawing conclusions about what he has observed. For some, what I am describing here is quite simply the process of careful, active reading itself. But it also reproduces with remarkable fidelity one of the most basic exercises of modern progressive education and a cornerstone of republican education reform: the object lesson, or in French, *la leçon de choses*.

First used in French nursery schools in the mid-nineteenth century and then gradually introduced at the elementary school level, object lesson pedagogy was, in essence, a rudimentary form of scientific inquiry. It trained the student to observe carefully ordinary objects found in the natural world. But following the defeat of 1870 scientific learning acquired a new, almost sacred status. This was France's Sputnik moment.[4] French leaders blamed the military debacle on weaknesses in the educational system and put their faith in science and scientific education as the means of improving the schools. In his landmark assessment of France's predicament in 1871, *La réforme intellectuelle et morale* (The Intellectual and Moral Reform), the philosopher Ernest Renan wrote: "Education must be above all scientific. As a result of his education the young man must know as much as possible about what the human mind has learned about the reality of the universe."[5] Over the next few decades, leaders of school reform not only sought to increase the role of empirical sciences at all levels of education but also applied new scientific insights to pedagogical practices.

As the schoolchild's initiation into the rudiments of scientific inquiry, object lesson pedagogy laid the foundation for the entire national project. "*Les leçons de choses à la base de tout*" (Object lesson pedagogy [must be] at the base of it all), Minister of Public Instruction Jules Ferry purportedly declared.[6] Indeed, the principles of empirical, active learning at the core of object lesson pedagogy were adapted for use in a wide range of disciplines. Republican educators often ascribed to it a value that surpassed the specific knowledge acquired by the student in the course of his lesson. This pedagogy, as they viewed it, trained students to think critically; it was meant to accustom the student to a mode of careful reasoning and judgment that educators believed to be characteristic of the republican mindset and that they hoped would become the intellectual habit of every citizen of the Republic. Discussions of object lesson pedagogy in late nineteenth-century France were also therefore vehicles for larger discussions about core republican values and their survival among future generations. In other words, object lesson pedagogy was — and remains — a microcosm for exploring the relationship between theories and practices of teaching and learning and a critical mindset underlying republican ideology. Debates about, and instances of, object lesson pedagogy offer the most important places for understanding the relationship between education and republicanism.

The Pedagogical Imagination goes even further. It connects the methods and rationales of object lesson pedagogy to the question of reading, meaning here the careful analysis of literature and film. Just as the concept of object lesson pedagogy was detached from its original function as a classroom exercise and turned into an idiom for speaking about republicanism more generally, so, too, can the *leçon de choses* be used as a model for theorizing the reader's and viewer's encounter with literary and cinematic form. In other words, object lesson pedagogy, a system of ideas about the cultivation of faculties of observation, analysis, and judgment in the service of republican ideals, also serves to explain in pedagogical terms the activity of interpreting works of art. It provides a model for describing the reader's engagement with form, his or her direct encounter with the arrangements of concrete, linguistic, graphic, textual, and visual materials by means of which artworks are read, viewed, and interpreted. Daudet's "La dernière classe" presents this idea in an abbreviated fashion. The works of Varda, Orsenna, Kechiche, and Bégaudeau that constitute the main chapters of *The Pedagogical Imagination* reveal it on a much larger scale. Their formal devices are more innovative, complicated, and extensive: they pervade the works in their entirety. In a bolder fashion than Daudet's brief graphic example, these works call as much attention to the material and linguistic techniques of their own construction — what Roman Jakobson famously called the work's "poetic function" — as they do to the (real or fictional) worlds to which they refer. They are themselves literary and cinematic object lessons. When understood as such, there begins to emerge, in my view, something "republican" about the act of reading them carefully and critically.

My insistence on intellectual autonomy and critical inquiry as products of republican pedagogy may surprise readers familiar with the view, prevalent since the 1960s, that the republican school founded at the end of the nineteenth century was primarily a state instrument for forming a docile citizenry and maintaining social order. Countless scholars from a range of disciplines have left us a considerable body of research intended to demonstrate that, in practice and despite the rhetoric of liberty, equality, and fraternity, the republican school perpetuated traditional class divisions and relied on age-old authoritarian teaching practices used in church-run schools.

An obvious landmark in this scholarship is Pierre Bourdieu and Jean-Claude Passeron's influential 1970 study, *La reproduction: Eléments pour une théorie du système d'enseignement* (*Reproduction in Education, Society and Culture*), a sociological analysis of the way educational institutions unwittingly maintain rigid class structures through a valorization of elite cultural norms that are nevertheless touted as democratic.[7] And, of course, Michel Foucault's *Surveiller et punir* (*Discipline and Punish*), though less exclusively devoted to the school per se, has also established itself as a classic reference for examinations of the inherent and often latent authoritarian nature of the school.[8]

A more recent work in this vein, and one that is more directly concerned with present-day perceptions of the legacy of the Third Republic's schools, is Christian Nique and Claude Lelièvre's *La République n'éduquera pas* (The Republic shall not educate) (1993). Subtitled *La fin du mythe Ferry* (The end of the Ferry myth), this semipolemical work by two of France's leading historians of education demythologizes the idea of the republican school founded by Jules Ferry in the 1880s as the fulfillment of the Enlightenment project. Nique and Lelièvre specifically reject the view that the Third Republic's school was the heir to Nicolas de Condorcet's call for a mode of public instruction that would eschew moral inculcation for the sake of promoting the skills of autonomous intellectual inquiry — that is, the fundamental skills required of every republican citizen. Ferry's primary concern, they write, "was not to make knowledge available to the people but rather to 'educate' the people. He was not the proponent of Enlightenment for all but rather the champion of the 'State as moral educator.' In this sense, and contrary to what the myth affirms, Ferry's policies did not mark a break with the political regimes that preceded the Republic but were in fact completely in line with them. For Ferry as it was for earlier regimes, the State must educate the people because the education of the people is useful to the State."[9]

With the insistence here on moral education as the primary aim of Ferry's school, Nique and Lelièvre recall the classic distinction in the history of French education between *éducation* and *instruction*. The words have come to symbolize the competing ideas regarding the function of public education debated before the Legislative Assembly of 1792 and associated most notably with the opposing arguments of Rabaut Saint-Etienne and Condorcet. The Calvinist minister Jean-Paul Rabaut Saint-Étienne, insisting on the importance of *éducation* ("*l'éducation nationale*") over Condorcet's view of *instruction* ("*l'instruction publique*"), contended that the former must fill a void left by the disappearance of the Ancien Régime and the clergy with their "catechisms, processions, ceremonies, sermons, hymns, pilgrimages and statues."[10] While *instruction* enlightens the mind, it is *éducation* that forms the "heart," and it is the latter, explains Rabaut Saint-Étienne, that must enjoy pride of place in the new system of national education. According to Nique and Lelièvre, Ferry's school belongs more properly to this moralizing tradition than to the rationalist, Enlightenment tradition of Condorcet. What mattered for Ferry, they argue, was not the spread of knowledge and learning but rather, as it was for Napoleon and Guizot before him, the training of a compliant citizenry devoted to the ideology of the state.

One of the most recent and original explorations of precisely this moralizing function of the Third Republic's schools is M. Martin Guiney's scrupulously documented *Teaching the Cult of Literature in the French Third Republic* (2004). Guiney argues that the school system established at the end of the nineteenth century, while presenting itself as a rival of Catholic education, actually imitated many of its methods.[11] The originality of Guiney's argument lies in his assessment of the role of language and literary studies as the disciplines that best served to disseminate the deceptive republican ideology. He develops this point through a comparison of the concepts of literariness and sacredness. Literature, and in particular its apotheosis in the form of a national canon, was accorded a sacred status under the Third Republic. This meant that France's great writers of the past were celebrated as the embodiment of republican values. As such, however, students did not actually learn to read the works critically: "The French literary canon operated as a type of scriptural authority for the secular power of the state."[12] One studied literature "as if it were nothing more than a guide to wisdom handed down through the centuries," and there was no "attempt to come to grips with the characteristics that distinguish it from other kinds of discourse." This practice made literature an "object of veneration" and "enhanc[ed] its aura as a pure, hermetic vessel for the unattainable Godhead."[13] In other words, though literary studies played an important part in the school's mission to forge a coherent national identity, students did not actually learn to analyze literature in the way that we understand that activity today. Instead of learning to "read" literature critically, the student learned to worship it and, consequently, glorify the nation as well. In a word, the republican school, at least insofar as literary studies were concerned, was no more emancipatory than the Catholic school that preceded it. For both Nique and Lelièvre and for Guiney, the Third Republic did little more than put old educational wine in new republican bottles.

The Pedagogical Imagination, however, takes a different view of republican pedagogy and its legacy. It aligns itself with recent scholarship in history, philosophy, and political science that provides a corrective to the perception of the republican school as only a rigidly traditionalist, authoritarian institution. The recent works of Yves Déloye, Pierre

Kahn, and Eric Dubreucq stand out in this regard. In *École et citoyenneté: L'individualisme républicain de Jules Ferry à Vichy* (School and citizenship: republican individualism from Jules Ferry to Vichy) (1994), Yves Déloye compares school manuals used in Catholic schools with those used in the new republican classroom at the beginning of the twentieth century to show that the republican schools were indeed training students to become self-reliant and independent thinkers in ways that traditional religious schools did not. Much of the historian Pierre Kahn's work, but in particular his *La leçon de choses: Naissance de l'enseignement des sciences à l'école primaire* (The object lesson: Birth of scientific education in the primary school) (2002), demonstrates that the grade school exercise of the object lesson and other elementary introductions to science provided more than merely basic practical training suitable only for the lower classes. He argues that this first introduction to scientific inquiry shared the same epistemological foundations as advanced scientific training offered in secondary schools and higher and should be understood as a genuine prologue to more sophisticated critical thinking. Eric Dubreucq's recent study of three towering figures in republican education reform (Henri Marion, Ferdinand Buisson, Émile Durkheim) examines the philosophical foundations of their respective ideas on education and pedagogy.[14] He concludes that despite their differences, these leading educators all viewed republican educational thought as a form of critical thinking that puts into question its own model and its own foundation. Moreover, argues Dubreucq, this intellectual principle survives today as a pillar of republican ideology. To this group of French scholars, we should add the work by the American historian Patricia Tilburg. Her recent *Colette's Republic* shows how the writer-performer's highly original and even audacious artistic experiments on the Paris music hall stage bear the mark of the progressive republican education she received as a girl in the 1880s.[15] Together this research indicates that the view of the republican school as only an oppressively authoritarian institution is skewed and that the educational reform pursued by republican leaders at the end of the nineteenth century was more emancipatory and less paternalistic than much late twentieth-century scholarship would have us believe. *The Pedagogical Imagination* lends its voice to this recent rehabilitation of the republican school's debt to the Enlightenment project. By examining the linkages between pedagogical doctrine and critical reading, it demonstrates, moreover, that literary scholarship has a part to play in the study of republicanism, a field often thought to be the preserve of historians and political theorists.

The Pedagogical Imagination is not a survey or inventory of contemporary works on French schools. Its ambitions are both more narrow and more profound. I have chosen to read works that demonstrate with particular force the relationship between republican pedagogical doctrine and artistic form. To take form seriously as an integral part of the act of reading and as an agent in the production of meaning requires deliberate examination of select works. This constraint, however, befits the topic at hand. For the very question of breadth versus depth — the quantity versus the quality of readings — resonates with issues at the heart of republican pedagogy. Republican pedagogues debated whether the object lesson served primarily to have students gain broad knowledge about the natural world or acquire the skills of painstaking observation and analysis. In a manner recalling Montaigne's famous distinction between a "well-filled head" and a "well-made head," they debated whether to prioritize *what* one learns or *how* one learns. Education leaders such as Ferdinand Buisson and Henri Marion, we shall see, insisted on the importance of the latter. By treating the works of Varda, Orsenna, Kechiche, and Bégaudeau as literary and filmic object lessons, it is only natural that I examine them accordingly — with the kind of scrutiny that is the cultural legacy of republican pedagogy.

My own reader might balk at my suggestion that critical reading be understood as an enactment of republican pedagogy and, by extension, a certain idea of republican ideology. After all, the practice of critical reading or close textual analysis is a centerpiece of humanistic inquiry in numerous fields that may have little or nothing to do with French much less republican traditions. What, then, permits me to propose so intimate a link between this type of reading practice and republicanism? Needless to say, I do not mean to suggest an exclusive relationship between the two. Of course critical reading as it is practiced by teachers and scholars and taught to their students owes its existence to a wide range of philosophical, intellectual, and cultural traditions rooted in, and traversing, different national and linguistic communities. Nevertheless, to acknowledge the overdetermined nature of critical reading does not in any way discount the value of exploring one particular strand of a complex weave or one particular branch of an ornate latticework. What is more, one could argue that the bond between language and literary studies and raison d'état is unusually pronounced in the case of France, that French regimes have nurtured this linkage in a sustained and concerted fashion that remains unparalleled. The Académie française with its extraordinary role in the shaping of French cultural policy over the centuries and across successive political regimes is an obvious symbol of this nexus between language, literature, and the ideology of the state. More to the point is the example of the *explication de texte*, the famous exercise in painstaking textual commentary and analysis that became the centerpiece of literary studies in the Third Republic's lycée.[16] A predecessor to later versions of close reading, the *explication de texte*'s rise in importance accompanied, and was a manifestation of, the scientification of teaching and learning throughout the French schools. It was thus, like the object lesson itself, a symbol of ascendant republican ideology. What is perhaps most remarkable about the *explication de texte* is that, to this very day, English-speaking teachers and students of literature continue to use the French term to refer to close textual analysis in general.[17] It would thus seem that there is something in the collective literary imagination of the Anglophone world that equates critical reading with this exercise issuing from the French republican tradition. In short, other nations and other traditions have certainly emphasized critical reading, but France has placed the concept at the center of an intense public debate about educational policy and woven it into the very fabric of government itself.

My insistence on form and especially formalist reading aligns my project with the recent trend in literary and cultural studies most commonly called New Formalism. This renewed interest in formal matters — the latest reminder that form does matter — arises out of what many perceive as an excessive concern in some New Historicist criticism with theme at the expense of form.[18] New Formalists, or at least those in the movement's "activist" wing, applaud the political engagement characteristic of New Historicism.[19] They lament, however, the tendency among New Historicists to treat texts as mimetic illustrations of historical and political reality and, consequently, to tolerate practices of reading that, in their neglect of formal complexities, undermine the very raison d'être of literary and cultural studies.[20] New Formalism refuses to treat works of art as mere "bundles of historical and cultural content."[21] It insists on reading practices that, in their attention to form, "constitute form itself as a meaningful content."[22] In the preface to his recent *Play and the Politics of Reading: The Social Uses of Modernist Form*, Paul B. Armstrong lays out with particular concision what is at stake in the New Formalist turn: "If reading itself is a site of important social and political activity, then the *how* of that experience is as important as the *what* of a text's mimetic commentary, and maybe more so. Asking questions about how formal textual strategies seek to engage a reader's assumptions and conventions is a specifically literary way to do the work of social, political criticism. This kind of close attention to the pressures and designs of the reading experience is something that we literary critics are (or should be) particularly skilled at."[23]

The Pedagogical Imagination asks these very questions. It examines the way the "formal textual strategies" on display in *Les glaneurs et la glaneuse*, *La grammaire est une chanson douce*, *L'esquive*, and *Entre les murs* "engage the reader's [and viewer's] assumptions" about republican schooling, republican pedagogy, and the historical and ideological forces residing therein. Of course, form is inseparable from content. We experience the one in relation to the other. As Ellen Rooney puts it, "reading is . . . corrosive of the facile opposition between form and content, because we must reinvent their relation in every new context."[24] The literary and filmic readings in these pages do just that. They investigate the necessarily dialogical relationship of form and content and reveal what this particular dialogue expresses that is not otherwise articulated by either of the "conversants" — the *how* or the *what* — alone.

Since all of the works I use to develop my argument have appeared since the year 2000, Daudet's story might seem an odd choice as an introduction to my topic. What could a relatively forgotten story from the 1870s have to do with this group of internationally successful and award-winning works from the start of the twenty-first century? More than one might think, I argue. One of this book's aims is to establish connections between present-day cultural production and the history of republican pedagogy, of which the early decades of the Third Republic, the years subsequent to Daudet's "La dernière classe," constitute a pivotal, defining moment. No matter how obviously rooted the works of Varda, Orsenna, Kechiche, and Bégaudeau are in questions of contemporary society and culture, they are concerned not only with events of the moment. They participate in an ongoing and century-old (if not older) conversation about republican education and pedagogical doctrine. Their richness and lasting interest can only be appreciated when situated in this broader context.

Chapter 1 develops the historical context outlined above by examining the way republican educators spoke and wrote about the new pedagogy, and the object lesson in particular, at the turn of the twentieth century. This "pedagogical revolution," as Durkheim called it, had its roots in a contest between scientific thought and the classical humanities reaching back to the Renaissance.[25] We also see how, at the hands of these educators, object lesson pedagogy and its parent concept, intuitive learning, became associated with rigorous rational inquiry, not an obvious connection given that learning through sensory perception was typically thought to be easy, spontaneous, and unaided by reason. Finally, the chapter highlights similarities between the language of object lesson pedagogy and that of twentieth-century formalist art and criticism. The purpose here is to bring together, within a single frame, these two distinct discourses — one about modern (literary and filmic) art and the other about modern pedagogy. Though each of these discourses is familiar enough in and of itself, the bridges connecting them remain relatively unexplored. *The Pedagogical Imagination* is an exploration of what one such bridge might look like.

Chapter 2's treatment of Agnès Varda's *Les glaneurs et la glaneuse* (*The Gleaners and I*) continues the historical contextualization begun in chapter 1. Of all of the works in this study, Varda's film documentary offers the most explicit and sustained look at the survival in the present of traces of older institutions, discourses, and practices. It is thus eminently pertinent for the relationship I am proposing between nineteenth-century republican pedagogy and its legacy today. A documentary study of the age-old practice of gleaning, the salvaging of leftover, unwanted food-stuffs, Varda's film might appear at first glance to have little to do with contemporary education. This changes, however, when we consider that it is framed by scenes of reading instruction and that gleaning itself, as Varda sees it, is a metaphor for the act of reading. The opening montage simulating a perusal of the Larousse dictionary prompts a reflection on Pierre Larousse (1817–1875) and his legacy. Not only a lexicographer, publisher, and ardent republican — a French Noah Webster — Larousse was also a teacher who developed innovative techniques for reading instruction that relied on the same principles we find at the heart of object lesson pedagogy. Varda's own cinematic technique of using word- and image-play instructs her own viewer to read digital visual media according to Larousse's methods. In sum, this chapter proposes that we see Varda as a kind of modern-day Larousse.

Gleaning, then, is not only about salvaging foodstuffs or other dis-carded objects. For Varda, it is a metaphor for recuperating and recycling all kinds of things, including fragments of the past, those forgotten or neglected chapters of history. By using her art to glean — or re-collect — these episodes, she also finds new purpose for them, thereby assuring their survival over time. This is precisely what her film does with Larousse and his method of reading instruction. It puts this forgotten chapter of republican education back into circulation. Varda breathes new life into Larousse's legacy by showing its applicability to the question of literacy in the age of digital visual media. Understood as a recupera-tion of the past, Varda's gleaning also serves as a metaphor for what is attempted throughout *The Pedagogical Imagination*. My return to late nineteenth-century republican pedagogical doctrine for the purpose of finding its resonance in twenty-first-century artistic treatments of education is a kind of historical gleaning à la Varda.

Erik Orsenna's *La grammaire est une chanson douce* (*Grammar Is a Sweet, Gentle Song*), discussed in chapter 3, is a philosophical tale in the moralist tradition and explicitly displays a debt to both Antoine de Saint-Exupéry and Jean de la Fontaine. It also gleans and recycles for its own purposes fragments of the republican past. It tells the story of an incredible journey taken by two schoolchildren to a magical land where the French language literally comes alive, where words and phrases are living, breathing, sentient beings. Having lost the ability to speak as a result of a shipwreck, the children embark on a fresh exploration of their native tongue. They rediscover the rules of grammar, acquire a rich and colorful vocabulary, and learn to combine words, phrases, and sentences to produce eloquent, imaginative prose. And, according to the logic of the story, the purpose of this linguistic reeducation is to acquire the skills enabling one to emulate the great literary authors such as La Fontaine, Proust, and Saint-Exupéry.

The children's tale is also a thinly veiled polemic against the gradual decline of traditional literary studies in the secondary school curriculum. If the story presents literary sensibility and prowess as the highest purpose of language study, this view is opposed to recent trends in French class that ignore the uniqueness of the literary work and train students to subject it to the same dispassionate semiotic analysis that one might apply to any "ordinary" text, such as a news article, an advertisement, or products of popular, "low" culture. Orsenna dramatizes this opposition in the opening classroom scene preceding the adventure story. Here, the children's kindhearted French teacher who uses nurturing methods to introduce students to the "magic" of the French language and its literature finds herself reprimanded by the inspector from the Ministry of Education for her failure to hew to the dry, technical, jargon-filled structuralist methods prescribed by the state. The story thus stages a Manichean opposition between the scientistic training in textual analysis and a more humanistic — and thus humane — exploration of the wonder and beauty of literary arts. It is, in other words, an opposition between cold, rational science and the affective experience of the humanities. Orsenna's tale would appear to take up unequivocally the cause of the latter.

I argue, however, that the story actually has a much more ambivalent relationship to the scientific tradition than the opposition of the opening chapter would suggest. We see this by comparing it not with La Fontaine or Saint Exupéry (to whom its debt is explicit) but rather with another famous story of the adventures of schoolchildren: G. Bruno's bestselling *Le tour de la France par deux enfants* (*The Tour of France by Two Children*) (1877), a quintessential monument to republican ideology. Like G. Bruno's story and instructional manual, Orsenna's children are separated from their home by a violent incident; a shipwreck in *La grammaire* serves a narrative function similar to the calamities set off by the Franco-Prussian war in *Le tour de la France*. At the end of their respective journeys, each set of children is reunited with family, defined in terms of a national community. In Bruno's manual, the nation is represented largely in geographic terms; for Orsenna, it is a matter of language and literary patrimony. The exploration of regions, industries, and products in Bruno is replaced in Orsenna by the discovery of parts of speech and grammatical rules. In a word, Bruno's *France* becomes Orsenna's *French*. What is more, both stories rely on a juxtaposition of text and image and expect their readers to "learn to look" in ways recalling the tradition of object lesson pedagogy. The similarities between the two works put the significance of their differences in greater relief. In Bruno's manual, a product of its positivistic epoch, the celebration of scientific progress and technological advances is accompanied by a denigration of works of fiction. It is precisely because it actually mimics the "tour of the nation" model that Orsenna's corrective to Bruno's mythophobia is so apparent. Orsenna, I argue, borrows the republican paradigm but reinvests it with a more humanistic message. It rewrites or, to borrow Varda's terminology, recycles *Le tour de la France par deux enfants* and places literature at its center. In other words, it reinscribes literature at the heart of the republican educational enterprise.

The work studied in chapter 4, Abdellatif Kechiche's film *L'esquive* (*Games of Love and Chance*) is about an ethnically diverse group of high school students in the working-class suburbs of Paris who are rehearsing for a school production of a classic French comedy of manners, Marivaux's *Le jeu de l'amour et du hasard* (*The Game of Love and Chance*). Like Orsenna's tale, it also addresses debates over literary education. But the principal conflict here concerns progressive republicanism versus traditional republicanism. For Kechiche, the primary question is whether traditional literary training rooted in the study of the national canon is consistent with the republican promise of providing an egalitarian education preparing all students, regardless of their backgrounds, for full integration into republican society. The topic revisits from a different angle the issues at play in Orsenna's tale. Since the 1970s, with the increasing democratization of French secondary schools, an ongoing topic of debate has been whether traditional literary studies serve the needs of students from immigrant and working-class families who, unlike many of their peers, do not acquire at home the cultural knowledge and language skills needed to succeed in this field of study, historically the preserve of elites. The debate has over time hardened into a dispute between rival camps. Traditionalists defend the national literary patrimony and its prominent place in the curriculum. Reformists have sought to transform literary studies into a general language arts curriculum that focuses on a variety of literary and nonliterary "texts" studied for the purpose of helping students acquire practical communication skills rather than literary culture per se.

My analysis centers on the scenes of formal classroom instruction and, in particular, the contradictory message of the French teacher who represents at one moment a progressive view that is suspicious of elite (and elitist) literary studies and, at a later moment, a traditionalist view that defends these selfsame studies in the name of republican universalism. The teacher, in other words, expresses opposing viewpoints in the longstanding debates about literary education. On the one hand, her disparaging remarks about the futility of the acquisition of literary culture amounts to a denunciation of the false republican promise that France's racial and ethnic minorities, through education and the learning of French cultural codes, can become fully integrated citizens in

French society. On the other hand and at a different moment, the teacher vigorously defends the possibility of self-emancipation gained through the imitation of a language and culture that is not one's own, a position in line with the doctrine of republican universalism. By situating this conflict of viewpoints in the figure of the teacher — that is, in one and the same person — Kechiche preempts facile readings of the teacher as merely an instrument of an authoritarian institution blindly committed to defending republican orthodoxies. The film "dodges" (*esquive*) such simple interpretations. The basic conflict of the film, then, is how to square the republican commitment to integrate France's multicultural population with a commitment to the value of republican universalism. The film sets up these rival camps — reformists and traditionalists — in a dialectical opposition. Its reluctance to choose between these alternatives illustrates one of the many ways in which the film remains true to its organizing principle captured in its title. But this dialectical structure is also a means by which the film passes the responsibility of judgment on to the viewer, and thereby also remains true to the republican message of intellectual autonomy so forcefully championed by republican educators a century ago. *L'esquive* nevertheless offers, albeit allusively (*en esquivant*), a way around the impasse it constructs. It proposes a rereading of the Marivaux play at its center by going outside the French tradition and using the interpretative lens of Farid al-din Attar's *Conference of the Birds*. The film's evocation of this twelfth-century Islamic poem not only produces a novel interpretation of the French literary classic but also affords a means of reconceptualizing the true universality of republican doctrine.

Chapter 5 examines *Entre les murs* (*The Class*), François Bégaudeau's novelistic chronicle of life in a troubled Paris middle school. While reactions to the book (and to its film adaptation) have praised its objective, impartial look at the problems of student underachievement and disobedience in today's classroom, this overwhelming interest in the docunovel's verisimilitude has been accompanied by a lack of attention to the work's form. Concern for the reality beyond the text, the external world to which it refers, has resulted in a neglect of the text itself, of its intrinsic properties. In short, the outside has eclipsed the inside. This is no small matter for a book whose title so clearly calls attention to the relationship between exterior and interior. On one level, of course, the title refers literally to the interior space of the school, a space of great concern to the general public, but whose actual goings-on remain largely hidden from view. When we attend, however, to the work's formal properties — its language play and innovative structure — we see that it contains a reflection that destabilizes the dichotomy of inside and outside with respect to both the literary work and the domain of education.

As with all of the works in this study, our reading of *Entre les murs* requires that we situate it in the context of contemporary debates and their relationship to the history of republican education. The issue that stands out in Bégaudeau's work, given its concern with the inside-outside binary, is the status of the school as a kind of "sanctuary." To what extent, if at all, should the school and its curriculum be susceptible to factors, influences, and forces existing in society at large — that is, in the world outside its walls? The question harkens back to the revolutionary period and (as mentioned above) Condorcet's conception of public instruction, which, according to hard-line defenders of *laïcité* (that uniquely French brand of secularism), lays the foundation for the idea of the school as a sanctuary. According to this view, the school is a site of pure rational, unimpeded inquiry in which the student cultivates his or her intellectual autonomy in a space protected from the influence of outside authorities such as religion, family, or other preexisting moral systems. Today the topic manifests itself most obviously in the question of whether and how the school should adjust its educational program and methods to the needs and abilities of an increasingly multicultural student body. How, in other words, should a student's particular cultural identity and background affect what is expected of him or her, with respect to both academic achievement and comportment, in the republican classroom? The question takes us right to the heart of republican doctrine and, once again, the ongoing conflict between, on the one hand, conservative republicans, defenders of orthodox universalism that makes few concessions to cultural particularisms, and, on the other hand, more progressive, multiculturalist republicans who call for a school that is more sensitive to and accommodating of the particular situation of students from immigrant communities or historically marginalized populations.

This chapter shows how all of these issues play themselves out through Bégaudeau's elaborate metaphorics of walls, a constant setting up of boundaries and frontiers — for example, between students and figures of authority, between rules of grammar and actual language use — that are invariably transgressed. This dynamic reappears in the work's form — for example, in Bégaudeau's extensive use of realia. The text is strewn with bits and pieces of authentic documents from the real world of the school (music lyrics, messages from the Ministry of Education, fragments of student assignments) that produce a disorienting effect for the reader. Paradoxically, then, those very moments when the real world most ostentatiously intrudes in the text are also moments that call attention to the surface of the text, to its textuality. They are object lessons and demand the reader's attention to the very act of reading. In other words, it is when the outside obtrudes into the reading experience that the reader becomes most aware of the intrinsic properties of the text. In the end our task is to show how this textual experience should be understood as a literary enactment of the dilemma, paradox, and contradictions at the heart of the republican concept of *laïcité*, a concept that Bégaudeau nevertheless wants to salvage insofar as it describes the reader's autonomous engagement with the literary text. Reading, according to *Entre les murs*, is a performance of *laïcité*.

The concluding chapter is more than a recapitulation. It insists on the role works of art and artistic analysis must play in the study of republicanism. Taking as its point of departure a recent remark by two eminent historians that "republican culture must rediscover its strangeness" if it is to be perceived afresh and in all of its complexity,[26] the conclusion argues that it is, indeed, through formalist reading of literary and other cultural artifacts that one can achieve precisely the kind of renewed vision of republican culture that the historians call for.

The foregoing chapter breakdown makes clear that the literary and filmic works featured in these pages approach the topic of education in distinct yet interrelated ways. They address many themes: reading and literacy, class difference, institutional authority, multiculturalism, science versus literature, progress versus tradition . . . the list could go on. These topics are some of the thorniest in past and present debates over republican education and the values of the Republic. Newspapers, periodicals, radio, and television report on them tirelessly, and they have staked out large territories in the blogosphere.

But the works of Varda, Orsenna, Kechiche, and Bégaudeau differ from these other media. As works of art, they do not report on or represent the reality of the school in any simple, mimetic fashion. They promote, I argue, a critical examination of schooling that comes into existence in the act of careful reading itself. Such reading, which necessarily attends to techniques of form, enacts core principles of republican schooling crystallized in the foundational exercise of the object lesson. As my discussion of Daudet's "La dernière classe" demonstrates, the most lasting lessons of these literary and filmic works reside not in *what* they depict but rather in *how* they depict, which, in turn, guides how we read. It is in this way that reflections *of* education become reflections *on* education.

I

A New Language of Learning

Object Lesson Pedagogy and the Modern Reader

This chapter recovers the way pedagogical doctrines were articulated at a founding moment in republican history and demonstrates the way the language of pedagogy served as an idiom for expressing a system of republican beliefs and values. Though we must look to the past, neither this chapter nor this book constitutes a history of republican education per se. My concern is pedagogical discourse and its ramifications. The school system constructed by Jules Ferry and his lieutenants at the end of the nineteenth and beginning of the twentieth centuries — regardless of whether one views it today as obsolete or a model to emulate — remains a touchstone for contemporary debate. One can hardly open a book on the topic without encountering a reminder of how Jules Ferry's words "continue to resonate today, 140 years later."[1] This discourse, when reconstructed, provides an indispensable historical frame of reference for examining what is most fundamentally at stake when we read or view present-day literature and film about the republican school. It is vital to an understanding of treatments of education in contemporary cultural production.

The discussion to follow consists of four parts. After a brief reminder in section one ("France 'Pedagogizes'") of the general context of education reform, the chapter turns more specifically to the topic of pedagogy and pedagogical discourse. Section two ("The Study of Real Things") privileges the object lesson (*la leçon de choses*) as the paradigmatic exercise in active, experiential learning. It represented the culmination of a gradual rise of empiricist, sensualist pedagogy that republican educators traced back through the Enlightenment to the scientific humanism of Rabelais. The third section ("Intuition and Autonomy") centers on the concept of intuitive learning as a theory of pedagogy closely related to object lesson pedagogy that insisted on cultivating the skills of observation and analysis leading to the student's intellectual autonomy. The final section ("Modern Learning and Modern Reading") explores the linkages between object lesson and intuitive learning, on the one hand, and, on the other, the question of modernist form and twentieth-century formalist criticism. The purpose here is to unearth parallels in the discourses of modern pedagogy and modern literary and artistic production and reception. This discursive intersection prepares us to see how the works of Varda, Orsenna, Kechiche, and Bégaudeau stimulate a reflection on republican pedagogy and republicanism that occurs through formal technique as well as through theme.

FRANCE "PEDAGOGIZES"

As Daudet's "La dernière classe" reminds us, France's longstanding concern with national education became a veritable obsession in the wake of the country's defeat by Germany in 1870.[2] French leaders blamed the military debacle and subsequent national disunity evidenced in the Paris Commune on weaknesses in the educational system. Indeed, the French defeat at the Battle of Sedan was said to be the victory of the German schoolteacher and German pedagogy.[3] Writing in 1871, Ernest Renan famously explained that "[i]n the struggle that has just ended, France's inferiority has been above all intellectual; it is not the heart but rather the head that has failed us. Public instruction is a subject of extreme importance; French intellect has grown weak; it must be strengthened."[4] This view was a commonplace in the early years of the Third Republic. Going to school became the first of the citizen's duties to the nation, before military service, paying taxes, and voting.[5]

There is no shortage of statements by contemporaries expressing the essential role that schooling at all levels played in strengthening the nation and preparing future generations to love and serve their country. Louis Liard, founder of the École pratique des hautes études and leading university reformer, observed that "[a]fter [1871], university reform was not only a question of science, it was a question of patriotism. We understood that this would become one of the centerpieces of our new system of defense."[6] As Liard's words indicate, the most prominent education reformers in France at the time put tremendous faith in science and scientific education as the way to modernize French education. Initiatives to restructure curricula, reorganize disciplines, and create new institutions for advanced research and for teacher training were all inspired by the ubiquitous scientific spirit. A cult of science permeated the culture of education. In a comment typical of the times, the eminent Hellenist Alfred Croiset observed: "Science is the indispensable foundation that must today serve as a support and guide to all other means of knowing."[7]

The sheer volume of laws, decrees, regulations and reports issued on matters of education policy indicates the degree to which the topic had become a focal point of government and political activity.[8] Of all the measures, none has come to symbolize the ambitions of republican education reform more than the Ferry Laws of 1881 and 1882. Named for Jules Ferry, minister of public instruction, the series of laws established free, obligatory, and secular elementary education for all French children between the ages of seven and thirteen. L'école Ferry did more than guarantee the spread of basic skills of reading, writing, and arithmetic to the masses. By wresting control of the school from the Catholic Church (and by extension monarchists and other defenders of the Ancien Régime), the new republican school was said to fulfill the ideological aspirations of the heroes of 1789. The tide of reform affected the secondary and university levels as well. Virulent debates in the 1880s and 1890s culminated in a historic reform of the lycée curriculum that placed modern, scientific studies on an equal footing with the classical humanities.[9] The Camille Sée Law of December 21, 1880 (named for its principal sponsor in parliament), established public secondary schools for girls. In order to train teachers for this new population of students, a university-level normal school for women was created in 1881 at Sèvres.[10] This era also witnessed the birth of the modern research university in France, symbolized by the inauguration of the New Sorbonne in 1896, newly equipped to become an advanced research center in the sciences.[11]

But the passage of laws, the training of teachers, and the creation of institutions are only part of the story. A new way of thinking about teaching and learning underlay the more conspicuous changes. A new intellectual ferment devoted to questions of pedagogy accompanied — and even drove — republican education reform. Félix Pécaut, republican education reformer and founder of the École normale supérieure de Fontenay-aux-Roses, famously remarked that a foreign visitor to France in 1882 wanting to describe the nation's greatest preoccupation at that time would jot down in his diary, "*La France pédagogise*" (France is pedagogizing).[12] As the year in which the most famous of the Ferry Laws was passed, 1882 is certainly a crucial historical marker in French education reform.[13] Pécaut's "*La France pédagogise*," however, refers to something other than the momentous legislation. It describes a current vogue for pedagogical questions in and of themselves. Marveling at the emerging abundance of new classes, training institutes, exams, books, manuals, and anthologies, Pécaut remarks that "there is no lack of things serving to cultivate or spread the art of education."[14] The idea of the "art of education" is of greater interest for purposes of the present study than specific reform measures, legislation, policies, or even teaching practices. Pécaut's "*La France pédagogise*" refers specifically to a heightened interest in process — theories, reflection, and debate about *how* to teach and *how* students learn. Pécaut observes an intellectual and cultural phenomenon that, while clearly related to what goes on in the schoolhouse, reaches beyond the school walls. The pedagogical fashion he describes circulated in essays, articles, speeches, and a tremendous outpouring of popular and middle-brow cultural production.

Pécaut's wording is strange. That he should resort to a neologism, *pédagogiser*, suggests that language was inadequate to describe the changing intellectual climate. His verbal invention underscores the novelty of the phenomenon — the extent to which this fascination with pedagogy was unprecedented. There is even something mildly jarring about Pécaut's new word; *pédagogiser* is as displeasing to the French ear as its equivalent, *to pedagogize*, is to the Anglophone ear. The word expresses an otherwise familiar concept in unfamiliar ways. It gives the reader pause. It is as if this awkward morphology were meant to have the reader conceive of pedagogy differently. I dwell on this lexical detail for its heuristic value. What Pécaut does with this one term the present study attempts to do with the concept of pedagogy more generally.

The Pedagogical Imagination has us reimagine pedagogy. It seeks to detach the concept from its usual association with the pedestrian practice of everyday teaching and learning and wash it of the stigma of post-1968 progressivism said by many to compromise the efficacy of today's education schools.[15] These pages aim to restore to the idea of pedagogy the theoretical value and intellectual eminence that it enjoyed at the end of the nineteenth century when the Third Republic's most influential thinkers used it to express an unapologetic commitment to autonomous rational inquiry.

THE STUDY OF REAL THINGS

The republican pedagogical imagination starts with the object lesson, the methodological foundation for the entire project of education reform at the turn of the twentieth century. "*Les leçons de choses à la base de tout*" (object lessons at the base of it all), Jules Ferry is said to have declared.[16] Whether the minister of public instruction actually uttered these famous words matters little.[17] They have come to represent an entire pedagogical mindset intimately bound up with the republican ideology of rational inquiry, scientific progress, and individual autonomy.

At a most basic level, object lesson pedagogy simply referred to an exercise of observation and discovery that was carried out in elementary school classrooms. First developed in the United States and England, object lesson pedagogy was gradually adopted in French nursery schools and later in republican primary schools thanks largely to the outspoken advocacy of the progressive educator Marie Pape-Carpantier.[18] The aim of this method was to accustom students to learn through sense perception. As opposed to passive book learning (*l'enseignement par les mots*) Pape-Carpantier advocated the more active "learning by looking" (*l'enseignement par les yeux*). In the entry on object lesson pedagogy in the 1887 edition of Ferdinand Buisson's *Dictionnaire de pédagogie et d'instruction primaire*, the educator and author of school manuals Narcisse Plâtrier described it as follows:

> The object lesson, as we understand it, consists of putting in the hand of the child, or before his eyes, any object, even the representation of an object, and of making sure that he knows how to understand it, how to observe it, how to use clear and precise language in describing its essential features. The object can be very simple: a ball, a cork, a sheet of paper, a stone, a piece of windowpane. It can be very complex, like a book, a plant or an insect. It is always the same method, and the child will have to indicate its characteristics of weight, form, dimension, color, the impressions it makes on our senses, etc.[19]

Nothing could seem more straightforward than the activity described here. It would appear to entail nothing more than putting ordinary objects before the child and having him or her accurately describe them.

But there is more here than meets the eye. If this unassuming exercise constitutes the foundation of the entire educational enterprise of the Third Republic — if it lies "*à la base de tout*" as Jules Ferry supposedly claimed — it is because the concept conveys much more than the elementary classroom task suggests. It summarizes an entire constellation of attitudes about the value of scientific learning, rational inquiry, and individual autonomy. While object lesson pedagogy would eventually be associated almost exclusively with the teaching of the sciences, many of its proponents, including its foremost champion, Marie Pape-Carpantier, saw it as a method that could be applied to a range of fields and all levels of learning.

Elsewhere in the *Dictionnaire de pédagogie* article on the topic, Plâtrier writes that object lesson pedagogy "does not apply only to primary schools. Normal schools, middle schools and high schools should also borrow its procedures and continue to use them, with the necessary modifications required by the specific milieu, until the end of formal studies."[20] In essays, articles, speeches, and official instructions from the period, one encounters the idea that scientific education, broadly understood as the skills of observation and analysis that promote active learning and autonomy, had implications extending beyond the immediate, practical considerations of specific classroom exercises or subject matter. As Elie Pécaut (Félix's son) put it, "this practical knowledge, however useful it may be, is but the least of the advantages that the scientific culture gives to the child. The truly invaluable benefit is that it arouses in him that critical mindset that is the soul of modern thought in all its forms without which he would be out of sync with his time and like a stranger in his own land."[21] Reformers such as Pécaut hoped that this culture of scientific instruction reaching beyond the classroom walls would introduce generations of French youth to the spirit of modern critical inquiry. The object lesson provided the foundation for this cultural edifice. As an introduction to scientific observation, it encapsulated republican ideology. It was, as the historian Pierre Kahn puts it, "a key to penetrating and understanding the republican imagination (*l'imaginaire républicain*)."[22]

The concept of object lesson pedagogy evokes a long history of tension between scientific learning and traditional literary education, a history that republican educators had in mind when they debated education reform a century ago. Of the many versions of that history that exist, it is the one delivered by Émile Durkheim as a lecture course on the "History of education in France" at the Sorbonne in 1904 that we review here.[23] The founder of modern sociological method and successor to Ferdinand Buisson as professor of the "Sciences of Education" at the Sorbonne in 1902, Durkheim played an incomparably influential role in shaping the intellectual landscape at the turn of the twentieth century in France. He stands out not only for his efforts in establishing scientific thought as a pillar of republican ideology but also for his part in elevating pedagogy as an area of serious reflection and inquiry.

In the second part of his course, a survey of pedagogical thought from the Renaissance to the beginning of the twentieth century, Durkheim describes the gradual shift from a pedagogy based on book learning and rote memorization to a more active method of study in which the student learns through direct encounter with concrete things in the natural world. For Durkheim, the history of pedagogical thought follows the trajectory of scientific thought in general: scholastic faith in metaphysics as a source of knowledge and the study of immaterial, unchanging rules, principles, and laws gave way over time to knowledge based on empirical observation. Durkheim recounts, in other words, the intellectual prehistory of republican pedagogy.

A binary opposition of abstract versus concrete learning structures Durkheim's discussion, and he sets up two major Renaissance figures — Erasmus and Rabelais — as representatives of the competing pedagogical poles. He portrays Erasmus as the principal architect of classical, literary humanism that dominates secondary school curricula in France (and elsewhere) until the end of the nineteenth century when it would be challenged (and partially displaced) by the growth of scientific education. For Durkheim, the central feature of Erasmus's pedagogy is its insistence on acquiring skills of felicitous verbal expression, or *l'éloquence*. He describes this education as "formalist" (abstract, immaterial) because of the importance it placed on the mastery of a "frozen, immutable form" of Latin dating from antiquity (227). It was formalist, moreover, insofar as the method for perfecting one's Latin required the imitation of select Latin (and to some extent Greek) literary models, or archetypes.

(A preliminary clarification is in order regarding the term *formalism*. What Durkheim describes as Erasmian literary formalism, a concern for abstract models of linguistic and literary perfection, is, as we see later in this chapter, different from the notion of formalism as it applies to textuality and the reader's experience of the text. This latter, more modern, and modernist formalism refers to the individual reader's immediate, "concrete" encounter with the textual object. Erasmian literary formalism — the "abstract" formalism that Durkheim associates with the classical humanities — should not be confused with the formalist reading that I argue enacts key features of active, experiential learning.)

Durkheim prefers Rabelais to Erasmus. The creator of Gargantua and Pantagruel represents what the sociologist calls the "encyclopedic" and "realist" current of pedagogical thought — "encyclopedic" because of Rabelais's emphasis on endless inquiry and insatiable search for knowledge and "realist" because of the writer's focus on the study of concrete things and the real world as opposed to literary models and abstract principles of oratory. The dominant idea running through Rabelais's work, explains Durkheim, is the rejection of rules and discipline and other obstacles to the free expression of one's desires, needs, and passions. At the core of this libertarian abandon is a celebration of nature (210). Durkheim sees Rabelais as a forefather of later empiricists, a harbinger for the rise of experimental sciences. If he describes Rabelais's thought as belonging to the *"courant encyclopédique"* (encyclopedic current) of intellectual history, it is because he aims to situate the Renaissance writer in a tradition that includes the French Enlightenment and its greatest monument, Diderot and d'Alembert's *Encyclopédie*. Rabelais's turn to the material world announces, for Durkheim, the Encyclopedists' preference for Baconian (a posteriori) experimentalism over Cartesian (a priori) rationalism — for the study of concrete things over abstract principles.[24]

Of all the *philosophes*, Rousseau stands out. Durkheim describes a filiation between Rabelais's focus on real things — *la chose* — and the educational doctrines of Rousseau. It is the author of *Émile*, Durkheim reminds his students, who "makes teaching by means of things the sole foundation of all instruction" (23). Indeed, Rousseau's *Émile* is in many respects one long pedagogical treatise advocating sensualist, "realist" learning; it is a paean to the child's direct encounter with the natural world and the study of real things, as evidenced by the following famous passage: "I detest spoken explanations. Youth pay little attention to them and hardly remember them. Things! Things! I can never repeat enough that we give too much importance to words: with our education based on prattle we produce nothing but prattlers (*avec notre éducation babillarde nous ne faisons que des babillards*)."[25]

Rousseau's statement boldly conveys the opposition between words and things that Durkheim traces back to the distinction between

Erasmus's literary formalism and Rabelais's unbridled discovery of nature. It also expresses, however schematically, an opposition at the core of nineteenth-century education reform. We find it, for example, in Marie Pape-Carpantier's conception of object lesson pedagogy that promoted learning by looking (*"l'enseignement par les yeux"*) over learning through words (*"l'enseignement par les mots"*).

Though Rousseau is famous for his radical distrust of literary education and book learning, most education reformers a century later did not take this preference for things over words nearly so far. No one fought to banish language and literary studies from the classroom. But the Rabelaisian-Rousseauist legacy did bring changes to the study of these topics. As many historians of education and literary studies have observed, it produced a scientification of literary culture, an application of scientific methods of active, experiential learning to the study of language and literature.[26] Michel Bréal, for example, the linguist and influential advocate of education reform after the Franco-Prussian War, advocated new methods of language instruction that would minimize the study of abstract rules of language in favor of a more active and practical use of real language: "Nobody speaks deliberately in order to apply a rule of grammar," he declared to a crowd of students at the Sorbonne in 1900.[27] He expresses a similar idea in his famous 1872 manifesto addressed to French schoolteachers, *Quelques mots sur l'instruction publique en France* (Some thoughts on public instruction in France): "To teach French to your students, have them speak, speak again and keep speaking."[28] This call for students to speak, speak, and speak some more is not as incompatible with Rousseau's attack on "wordy" learning as it might first appear. What matters for both of these pedagogues is that learning occur through real, lived experience. By valorizing the subjective experience of the student, the teaching of French promoted by Bréal falls squarely in line with the empiricist pedagogy typified by the object lesson.

The spirit of scientific inquiry also left its mark on literary studies in the secondary program. The traditional humanities curriculum rooted in the study of rhetoric and the imitation of classical authors gave way to modern literary education that placed greater emphasis on skills of close reading and opened the field of study to a larger canon. The idea of the literary text as a model to be imitated was replaced by a view of the text as an object to be explicated. Exercises of close textual analysis (*l'explication de texte*) and expository compositions (*la dissertation littéraire*) designed to train students to observe and analyze the literary object according to modern scientific principles gradually displaced exercises of style and literary amplification. A "culture of commentary" replaced a "culture of rhetoric."[29] To put it bluntly, reading replaced writing. At the university it was Gustave Lanson's new literary history that would lend new, scientific rigor to modern literary studies. The new method, "lansonism," required that the student-researcher account for the literary text in a precise and exhaustive manner by using research in paleography, philology, biographical information, and the study of sources. The underlying forces driving these new practices in literary education were still the basic principles of active, experiential learning emblematized by object lesson pedagogy. Even words, the twentieth-century sciences of language and literature remind us, could be studied like things.

Such faith in scientific learning strikes many of us today as naive. The dreadful events of the twentieth century occurring under the banner of scientific progress have taught us, with the guidance of Frankfurt School theorists and others, to distrust nineteenth-century celebrations of science, progress, and reason. We now hear such old-fashioned shibboleths as expressions of a rigid, dogmatic cult of reason and not that of genuine rational critique.[30] Republican leaders did indeed display excessive, "unreasonable" pride in the achievements and promises of science. French colonial policy under the Third Republic and its *mission civilisatrice* (civilizing mission) are but the most flagrant signs of this Enlightenment-inspired complacency. But alongside such arrogance there remained a pronounced commitment, also in the name of science and the Enlightenment legacy, to restraint, modesty and intellectual prudence. One need only look to the Dreyfus Affair — in particular, to the role of university professors in the Zola trial — to find evidence of a more balanced, self-critical application of these principles.[31]

A similar scrupulousness predominates in the final lessons of Durkheim's course on the history of French pedagogical thought. His last word to his students, aspiring secondary school teachers, insists on the circumspection inherent in true scientific inquiry. Most interesting for our purposes is how Durkheim's vision applies to the humanities. It is necessary to "transform the humanities," he says, "by animating them with new ideas" (380). Durkheim lends his support to the scientification of literary studies already underway. This scientification, however, has implications for the student's understanding of the object of study. Durkheim's main objection to the classical humanities lies in their presupposition that human nature is immutable, thus giving the student a false and oversimplified idea of humanity (384). Modern science renders this premise untenable. The research of anthropologists, linguists, archeologists, and historians presents a different idea of humanity: "it constructs, deconstructs, and reconstructs itself constantly (*elle se fait, se défait, se refait sans cesse*); hardly uniform, it is infinitely diverse, in time and in space" (372). To apprehend *real* humanity, the student must see it as the ever-changing and multiform *thing* that it is. He must observe the "*chose humaine*" (human thing) just as he would the material world: "[W]e must treat ourselves," says Durkheim, "in the same way that we do external things in nature, according to the objective facts that express them . . . we must see ourselves as an unknown reality (*il faut se traiter soi-même comme une réalité ignorée*)" (379).

By expecting the student to approach humanity empirically, treating it as an "unknown reality," Durkheim brings man down to earth. His proposal for a transformed, scientific humanism demotes man from the privileged, central place he holds in classical humanism and resituates him on a par with the natural world. An element of humility accompanies this view of mankind. No longer an exalted figure, he is considered with the same disinterest and impartiality with which one considers any other object of nature. From Durkheim's repeated insistence on the "irreducible complexity and diversity" of the "human thing" emerges a curious conceit about humanity as an object of study. Humanity must appear to the student as something strange, almost foreign. The study of this "unknown reality," says Durkheim, should "disorient" (*dépayser*) the student (380). By this Durkheim means specifically that the student must learn "other ideas, other customs and moral codes, other political systems and domestic arrangements" (384). But his language, *dépayser*, suggests a certain unease in this learning process. It depends upon the student's encounter with the unfamiliar, with the unexplored perplexities of nature. Durkheim welcomes — celebrates even — the discomfiting effect that such learning entails.

It is particularly fitting, given the broader purpose of *The Pedagogical Imagination*, that Durkheim should conclude his discussion of realist pedagogy by insisting on the student's encounter with the object of study as a disorienting experience, as an encounter with an unfamiliar object. As explained in the introduction, one of the goals of this book is to explore the intersection between the discourse of pedagogy and that of literary form, and the very notion of unfamiliarity indicates an important point of convergence. After all, that the literary work has a disorienting effect, that it provokes a fresh, unfamiliar look at an otherwise ordinary object or circumstance, is an idea that was first made famous by the Russian Formalist Victor Shklovsky at the start of the twentieth century. [32] It has become a standard disciplinary concept for almost every student of literature since. In a word, defamiliarization is a central feature of modernist literary form and a basic tenet of modern formalist theory. It is at play when we pause to consider Daudet's formal technique, namely, his curious manipulation of the words VIVE LA FRANCE and the novel connection these words reveal between reading and patriotic duty (which is not to say, however, that Daudet qualifies in general as a "modernist" writer). It is at work in the chapters below in the way the authors and filmmakers use formal experiment that provokes an unusual look at — while also enacting — republican pedagogy and ideology. The question reappears in the conclusion when, in response to the historians Vincent Duclert and Christophe Prochasson's remark that republican culture needs to rediscover its "strangeness," we reply that it is precisely by attending to the defamiliarizing effects of works of art that such a rediscovery can occur. The point to retain for the moment is simply that at the conclusion of his survey of empiricist, realist pedagogy,

Durkheim advocates a principle of modern learning (defamiliarization) that resonates uncannily with formalist conceptions of literary production and reception. Pedagogical theory and literary theory thus appear more closely related than one might ordinarily assume.

INTUITION AND AUTONOMY

The object lesson crystallizes in pedagogical terms a complex set of beliefs and values at the core of republican culture. It is, once again, as the historian Pierre Kahn puts it, "a key for penetrating and understanding the republican imagination."[33] To grasp the full significance of this idea, however, we must understand its relationship to its parent concept, intuition, or the intuitive method. For some nineteenth-century educators, the intuitive method was a general term for any clever teaching device that captured student attention; it was practically a synonym for object lesson pedagogy. For others, however, it was a weighty philosophical notion, "almost a metaphysical key for understanding the relationship between humans and the world."[34] A closer look at intuition will help us perceive the intellectual and ideological stakes inherent in republican pedagogical discourse.

Ferdinand Buisson's article on the topic in the *Dictionnaire de pédagogie et d'instruction primaire* (of which he was the general editor) stands out here.[35] A philosopher by training and inspector general of primary education appointed by Jules Ferry, Buisson was "one of the most representative figures of the Third Republic, in particular with respect to the domain of education."[36] His discussion of intuitive learning is important not only because of his status as one of the masterminds of republican education reform. It also makes explicit the connections between pedagogy and republican ideology inherited from the Enlightenment that places a premium on rational inquiry and intellectual autonomy.

What is striking in Ferdinand Buisson's discussion is his determination to distinguish the intuitive method pertaining to French education from more widely accepted understandings of the term. Buisson's intuition resembles — and yet, he argues, must not be confused with — the Lockean idea of spontaneous knowledge resulting from direct observation of incontrovertible fact. Nor does it neatly correspond to the German concept of *Anschauung* (intuition) referring to the perception of sense data requiring little or no rational interpretation. Buisson shows particular discomfort with the French philosopher Victor Cousin's presentation of intuition as an "act of human intelligence [comparable to vision that] requires no effort, nor reflection, entails no hesitation, takes no significant amount of time insofar as it occurs easily and naturally" (1374). Intuitive learning may be spontaneous and natural, says Buisson, but this does not render it passive or effortless. Disputing the common association of intuition with ease, the educator seeks to link the notion with intellectual rigor and industry. The opening line of the article reveals Buisson's ambivalence. From an etymological perspective, he admits, the word *intuition* signifies vision, a type of vision that is "immediate, certain, easy, distinct and achieved in the blink of an eye (*d'un seul coup d'oeil*)," but this is neither "cursory" nor "superficial" ("*pas une vue sommaire et superficielle*") (1374). Buisson's word choice indicates the kind of nuance he is after: this vision may be simple to perform, but it is not simplistic.

Buisson invokes Descartes, the philosopher most famous for his distrust of sensory perception, to help him make his point. Citing a passage from the *Regulae*, Buisson observes that for Descartes, intuition is "not the unreliable testimony of the senses, nor the misleading judgment of the imagination, but the conception of an attentive mind (*esprit attentif*), so distinct and clear that there remains no doubt as to that which it understands" (1374). The key words here are *esprit attentif*. They signal Buisson's intent to recast intuition more as a painstaking rational activity than a form of spontaneous knowledge. The words even suggest that intuition, as seen by Buisson through this Cartesian lens, conveys a sense of slowness rather than rapidity. For the attentive mind is one that literally "attends" or waits; it moves in a deliberate, unhurried manner. Whether Buisson's ideas conform to the prevailing philosophical thought on intuition is unimportant. What matters are the likely ideological motives for Buisson's argument.

A concern for republican principles rather than the details of intellectual history drive the educator's thinking. He must promote intuitive learning as an active, rationalist endeavor because the suggestion of passive learning and the bypassing of reason raises the bugbear of the Republic's rival in education, the Catholic Church, and its "catechistic" mode of learning decried by republicans as relying on the passive acceptance of received and unverifiable truths.[37] The invocation of Descartes serves to bolster the rationalist pedigree of republican pedagogy. If Buisson associates the concept of learning through sense perception with the rationalist philosopher par excellence who is remembered for his distrust of the senses it is because he seeks to place intuitive learning alongside the cogito as an emblem of France's rationalist philosophical heritage.

Buisson also invokes Rousseau in order to dispel the idea that sensualist learning is effortless and precludes rational activity. He cites the often-quoted line from Book 11 of *Émile*: "[W]e do not know how to touch, see, or hear, other than as we have been taught" (1376). While the human capacity to perceive by the senses may be inborn, the individual's ability to use these faculties to any effect requires practice and instruction. The same passage from Rousseau, moreover, insists that one does not just exercise the senses in order to hone those skills for their own sake: "To exercise the senses is not merely to make use of them, but it is to learn how to make judgments effectively with them" (1376).

At every turn Buisson insists on the penetrating nature of this activity. The exercise of object lesson pedagogy or other exercises using intuitive methods do not only sharpen, refine, and strengthen faculties of external perception for the sake of developing the senses. They also develop faculties of judgment. They are, says Buisson, a form of "intellectual gymnastics." The child who has benefited from this learning "is not only able to see and hear, he can look and listen. He no longer experiences sensations passively or undergoes [submits to] them. He arouses them, guides them, compares them, distinguishes them, measures them, analyzes them: he observes" ([*il] ne subit plus des sensations, il sait les faire naître, les diriger, les comparer, les distinguer, les mesurer, les analyser; il observe*) (1376). Buisson's wording is arresting. The language he uses to describe learning by sense perception insists on the volition and agency of the perceiver. This student-observer is also a creator; he produces or even, according to Buisson's curious formulation, "gives birth to" (*faire naître*) sensations. Buisson's string of verbs, moreover, has an almost incantatory force. These various activities, all elements of investigation, build in Buisson's thinking to a crescendo that ennobles the act of observation beyond any ordinary sense of the term. It becomes for Buisson the most rigorous and penetrating form of scrutiny.

For Buisson it is process, not substance, that is crucial. It is not the knowledge acquired about a particular object in and of itself that counts but rather the training the student gains in the skills of observation. The object lesson exercise can disappear, says Buisson, without the intuitive method disappearing with it. In Buisson's mind the intuitive method describes almost any kind of learning experience that fosters in the student his own autonomous intellectual activity: "Even if one does not show the student objects or images, it can be said that one teaches by intuition [i.e., the intuitive method] whenever, instead of having the student follow his teacher passively and submissively repeat a ready-made lesson, one causes him to search, one helps him find, one puts him on the right track [. . .] letting him take a few steps on his own." And then shortly after: "The intuitive method succeeds at making the child think because it lets him think on his own instead of obliging him to think as we do, because it has him go at his own pace instead of the teacher's" (1376).

Buisson expresses one of the most widespread refrains of republican pedagogical discourse. Republican education reformers emphasized the importance of methods cultivating intellectual autonomy. The teacher was expected to be more of a guide than a master, a pedagogue in the etymological sense of the word. A Rousseauist conception of the teacher-student relationship clearly underlies republican pedagogy. Indeed, one hears throughout these discussions of pedagogy echoes of Rousseau's instructions to Émile's preceptor to minimize his control of the youth's education: "[I]t will be necessary to guide him a little; but very little, without it seeming so. If he makes a mistake, let him; do not correct his errors; wait in silence for him to be able to see his mistakes and correct them on his own."[38]

Marie-Pape Carpantier in an 1868 lecture on object lesson pedagogy explained that its success relied on the principle that the student must be "[an] intelligent collaborator in the lessons he receives from his teacher."[39] In Minister of Public Instruction Jules Simon's landmark 1872 circular to secondary school principals, a blueprint for republican education reform over the next several decades, we hear a similar appeal for a more egalitarian relationship between teachers and students. In a manner recalling the Rabelais-to-Rousseau tradition of experiential learning discussed by Durkheim, the minister of public instruction celebrates an intellectual freedom to explore that liberates the student not only from the confining routine of traditional education but also from the educator's firm control. According to Simon, as the student's autonomy increases, his traditional deference or perhaps even submission to the "*maître*" appears to ebb: "Teachers can never do enough to make the class an active exercise rather than a passive one. In our schools, the teacher is the only one who speaks, the students only listen. But they must speak in class."[40] Again the emphasis is on the student's action and activity; class should be a place where the student does not merely listen passively to the professor but also speaks and participates actively in the lesson. The *maître* should not preach but rather should stimulate or "provoke the student's own observations and discoveries" (224). "The lesson should be a dialogue," he says (224). Learning is not a unilateral process, argues Simon; it depends on a give and take between student and teacher. Short of calling this dialogue an exchange between two equals, Simon nonetheless seems intent on correcting an imbalance between *maître* and *disciple* and promotes the significance — and perhaps even authority — of the student's own voice.

Ferdinand Buisson, in 1903, insisted on the student's intellectual independence in the strongest of terms. Republican education should train the student to question the traditional authority of teacher, *maître*, or mentor of any kind: "[I]t is necessary to take a human being, however young and humble, [...] and have him understand that he must think on his own, that he need not put his faith in, or be obedient to, anyone, that it is up to him to seek truth on his own and not receive it already made from any teacher, director or leader whatsoever, temporal or spiritual."[41]

Buisson's words — an anthem to critical thinking — read like a republican pedagogical credo. They pay tribute in no uncertain terms to Enlightenment values of rational inquiry and individual autonomy, and they express an allegiance to the legacy of the Revolution. But Buisson's words also anchor this ideological imperative in a particular pedagogical project. They endorse methods of teaching and learning that have the child, "however small and humble," seek truth himself rather than receive it from another. As we have seen, republican educators turned to theories of active, experiential learning modeled on scientific inquiry to achieve these ends. One could object that these Rousseauist, "realist" theories were inadequately translated into actual classroom practices. To be sure, such progressive pedagogy does not fully become the academic order of the day until the end of the twentieth century in the wake of the cultural revolution of the 1960s and the rise of a new generation of education administrators and teachers. My point is simply to remind us that this pedagogical thought is already in place at the founding moment of the republican school at the end of the nineteenth century. It was already making its way into the culture of education through various adaptations of object lesson pedagogy and intuitive learning. This scientific learning, moreover, spread beyond the sciences. It infused all of the disciplines and reached every level of education. If the object lesson was "at the base of it all" (à la base de tout), as Jules Ferry purportedly declared, it is because the pedagogical principles that it represented structured an entire vision of learning in the Republic.

MODERN LEARNING AND MODERN READING

As important as Jules Ferry's "*les leçons de choses à la base de tout*" is for our understanding of republican pedagogical discourse, another of his catchphrases is equally so: "*la méthode, c'est la réforme même*" (method is the essence of the reform).[42] What Ferry means is that technique outranks content; *how* one learns is more important that *what* one learns. This is of course a classic opposition in debates on education. Again, it recalls Montaigne's estimation of the "well-made head" (*la tête bien faite*) over the "well-filled head" (*la tête bien pleine*).[43]

We have already encountered this idea in Ferdinand Buisson's remarks on object lesson and intuitive learning. The student does not only learn about the object in question; he also learns how to observe. This pedagogy is not about the object per se but rather the honing of skills of observation and analysis occasioned by the study of the object. Henri Marion's 1889 survey of contemporary pedagogical currents, *Le mouvement des idées pédagogiques en France depuis 1870* (Trends in pedagogical thought in France since 1870), provides a particularly powerful expression of this idea. Marion, a philosopher by training and the first professor to hold the new chair in education (*"Sciences de l'Éducation"*) at the Sorbonne, reminds his reader in the opening pages that the purpose of the school goes beyond the mere transmission of knowledge. Such instruction, he explains, is only of value insofar as it contributes to the fashioning of free men (*"qu'[elle] contribue à faire des hommes libres"*). It does this, he says, "much less through its content than through its form, by its invigorating effect. Another feature of our pedagogy is that it has once and for all understood this truth and increasingly substituted for its misguided faith in programs a concern for methods and discipline, making the final goal not knowledge but culture."[44]

Marion repeats the opposition between *how* and *what* that we have already seen. But he adds an explicit political dimension to it. The concern for method over content has an emancipatory effect. If the purpose of the school is to produce free individuals, it achieves this by the "invigorating action" (*action vivifiante*) of learning methods — what Marion calls "form" — rather than by the transfer of knowledge.[45]

Though Marion uses the word *form* as a synonym for pedagogical method, the opposition between form and content with respect to schooling bears an affinity with the form-content opposition in literary studies and the arts. For Marion, of course, form is about a mode of cognition, a practice of observing and analyzing. Marion's *form* does not explicitly concern aesthetics. It is not a matter, as it is for twentieth-century theorists, of the arrangement of linguistic or visual signs serving to present a certain *what* or thing.[46] And yet, we cannot disregard the similarities between Marion's concept of form used in the context of republican pedagogy and the concept of form as it pertains to the work of art. The *how* versus *what* dichotomy is fundamental to both. In both pedagogy and literary and artistic criticism, the concern for form suggests a shift of focus away from the message or information delivered in an act of communication and toward the procedures — techniques, means, methods — by which such information is delivered and received. In both cases there is a reorientation of attention from message to medium such that, to borrow McLuhan's coinage, the medium is the message.

We have already encountered this opposition in a literary context. It brings us back to the discussion of Alphonse Daudet's "La dernière classe" that introduced this study. There we saw that the fictional character Monsieur Hamel's inscription on the blackboard takes a particularly striking form on the page. The arrangement of graphic signs directs the reader's attention to the techniques and materials by means of which the events of the story are communicated. It turns his focus, in other words, from *what* is being narrated to *how* it is narrated. In so doing, it also throws into relief the reader's own activity of reading. What is more, the formal maneuver projects the reader *en abyme*. It repositions the reader's own enterprise within the space of the story and informs him that he, too, partakes in the fictional teacher's lesson that equates reading with service to the nation. The lesson, in other words, is not only communicated by means of — or through — the language appearing on the page; it resides in that appearance itself, in the kind of reading that such appearance stimulates.

The concepts of form and formalism have changed over the course of this chapter. They no longer connote the abstract formalism Durkheim associated with the literary formalism of Erasmus and the classical humanities. This more modern — and modernist — formalism emerges from the intellectual history that Durkheim recounts. It belongs to the rise of empiricist thought and method that the sociologist calls "realism." In the context of literary production and reception in the twentieth century, a concern for form is above all a concern for the concrete "stuff" with which art is made. It goes hand in hand with the "crisis of representation" of modernist aesthetics, a shift among artists, writers, and critics away from a concern with the mimetic function of art to a preoccupation with the techniques and materials of its own construction. Modernist art, Pericles Lewis reminds us, is an "art that examine[s] its own conventionality, that put[s] the conventions of art on display, an art that put[s] art itself in question."[47] Such art is formalist insofar as it proposes its own formal properties as objects of study in their own right. While we tend to associate this formalism with the literary and artistic experiments of the early twentieth-century avant-garde, it has remained a fixture on the cultural landscape ever since. The *nouveau roman*, New Wave cinema, and later postmodern literature and art continue to draw on this formalist aesthetic. Twentieth-century literary criticism and theory parallel these aesthetic developments. Most of the major critical movements of the past century — Russian Formalism, the American New Criticism, structuralist poetics, and poststructuralism — rely on the idea of form and structure as an integral as opposed to accessory component of the work of art. It has returned to the center stage of literary and cultural criticism most recently, as we saw in the introduction, under the banner of New Formalism.

I have digressed from Marion's remarks about form and pedagogy in order to establish connections between what might at first appear to be the unrelated domains of education and cultural production and criticism. I do so, however, to underscore the simple but relatively understudied point that an empiricist imperative underlies both modern pedagogical thought and modern formalist practices of producing and studying art. Or, to put it in terms more closely related to the literary concerns of the present book, theories of active, experiential learning typified by object lesson and intuitive pedagogy share philosophical, methodological, and even political foundations with staple twentieth-century concepts of cultural production and reception. The discussion of *Les glaneurs et la glaneuse, La grammaire est une chanson douce, L'esquive,* and *Entre les murs* aims to bring this nexus into sharper focus.

I propose, in other words, an intellectual and cultural genealogy that leads from the "pedagogical revolution" of the Third Republic to literary and filmic treatments of republican schooling today. To see this lineage, we must recall the way the scientifico-pedagogical discourse of the Third Republic merges with formal experiments in literature, art, and twentieth-century formalist criticism. It is thus useful to turn our attention to Gérard Genette, who already alerted us decades ago to the linkages between republican pedagogy and modernist literary form.[48]

Reflecting on the transformation of literary studies in the French secondary schools at the end of the nineteenth century, Genette's 1966 essay, "Rhétorique et enseignement" (Rhetoric and education), examines the transition from literary education grounded in the study of the classical humanities to modern literary studies. He describes the replacement, already discussed in this chapter, of a "culture of rhetoric" with a "culture of commentary." A more scientific practice of commenting on, or explicating, literary works and establishing their historical significance gradually supplanted exercises intended to hone, through the imitation of the style of past literary masters, skills of literary eloquence. The new "science" of literature, deemed more rigorous in the eyes of reformers than the antiquated activities of imitation, taught the student to speak and write about literature rather than create it. It trained critics rather than poets, readers rather than writers of literature. Genette argues, however, that rhetoric does not entirely vanish with the decline of the classical humanities. It changes and reappears in other, less obvious guises. The new exercises of expository writing and literary commentary, though touted as stylistically neutral because scientifically objective, relied on an undeclared rhetoric of composition (*dispositio*). This more concealed rhetoric, with its strict rules of argumentation, was just as much a tool of linguistic persuasion as had been the rhetoric of eloquence (*elocutio*) in the past. Genette, in other words, detects continuity beneath the semblance of change: an older, traditional, "imitative" kind of literary studies persists at a moment when a new type of literary studies declared its break with the past.

Genette's essay has deep implications for the circulation of republican pedagogical discourse beyond the classroom walls. A subtle move in its conclusion directs our attention from literary studies in school to the cultural sphere more broadly conceived. Genette observes that the hidden rhetoric of scientific literary analysis shows up in the form of a discourse on literature inscribed in modern literary works themselves:

> Has rhetoric disappeared from our culture, however? Certainly not, for at the very moment that rhetoric became hidden from view in teaching, it reappeared in a new form in literature itself, insofar as literature, with Mallarmé, Proust, Valéry, Blanchot, strove to take on the task of reflecting on itself, recovering in an unexpected way the coincidence of the critical and the poetic functions: in a sense our present-day literature is fundamentally, and despite its principle of anti-rhetoric, [. . .] entirely a rhetoric, because it is at the same time literature and a discourse on literature.[49]

According to Genette, the "discourse on literature" originating in the classroom has become an integral part of literary production. This unavowed rhetoric, he says, manifests itself in the self-reflexive nature of present-day literature (again, Genette is writing in 1966). Mallarmé, Proust, Valéry, and Blanchot are Genette's representative "rhetoricians": their work epitomizes the self-reflexivity of contemporary writing. It is a literature about literature. Genette's evocation of these paragons of French literary modernism points up a linkage between the new "scientific" discourse of literary criticism and modernist aesthetics. Modernist literature, in other words, proposes itself as an object of study as much as, and sometimes even more than, what it represents. Autotelic art calls attention to its own form, to what Blanchot (and many others) call the "materiality of language," "verbal facts," and the "palpability" of narrative texture.[50] It turns our attention away from the represented reality, which now appears abstract and distant in comparison with the literary thing immediately before us.

More significant than what Genette says, however, is what he does not say. Nowhere in the essay does he refer to the Third Republic or republicanism. And yet, their presence is strongly felt. The transformation of literary studies, its scientification and the rise of a discourse on literature, rests on a broader pedagogical foundation that has everything to do with the ideology of the Republic. Changes in the study of literature are motivated by the same spirit of scientific inquiry that drove school reform more generally. The principles of object lesson pedagogy and intuitive learning underlay the entire project. Once again, we recall Jules Ferry's "*Les leçons de choses à la base de tout.*" Republican educators attempted to implement in all disciplines and levels of education notions of active, experiential, autonomous learning crystallized in this deceptively simple classroom exercise. They turned to these pedagogical doctrines as a vehicle for diffusing republican ideology rooted in the Enlightenment tradition. In so doing they aimed to fulfill the ambitions of the heroes of 1789 and assure the survival of the republican legacy. Therefore, when Genette describes the mutation of rhetoric into a (scientific) discourse on literature and traces the permeation of this discourse in the cultural sphere defined by Mallarmé, Proust, Valéry, and Blanchot, the discussion implicitly suggests a genealogy connecting republican ideology to modernist form.

The rise of the modern, autonomous reader is a corollary of modernist autotelism; it flows naturally from the appearance of a "discourse on literature" within literature itself, which, Genette suggests, is a cultural manifestation of the scientifico-pedagogical discourse of the modern classroom. It is in Roland Barthes's "*La mort de l'auteur*" (*Death of the Author*) that we find one of the most memorable formulations of this staple concept of twentieth-century literary studies.[51] For Barthes's idea of the emancipated modern reader — whose birth comes at the expense of the author's death — arises from an understanding of the text as an object of study independent of authorial intention. His line of reasoning and the language of emancipation he uses to advance his argument root his thinking in the same ideological foundation that we have seen in republican pedagogical discourse.

Barthes begins precisely where Genette leaves off, with the giants of French literary modernism: Mallarmé, Proust, and Valéry. For Barthes the end of the author's control over the work's meaning (his "death") and thus the inception of modern textuality and the autonomous reader originates in France with Mallarmé's understanding of the independent status of language itself: "In France, Mallarmé was clearly the first who saw and foresaw the vast importance of the need to substitute language itself for the person who until then was supposed to be its owner; for him, as for us, it is language that speaks, it is not the author" (492). Mallarmé's insight would be pursued, says Barthes, in various ways by Valéry and Proust and through Surrealist experiments with automatic writing. It receives its most scientific treatment through structural linguistics and the idea of the act of enunciation (*l'énonciation*) whereby the relationship between receiver and sender of a message is no longer determined by the intentions of real persons. Rather, it is established by means of the way the language system functions in the text. As opposed to the "work," a product of a flesh and blood historical author, the text is a meshwork of different linguistic and cultural codes that precede and exceed the existence of the individual who sets pen to paper.

Barthes likens the text to a space or surface one traverses as opposed to a veil one penetrates in the search for hidden a priori meaning: "the space of writing is to be travelled, it is not to be pierced" (*l'espace de l'écriture est à parcourir, il n'est pas à percer*) (494). The reader, as the surveyor of the network of codes, becomes the site where the text is realized: "[T]here is a site where this multiplicity comes together, and this site is not, as it has been said until now, the author, it is the reader: [...] the unity of the text is not in its origin but in its destination" (493). The text is that which is experienced by the reader, and the act of reading brings forth the text.

This idea of the text as a space, terrain, or surface the reader explores resonates with themes we have already discussed regarding pedagogical discourse. Barthes's "newborn" reader, emancipated from authorial control, resembles an adventurer, and the text becomes the territory over which he freely wanders and observes. In "De l'oeuvre au texte" (From Work to Text), Barthes explicitly compares the reader's encounter with the text to that of a traveler crossing through an unfamiliar valley. He purposefully describes the valley as a "wadi" (*oued*) to underscore the "disorienting" (*dépays[ant]*) nature of the experience. "What the reader sees is multiple and irreducible; it emanates from heterogeneous and disconnected substances and levels: lights, colors, vegetation, heat, air, bursts of noise, high-pitched bird calls, children's cries from the other side of the valley."[52] Reading, in other words, is a traversal of a textual wilderness.

It is instructive to observe the way Barthes's notion of reading as an adventure, and the reader as solitary wayfarer (à la Rousseau), echoes the conception of reading found in Jules Simon's famous 1872 circular, one of the seminal documents of republican education reform. The republican leader advocates reading as a liberating alternative to the tedium of traditional writing assignments typified by Latin translation exercises (*thème*). "I would prefer," writes Simon, "that the student's mind, like his body, be able to move more freely; that it, too, have its excursions and promenades; [I would prefer] that the book replace a little more often the pen, and that individual inquiry be substituted for the routinized exercises of the Greek and Latin dictionary."[53] In contrast to the unimaginative routine of written translation, indicated metonymically by the pen, Simon proposes reading as an activity that will do more to stimulate the student's mind. The intellectual "excursions" and "promenades" promoted by Simon evoke Emile's famous adventures out-of-doors and his discovery of the natural world. Simon's point is that the mind, too, must have its outings, journeys, and peregrinations. The minister of education celebrates an intellectual freedom to explore, and perhaps even wander, that not only frees the student from the confining routine of traditional education but also from the educator's firm control. Simon proposes reading over writing in the language of active, experiential learning that both reminds us of Rousseau and heralds Barthes.

Reading for Barthes is a fundamentally democratic endeavor. The reader enacts the principles of progressive, egalitarian politics; he "collaborates" with the text; he is its "co-author." By positing the reader as a producer of the text, Barthes puts forward a radical shakedown of traditional literary roles. Since every text is "written" in the present through the act of reading (*"Tout texte est écrit éternellement ici et maintenant"*) (493), reading becomes a "revolutionary" activity. It is "anti-theological" (*contre-théologique*) because it rejects the idea of ultimate meaning originating in, and guaranteed by, the intentions of an absent author. The refusal to fix meaning is thus, for Barthes, tantamount to "repudiating God" (*refuser Dieu*). In other words, Barthes paints the birth of the reader as part of a historical development that parallels the republican renunciation of institutions, traditions, and beliefs associated with the Ancien Régime. Barthes's reader resembles Buisson's republican student, the humble human being, we recall, who must "seek truth on his own and not receive it already made from any teacher, director, or leader whatsoever, temporal or spiritual." Though Barthes would not use the word *truth* in this way (opposed as he is to absolutes and ultimate meaning), he would most certainly subscribe to Buisson's pedagogical method, its anti-authoritarian spirit and emancipatory effect.

The essays of Genette and Barthes reveal the intellectual and cultural continuities running from republican pedagogical discourse rooted in active, experiential learning to basic twentieth-century conceptions of modernist form and formalist, structuralist reading. Despite the underlying philosophical differences between nineteenth-century empiricism and later structuralist approaches to language and texts, a common thread unites them. Both insist on the direct observation and analysis of real, concrete things and reject learning that relies on the passive reception of abstract notions. The idea of "real, concrete things," of course, changes from one century to the next. If for Lanson's generation this meant the solid historical facts (paleographical, biographical, philological) explaining a literary work, these "facts" would be rejected as mere abstractions by later structuralists such as Barthes and Genette. For them the "concrete" object of study becomes the linguistic materiality and structure of the text. The textual surface, its form, is what the twentieth-century reader encounters most concretely and thus on his or her own.[54] Underlying these different conceptions of the literary object, however, lies a similar imperative. The student of the artistic "object" studies it according to the same methodological principles derived from the "realist" tradition that Durkheim traced from Rabelais to the Third Republic. It is a tradition that, as we have seen, became fused with a republican ideology of autonomous, rational inquiry, an ideology crystallized in object lesson pedagogy.

Les glaneurs et la glaneuse, *La grammaire est une chanson douce*, *L'esquive*, and *Entre les murs* are literary and filmic examinations of how these cultural and pedagogical traditions play themselves out. They are works that remind us that the contemporary question of education in France — many would say "crisis" — reaches deep into the republican past. Agnès Varda's film develops most explicitly the historical framework required for viewing the present. For this reason we turn to her film first. The concept of gleaning, which for Varda means (among other things) salvaging fragments of the past, serves as a metaphor for grasping how the works of Orsenna, Kechiche, and Bégaudeau recuperate and rework an older discourse in order to reexamine republican education today. But again — and as they themselves make clear — the historical significance of *Les glaneurs et la glaneuse*, *La grammaire est une chanson douce*, *L'esquive*, and *Entre les murs* does not reside in their thematic content alone; it is not only found in their depictions of classrooms, teachers, and students. The attention they draw to their own formal properties — to their "textuality," Barthes would say — reminds us that the reflections they propose exist also in the activity of literary and filmic reading. The reader and viewer most directly encounter the art object itself through reading and screening that is attentive to form. Herein lies the most immediate — "real" and "concrete" — experience with the actual work. To put it another way, it is in formalist reading that the reader's enterprise becomes active and experiential in terms that resemble the republican pedagogical imperative. *Les glaneurs et la glaneuse*, *La grammaire est une chanson douce*, *L'esquive*, and *Entre les murs* are literary and filmic object lessons because it is this kind of reading that they demand.

2

Visualizing Literacy:

From Pierre Larousse to Agnès Varda's
Les glaneurs et la glaneuse

As its title indicates, Agnès Varda's *Les glaneurs et la glaneuse* (*The Gleaners and I*) is a film about the custom of scavenging for discarded, leftover foodstuffs. Video camera in hand, Varda records the lives of those who, still today, like the indigent peasants of centuries past, gather unharvested fruits and vegetables in the orchards and fields of rural France. She also captures modern variations on this age-old theme, showing us urban gleaners rummaging for produce in trash cans, dumpsters and piles of refuse on the marketplace floor. Not all of Varda's gleaners are downtrodden: some of them are ordinary citizens who, in the spirit of conservation, salvage unwanted comestibles so that nothing should go to waste; others are volunteers collecting food surplus for local soup kitchens. As a general study of consumption, waste, and recycling practices in contemporary France, *Les glaneurs* occupies a place among the most important ecology films of recent years.[1]

But little attention has been paid to the film's concern with reading, the very topic with which the film begins. The opening sequence lingers on the dark leather binding of the Larousse dictionary. The camera homes in on the spine of a volume displaying the letter *G*. As the book opens and the pages begin to turn, a voiceover pronounces the film's first words: "G is for gleaning" (*G comme glanage*). We have all heard sentences like this before. They bring to mind the alphabet primers we used in our earliest introduction to reading. While the camera scans the words on the page,

FIG. I. (1a., 1b.) Close-up shots of spine and page of the *Nouveau Larousse illustré* in Agnès Varda's *Les glaneurs et la glaneuse*.

the voiceover reads aloud the definition of the verb *to glean* (*glaner*): "to glean means to gather up after the harvest" (*Glaner, c'est ramasser après la moisson*). Still accompanied by the camera, the voiceover moves to the entries for *glaneur* and *glaneuse*, guiding the viewer, as one might a pupil, through what resembles a lesson in morphology. The opening sequence looks and sounds like a reading lesson.

Why begin a film documentary about gleaning with this pause over the dictionary? What is the relationship between gleaning and reading, or, more precisely, between gleaning and *learning* to read? Searching for words in the dictionary — neglected, underused, or little-known words — can of course be likened to gleaning. It is a kind of lexical gleaning. But I would submit that even more is suggested by this methodical look at the pages of the Larousse.

I argue in this chapter that the dictionary — specifically, the Larousse dictionary — in the opening sequence is an indication of a fundamental and often overlooked reflection on reading and learning to read that frames the entire film. We shall see that Varda's distinctively logophilic style, on display from the start, is tantamount to a kind of reading lesson redolent of a tradition of republican education. The way Varda uses wordplay and associations between words, images and concepts to stimulate the viewer's critical activity bears a striking resemblance to the methods of language and literacy instruction, known as *lexicology*, developed in the mid-nineteenth century by that staunch republican Pierre Larousse. And Larousse, we should recall, was a schoolteacher and writer of school manuals before becoming a famous publisher, editor, and writer of dictionaries and encyclopedias. Therefore we must not read Larousse's name on the spine of the dictionary, the *Nouveau Larousse illustré*, in the opening sequence of the film as a mere passing reference. It signals that Varda's film is engaged with a tradition of republican education characterized by a commitment to the spread of literacy and universal access to knowledge. Varda's film "gleans" from that tradition, recycles its idioms and rhetoric, and brings it up to date for our age of digital visual media.

That the question of reading and literacy are typically neglected in discussions of the film is particularly fitting given what appears to be the film's main subject matter.[2] If gleaning is fundamentally about attending to those things that others have left behind, then the pursuit of this understudied topic is to approach the film in the very spirit of the film's subject.

The concept of gleaning may be pushed further still. I propose to ascribe to it a metaphorical significance that departs from the film's immediate concerns and speaks more directly to the entire project of *The Pedagogical Imagination*. As discussed in greater detail below, gleaning for Varda is about much more than salvaging food items or sundry objects. It is also about looking to the past. It is about combing through the debris of history and putting back into circulation forgotten or neglected episodes, events, or figures that no longer retain our attention. Just as Varda's film, through the portal of the Larousse dictionary, recovers a forgotten chapter from the history of reading instruction and renews its relevance for today's discussions of visual literacy, so, too, do all of the works studied in these chapters pick through the history of republican education and find a place for fragments of older debates and pedagogical methods in their treatment of modern-day schooling. In other words, all of the works in this study practice the art of gleaning with respect to republican education. They recycle the republican past for their present purposes. Our discussion of *Les glaneurs*, therefore, is also a way of preparing the ground for the chapters that follow. It is a model of the pedagogical imagination at work.

Before delving further into the film's treatment of reading and its recuperation of Larousse's legacy, let us briefly recall several of the more obvious metaphorical possibilities Varda finds in the concept of gleaning. She discovers gleaning in the most ordinary cultural and social practices. As the film's soundtrack occasionally reminds us, rap music, with its tradition of sampling other music and looping, puts back into circulation, or recycles, bits and pieces of sound fragments discovered elsewhere; it is a kind of sonic gleaning. Another example, and a recurring topic in the film, is Varda's fascination with the art of bricolage. She interviews and explores the work of several bricolage artists who, with their keen eye for hidden beauty, are themselves gleaners of those seemingly insignificant images and objects neglected by — or rejected by — the rest of society.

Most importantly, gleaning is a metaphor for Varda's own artistic process, a kind of cinematic bricolage. She turns her handheld video camera on a random assortment of objects — an oddly shaped potato unfit for the marketplace, mold on her ceiling, a broken clock lying in a pile of bulk trash — and collects the stories of various and sundry real-life gleaners. By giving them a place in her film, she puts these forgotten, marginalized things and people back into circulation, recycling them for her own politico-esthetic purpose.

Varda's interest in the past and its metaphoric potential is not limited to the specific legacy of Larousse. The film demonstrates an abiding fascination with history, both distant and near. Her journey, for instance, leads her to consult a lawyer who reads to her from a sixteenth-century edict sanctioning the practice of gleaning. She visits the hôtel de ville in Beaune to view van der Weyden's *Last Judgment*. Contemplation of the fifteenth-century altarpiece brings sweeping historical perspective to her cinematic reflection on gleaning. It asks the viewer to reflect on the relationship between the seemingly commonplace act of salvaging random objects and a bimillenial Judeo-Christian preoccupation with salvation, the salvaging of souls. And one of the most recurrent demonstrations of Varda's historical sensibility appears in the filmmaker's fascination with her own life and career. She incorporates allusions to her earlier films and repeatedly turns her camera on parts of her own body. Snapshots of wrinkled skin, liver spots, and graying hair — bits and pieces or fragments of her "historical" self — gleaned with the camera mark the passage of time and the passing of her life at the same time that they keep this past alive, memorializing it on screen. And yet, all of this — from the Beaune Altarpiece to rap music to Varda's own self-study — is introduced through Larousse. If critics mention the Larousse dictionary at all, it is usually in passing. It is treated as a kind of provisional device intended to guide us toward the film's more central concerns, namely visual images such as Jean-François Millet's famous 1857 painting of gleaners or Jules Breton's 1877 treatment of the same subject.[3]

There is substantial support for this reading. The critics are justified in privileging such visual images over the written text and for reasons that go beyond the simple fact that we are concerned here with a work of visual media. The opening grammar exercise ends when the camera, still moving down the page of the Larousse dictionary, comes upon a black-and-white reproduction of Millet's painting. From there, the film cuts to the original Millet painting on exhibit at the Musée d'Orsay, a cut from text to image. In so doing, by moving from the dictionary reproduction to the "original" work of art, as the voiceover observes, the film might appear to arrive at a true, more natural starting point. The preliminary shots of the dictionary's leather binding, moreover, provide the background for the film's opening credits, reinforcing the idea that words are mere prefatory matter. It might be argued that they are a pretext, and we are naturally expected to get beyond them and turn our attention to what really counts: images. After all, Varda, who began her career as a photographer, is a lover of images and, especially, as she says herself, painting.[4] The filmmaker is a kind of modern-day Millet: she is a painter of gleaners who has traded the canvas and paintbrush for the digital video camera. Given the attention the film will pay to images, visual artists, and vignettes or portraits of real, live gleaners, it is surely defensible to view the opening cut from Larousse to Millet — from dictionary to art gallery, from book to painting — as a turning of our attention to what the film is more centrally about: seeing, not reading.

And yet, I contend that *Les glaneurs et la glaneuse* is as much about learning to read as it is about learning to look and that Varda is a modern-day Larousse. In fact, as becomes evident, the film is not only about reading visual images. It is also about visualizing or observing the act of reading itself.

The dictionary motif runs through the film. Varda's camera and the voiceover repeatedly return to the pages of the Larousse. One of the bricolage artists she interviews, Louis Pons, refers to his bric-a-brac, the raw materials of his art, as his "dictionary." The film's fascination with words, reading, and learning returns most strikingly, however, in the penultimate sequence about Alain Fonteneau, a hawker of street newspapers by day who scavenges for food in the streets of Paris. In the evenings he volunteers to teach immigrants to read in a makeshift classroom on the outskirts of the city. Varda's film, in other words, is bounded by scenes of reading and learning to read.

The symmetry between the beginning and the end of Varda's film, and the rootedness in reading and learning that animates them both, is accentuated even further by the fact that Fonteneau teaches literacy to African immigrants. This brief reminder of France's relationship to former colonies is redolent of the nineteenth-century republican imperative to spread literacy skills to the provinces — that is, to the periphery, to the margins. In other words, it is not only a question of reading instruction that frames the film. It is a question of teaching *everyone* to read. Both Pierre Larousse and his perhaps unlikely counterpart, Alain Fonteneau, represent a fundamental republican tenet of universal education, of spreading literacy to all.

But again, why? Why frame this film that is ostensibly about gleaning with these two scenes of reading instruction? What does reading have to do with gleaning?

Varda's study of gleaning is fundamentally, as Mireille Rosello rightly observes, a reflection on society's practices of collection and waste — about what we keep and what we reject, what we value and what we disregard.[5] Varda's concern with reading is similarly engaged. Indeed, a reading of Varda's film as a reflection on reading does justice to her principal theme. If gleaning is all about attending to the margins or fringe elements — about picking through and selecting among the rejected, overlooked, and neglected food, bric-a-brac, random objects, and images of everyday life — then to be mindful of the topic of reading in *Les glaneurs et la glaneuse*, an understudied fragment of an award-winning film, is to read or view the film as would a gleaner.

This observation raises certain difficulties. After all, how does one discuss the *central* question in a work that is so preoccupied with the margins, marginalia, and seemingly trivial things? The problem, however vexing, is crucial to an understanding of the film. And it has everything to do with reading. Varda's film, in fact, explores a longstanding tension in a centuries-old debate about reading, literacy, and literary education. We can summarize it with a series of queries: What deserves to be read? What can be salvaged or recuperated as legitimate reading material? Which elements in a given work are significant and deserving of attention? Which details are central — and which are peripheral — to the act of interpretation and of making sense? What kinds of works belong in our curriculum, on our bookshelves, in film and music collections? How should we read and, more importantly, teach our students to sort through and read this vast array of materials?

Such questions pitted republican education reformers against defenders of more traditional and often more elite language and literary studies in late nineteenth-century France. Defenders of the classical humanities curriculum, based on the study and stylistic imitation of a limited number of Latin authors, models of formal decorum, were often opposed to the changes that republican educators introduced in the literature curriculum. Traditionalists complained that the introduction of (pseudo) scientific methods of literary analysis were excessively concerned with philological and historical minutiae and neglected the more important *central* task of reading a work for moral guidance or honing one's skills of moral and esthetic judgment. These are debates, needless to say, that continue today as schools and universities attempt to determine the relationship that, say, cultural studies, visual studies, media studies will have with traditional literary studies. We return to these debates below, both later in this chapter and in the next when we consider Erik Orsenna's critique of the structuralist tendency to minimize the distinction between great literary works and other kinds of texts and of the influence of this view on literary education.

Varda's film approaches this historical dimension by using the very reference to Pierre Larousse that she provides at its outset. Again, while critics have mentioned the appearance of the Larousse dictionary, few if any have considered its significance as a structuring device for the film as a whole. A review, however, of some of Pierre Larousse's methodological innovations for reading instruction — in particular, what he called *lexicology* — reveals that his work provides a particularly apt lens for explaining the conceptual connections and verbal and visual slippages that Varda's film expects its own viewers to perform. It also points up the ways in which Varda's own artistic project has ties to a republican pedagogical tradition.

PIERRE LAROUSSE AND LEXICOLOGY

Today when we think of Larousse and his legacy, we think of a hugely successful publishing house and its products, an impressive array of dictionaries, encyclopedias, and countless other specialized reference works. Of the approximately forty titles published in Larousse's own lifetime, it may be only the monumental *Grand dictionnaire universel du XIXe siècle* that we can identify, in part because it has earned a place in Pierre Nora's pantheon of sites of memory.[6] Pierre Larousse, however, began his professional life as a teacher, earning a teaching certificate (*brevet supérieur*) after completing his studies at the Normal School of Versailles in 1834. His second career as a lexicographer and publisher of schoolbooks grew naturally from his passion for studying words and language and his pedagogical innovations in the classroom.[7]

As a provincial schoolteacher under the July Monarchy and then later as a French and Latin teacher in Paris, Larousse experienced firsthand the inadequacy of instructional materials and the futility of prevailing teaching practices that relied excessively on parrotry and rote learning. As one contemporary observed, the tendency was to turn students into "talking machines rather than intelligent thinkers" (*des machines parlantes et non des intelligences pensantes*).[8] Using his own classroom as a kind of experimental laboratory, Larousse devised new methods for teaching that developed the faculties of observation and demanded more of the student's own intelligence. Influenced by a long line of innovative educators going back to the sixteenth century (including Comenius, Pestalozzi, and Jacotot), Larousse promoted active, autonomous learning, the importance of play in learning activities, and the use of images in the learning of language. His views on teaching and learning belong to a heritage of pedagogical thought that would become doctrine for education reformers under the Third Republic.

Larousse's biographer, André Rétif, describes him as an "intellectual bulimic," whose appetite for learning was "encyclopedic" and "gargantuan."[9] In the 1840s in Paris Larousse attended public lectures on any and every topic; he frequented all of the municipal libraries and was, in particular, a fixture at the Sainte-Geneviève library. Larousse's insatiable curiosity was matched by a zeal for the diffusion of knowledge. A supporter of the creation of public lending libraries and evening courses for the working class, he embodied the republican commitment to universal education. One need only recall the Larousse logo — the sower who blows the seeds of knowledge in every direction — to grasp in a single image this republican pedagogical imperative.

The method of language study that Larousse called lexicology was an elaborate series of different exercises all of which were, at the core, about playing with words. It trained students to make connections among words and draw distinctions between them. Many of Larousse's exercises presented students with individual words and then required that they find related terms on their own. In one exercise, for example, Larousse would give the student a common term such as *cemetery* and ask him to find a more technical or scientific equivalent, such as *necropolis*.[10] In other exercises, the student would turn nouns into adjectives or identify verbs and adverbs derived from a common word (*actualiser, actuellement, actualité*). The teacher might also have students turn singular forms into plural forms or masculine into feminine forms. "With the lexicological method," wrote Larousse in the preface to the instructor's manual of the *Grammaire élémentaire lexicologique* (1850), "the student will learn not only to spell words but also to weigh their value, to recognize their etymology, to distinguish their literal meaning from their figurative meaning, to identify their antonyms and synonyms, etc. This double study will be the result of a method of grammar study that has only produced until now dictation exercises and analyses of parts of speech. This is, in our opinion [...] the only way to lead students to write compositions."[11]

This passage evidences Larousse's view that language study must entail more than learning to spell and identifying parts of speech. He impugns the passive and potentially tedious exercises of memorization and the application of abstract rules ("dictation exercises and analyses of parts of speech"). The student of lexicology must "weigh the value" of words, understand their history, appreciate nuances of meaning, and ascertain relationships of synonymy and antinomy. In short, Larousse's lexicology aimed to rouse the student's intellect and engage his skills of discernment and judgment.

In the entry for "Lexicologie" in the *Nouveau dictionnaire de pédagogie et d'instruction primaire*, Léon Flot, professor of French at the Lycée Charlemagne, describes Larousse's method as the study of "word families" (*familles de mots*) or relationships between different words sharing a common radical. He goes on to write that lexicology is "a methodical and sustained study of the variations of meaning produced by a single expression or the relationships of meanings appearing in different terms."[12] Flot, in other words, sees Larousse's program as an introduction to the study of polysemy and analogy, two cornerstones of the then-burgeoning field of lexical semantics.[13]

The preface to the teacher's edition of another of Larousse's manuals, *Analyse et synthèse logique* (1853), most boldly asserts the idea that lexicology aims to encourage the student's intellectual independence: "Our constant goal is to contribute to the student's intellectual development by guiding him to compose, invent [and] construct on his own.

This method produces a veritable gymnastics of the intellect: the young student goes back in some sense to the sources of the French language; he studies it; he probes it with scalpel in hand; and, freed from the restraints of mechanical routine, he examines, compares, reasons, learns."[14]

Although such insistence on active, student-centered learning may sound hackneyed today, it is important to recall that in mid-nineteenth century France when most elementary reading instruction was designed to train students to read the Bible and relied on methods described as catechistic, discussions of pedagogy in these modern terms were perceived to be truly innovative.[15]

It is not easy to assess the legacy of Pierre Larousse's pedagogical innovations. Though Larousse himself was convinced of their widespread influence, André Rétif observes that Larousse's name is surprisingly absent from the history of nineteenth-century education. A significant exception, however, is found in a letter written in 1880 by Ferdinand Buisson, who, as we saw in the previous chapter, was one of Jules Ferry's most influential lieutenants. In a letter to Larousse's collaborator, Auguste Boyer, Buisson writes: "How can one fail to notice that the method for teaching grammar used by Larousse thirty years ago is, except for differences in execution, fundamentally the same method that inspires almost everywhere and in every way primary education?"[16]

In the context of a discussion of Varda's *Les glaneurs et la glaneuse*, it is particularly fitting that Larousse's contributions should be relatively absent (Buisson's comments notwithstanding) from the history of education. As a pedagogical method that has been ignored or overlooked by scholars, Larousse's lexicology is the perfect trouvaille for Varda's study in gleaning. Like the other sundry objects, images, and life stories that the film gleans and recycles, Larousse's legacy is given new life through Varda's art. The linguistic, visual and conceptual associations and slippages pervading Varda's film require her viewer to study, to paraphrase Flot, "variations and relationships of meaning," as if engaged in a lexicological exercise à la Larousse.

The wordplay in its title reveals at once the importance that word associations redolent of Larousse's lexicology will have in the film. The

contrasting inflexional suffixes — the plural, masculine *glaneurs* juxtaposed to the singular, feminine *glaneuse* — draws attention to an uncertain
relationship between the film's two main themes. To what extent, these
near synonyms seem to ask, is it even permissible to compare gleaners
who scavenge for food with artists such as Varda herself? The seemingly trivial difference of morphology draws attention to weighty moral
questions regarding the relationship between art and social issues such
as poverty and hunger. (While not all of Varda's gleaners are destitute,
several most certainly are.) In short, the wordplay in the title is no mere
game. It alerts the viewer to the kind of ethical stakes inherent in Varda's
project. As if she had read Larousse's textbooks from the 1850s, Varda
challenges her audience to "weigh the value of words," "distinguish literal from figurative meanings," and engage in what Larousse called a
"veritable gymnastics of the intellect."

VARDA'S LEXICOLOGICAL IMAGINATION

It is well known that Varda, who coined the term *cinécriture*, is a particularly "logophilic" filmmaker. Her films are peppered with playful
and suggestive word associations. In her own autobiography, *Varda par
Agnès*, we find in particularly concise form evidence of the filmmaker's
extreme sensitivity to — even obsession with — language and wordplay.
In lieu of an ordinary introduction, for example, Varda proposes what
she calls an "introductory synonym" (*synonyme d'introduction*), a ludic
survey of terms — *foreword, announcement, notice, preamble, prologue,*
and so forth — that might serve, each rather imperfectly, to describe the
purpose of those first crucial pages intended to present her book to her
reader.[17] Published only a few years before the release of *Les glaneurs,*
her autobiography offers a foretaste of the pedagogical imagination at
work in the film. In fact, *Varda par Agnès* is a simulacrum of an instructional manual. Varda says as much when she describes it at one point
as an "abecedary" (*abécédaire*).[18] The entire book is constructed so as
to resemble an elementary textbook. Varda organizes her recollections
alphabetically rather than chronologically. Anticipating the "G is for
gleaning" (*G comme glanage*) at the start of *Les glaneurs*, the individual

entries of her autobiography, each signaling a particular episode or aspect of her life, recall the language of alphabet primers and elementary school readers: "A as in Agnès," "A as in Anamorphosis," "A as in Angels," "A as in Artists," and so on through to the letter Z. As if this were not enough to convince us of Varda's deep attachment to her earliest encounters with language and reading, in the entry "*C comme Cahiers*" ([approx.] N is for notebook), Varda reminisces about the school notebooks that her mother brought with them as the family fled Brussels in 1940. The filmmaker's own schooling has left an explicit and lasting mark on her own artistic imagination.

In addition to letting us examine her lexicological mindset and its deep connection to her own experience of schooling, Varda's autobiography exposes her fascination with word-image associations. The margins of *Varda par Agnès* are filled with reproductions of assorted photographs, maps, paintings, drawings, documents (e.g., her certificate of completion of training as a photographer, a page from a school notebook) that complement and interact with the words on the page. The entry "C as in Cats" (*C comme Chats*) provides a particularly concise and playful example. The text reads: "*Je les aime en poils et en os et en dessins de Siné. Voyez plutôt le chat-thon et le Chat-plin, ciné Siné oblige!*" (I like them in fur and in bones and in sketches by Siné. Look instead at the cat-tuna [*thon* means "tuna" in French; *chaton* means "kitten"] and the Cha-plin).[19] The words direct our attention to the page's margin where we find sketches of two cats by cartoonist Maurice Sinet, alias Siné. One of the cats sports the characteristic bowler hat and mustache of Charlie Chaplin. The playfulness here depends of course on the homonymic "*chat*" — both the word for cat and the first syllable of Chaplin's surname. But more important for our purposes is the to-and-fro movement between word and image — between marginalia and the main body of the text — and the resultant interdependence of the two. It is this kind of to-and-fro movement, back and forth between word and image, that Varda puts to even greater pedagogical purpose in *Les glaneurs*.

That this word-image interplay should take place on the page of a book that so deliberately resembles an alphabet primer serves to remind us of the important place that word-image associations have occupied in the history of pedagogy and in particular in the teaching of reading and language acquisition.[20] As the historian of education André Chervel observes, object lesson pedagogy, sometimes called "learning by looking" (*l'enseignement par les yeux*) was considered by many nineteenth-century republican pedagogues as a valuable exercise for learning vocabulary.[21] We should recall, moreover, that Pierre Larousse's *Nouveau petit dictionnaire de la langue française* (1856), a forerunner of the *Petit Larousse illustré* (1905) and intended for schoolchildren and their teachers, was the first illustrated dictionary in France.[22] In sum, as the design and structure of her autobiography suggest, the word-image manipulations that inundate *Varda par Agnès* have deep roots in the history of republican pedagogy.

A REPUBLICAN INSTRUCTION MANUAL

When we turn to the film, we find that the lexicological imagination already at work in *Varda par Agnès* reaches a new level of both playfulness and complexity. It also becomes decidedly political. To see this we must follow Varda as she returns to the pages of the Larousse, still near the film's beginning. This time her camera lights on another dictionary reproduction of a painting of nineteenth-century gleaning, Jules Breton's heroic *La glaneuse* (1877). This moment sets off a chain reaction, a play of associations, that takes us from Larousse, the nineteenth-century pedagogue and lexicographer, to a statement about learning to read and write with today's digital media. The sequence thus shows how Varda's creative project, linking past and present, is put in the service of a pedagogy that is distinctly republican.

Once again, as with Millet's *Les glaneurs*, the dictionary reproduction prompts Varda to seek out the original, and she travels to the museum in the city of Arras where Breton's painting hangs. Standing next to the painting with a bundle of wheat on her shoulder, Varda strikes almost the same pose as the figure in the painting (figures 2a and 2b). She drops the wheat, however, and replaces it with her own video camera. The gesture enacts the point made in the film's title. It draws attention to the way Varda is both like and simultaneously unlike the real gleaner of wheat in

FIG. 2. (2a., 2b., 2c., 2d.) The filmmaker's visit to the Musée des Beaux-Arts in Arras to see Jules Breton's painting, *La glaneuse* (1877) in Agnès Varda, *Les glaneurs et la glaneuse*.

the realist painting. Furthermore this sequence reinforces the idea that Varda is both gleaner of images *and* object of her gleaning. She is both artist and subject of her art. This point gains significance in her next move. She slightly twists her body, thereby turning the camera directly on her viewer (figures 2c and 2d). She looks directly at the viewer while the viewer looks at her. Her gesture calls attention to the viewer's own status as viewer and thus explicitly includes him in the film. We could even say, using the film's own terminology, that Varda gleans the viewer like so many other overlooked objects that the film puts back into circulation. She moves the viewer from the margins to the center. In any event, this gesture identifies the viewer, like Varda herself, as both subject of the film (the object of her gaze) and also a potential gleaner in his own right (as a collector of images by dint of viewing the film). The *mise en abyme*, by establishing an identification between the viewer and Varda herself, informs the viewer that his activity is not — or at least should not be — one of passive spectatorship but rather, like the model gleaner of images that Varda herself is, should be one of active and careful observation of detail.

What is gained, one might ask, by recognizing Varda's involvement of her viewer as part of a chain of associations that begins on the pages of the dictionary? Wouldn't the point here — the activation of the viewer's participation — have been made just as well with the maneuvering of Varda's camera alone? What purpose is served by the complicated montage rooted in the dictionary? The logic of the Breton sequence, taken in its entirety, supplies the answer.

In the continuation of the sequence Varda demonstrates the capabilities of her marvelous new camera. In so doing, she continues the effort to transform the passive spectator into an active observer. As we shall see, the filmmaker does all that she can within the limits of her art form to place the camera in the hands of her viewer. There is a democratizing gesture here, an effort to say to her viewer, "You, too, can learn to be a filmmaker/gleaner." There is also something doubly republican here. First, there is her effort to democratize or popularize the art form. Second, she makes her point through word-image associations that recall Larousse's lexicology. The voiceover communicates her amazement with the new technology: "These new little cameras, they are digital and they are fantastic; they allow us to produce effects that are stroboscopic, narcissistic and even hyper-realistic" (*Ces nouvelles petites caméras, elles sont numériques, elles sont fantastiques, elles permettent des effets stroboscopiques, des effets narcissiques et même hyper-réalistiques*). As we listen to this playful, comical rhyme, made to sound almost childish through the simplistic repetition of suffixes (-ic, -ic, -ic), she shows us the special effects she can produce by manipulating the controls of her camera (she

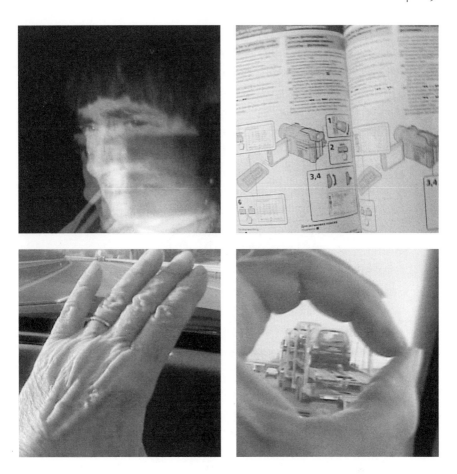

FIG. 3. (3a., 3b., 3c., 3d.,) Various shots illustrating the filmmaker's ludic manipulations of her camera. Agnès Varda, *Les glaneurs et la glaneuse*.

plays back, for instance, her recording in a highly pixilated mode). She appears most impressed by the camera's lightness and maneuverability, which she demonstrates by holding the camera at arm's length in one hand and turning it back on herself so as to film herself in the act of filming (figure 3a). The shadow of the camera's L C D screen places the camera in the viewer's space. It is as if she has put the device in our hands.

Varda includes in this presentation of her equipment a shot of a page from the camera's user's manual (figure 3b). There we see drawings of the camera surrounded by written instructions and diagrams with arrows explaining the function of the device's specific parts. It is impossible, in this film rooted as it is in word associations and lexicology, to ignore the wordplay suggested by this image of a *manual*, or user's guide, of a handheld or *maniable* camera. But there is greater significance here than this apparently superficial lexical game first suggests. For in showing the user's manual, Varda demystifies the art of filmmaking. Anyone in this technological age, the montage suggests, can glean images like the gleaner/filmmaker herself — anyone, that is, who can learn to use this widely available and relatively inexpensive equipment. As the instructional manual reminds us, it is a matter of learning. And learning, we are also reminded, is a matter of reading both word and image.

The sequence has come full circle because the user's manual recalls the Larousse dictionary with which the sequence began. This is the case not only because the dictionary — it, too, an instructional book — requires a reading of both text and image, but also because, as we have seen, Larousse, both innovative pedagogue and publisher of dictionaries, was instrumental in producing numerous instructional books or reading *manuals*. We might even view Larousse's magnum opus, *Le grand diction-naire universel*, or any and every dictionary for that matter, as a manual par excellence, not in the strict sense of a textbook or reader to be used in the schools but rather in the larger sense of a book intended to make knowledge available to all, to place knowledge in everyone's hands. Larousse says as much in his presentation of the *Grand dictionnaire*: "A universal dictionary, which contains everything that has been said, done, written, imagined, discovered, invented, is thus a highly useful work, destined to satisfy an enormous need; for such a dictionary places, so to speak, *in the hand of everyone (sous la main de tout le monde)*, the exact object of every kind of research that one might need to do" (my emphasis).[23]

This is perhaps the moment to acknowledge that the dictionary Varda uses in her film, the *Nouveau Larousse illustré*, published under the direction of Claude Augé in 1898, almost twenty-five years after Larousse's death, is actually a shorter version of Larousse's seventeen-volume *Grand Dictionnaire*. Though the newer *Larousse*, as Augé explains in its preface, aimed to maintain the basic encyclopedic scope of its predecessor, its reduced size was intended to make its contents accessible to an even wider audience than that reached by Larousse himself. Unlike the scientist or intellectual, the general public for whom the *Nouveau Larousse* was created, explained Augé, has little free time to read pages and pages in order to find a simple date or fact: "There is good reason to provide this audience with a midsized encyclopedia, as complete as possible, and that might become the basic reference book in every library, for every family."[24] The *Nouveau Larousse* is, therefore, even more of a manual than the *Grand dictionnaire*. Both by emphasizing the relative ease with which one can handle a modern video camera and by showing the instruction manual with which one — almost anyone — might learn to use it, Varda situates her own cinematic project in a tradition, signaled by the dictionary/manual serving as her point of departure, of making learning and research accessible to all.

The coherence of the sequence beginning with Jules Breton's *Gleaner* depends on our recognition of a play on the words *hand, handheld, maniable,* and *manual,* which, as we have seen, connect, by lexical association, the user's manual to the video camera to the *Nouveau Larousse illustré.* Varda completes this lexicological game by frequent close-ups of her own hands. The ease with which she can film herself with one hand while showing us the signs of age on the other, liver-spotted hand brings together and crystallizes in one image several of the film's complementary themes. With time, technological progress makes potential gleaners of us all. The very last image of the sequence is of Varda's wrinkled hand resting on the dashboard of the car as she leaves Arras and heads for her next destination (figure 3c). This image forms a natural segue to one of the most memorable sequences of the film, the hand-iris sequence.

During one of the film's many on-the-road segments — segments shot while traveling on the highway — Varda discovers a game in which, by touching her fingertips to her thumb, she forms with her hand what resembles a camera lens or iris diaphragm (figure 3d.). Using nothing more than her own hand, she has made the ultimate handheld camera — the manual camera that needs no manual. Looking through this make-believe device, Varda captures — or "be-holds" — passing trucks on the highway. She is merely playing, says the voiceover, but "play" in this film of wordplay is hardly innocent.

The chain of associations that Varda has created embraces much of the republican pedagogical ethos. From the Larousse dictionary, an emblem of a tradition of putting knowledge in the hands of the people to the digital handheld camera and its owner's manual, which tells us that there is a potential gleaner-artist in every citizen, to this sequence in which Varda, like a child on a family holiday, beholds passing trucks by looking through her own hand-made camera, the filmmaker insists on the popularization and vulgarization of the skills needed for gleaning images and thus reading the world. And she accomplishes this through a game of association that recalls Larousse's lexicology and an almost two-hundred-year-old republican tradition of teaching people to read.

ENCYCLOPEDIC RESTRAINT

Varda makes a point of showing us the roads and highways she travels in her search for modern gleaners. These roads connecting different regions of France and different segments of her film can be said to be an outward, concrete expression of the lexical and iconic connections conveying the viewer from one concept to the next. At times one has the impression that Varda is as interested (perhaps *more* interested) in the connections, analogies, and relationships that she establishes between the sundry objects and topics she collects than in the items themselves. It is here that Varda's film invites comparison not with the Larousse as a language dictionary (*dictionnaire de langue*) but with its other function as an encyclopedic dictionary (*dictionnaire encyclopédique*) or even, reaching further back in time, with Diderot and d'Alembert's *Encyclopédie* to which Larousse saw his own project as the successor. Varda's persistent, almost obsessive, pursuit of linkages across word, image, and concept suggests an intellectual debt not only to Larousse's lexicology but also to the extensive system of cross-references (or *renvois*) that, Diderot and d'Alembert explained in their Preliminary Discourse, link together (*enchaînent*) all of the arts, sciences, and trades. Likening areas of knowledge to geographic locations, d'Alembert described the *Encyclopédie* as "a kind of world map which is to show the principal countries, their position and their mutual dependence, the road that leads directly from one to the other."[25] Varda's membership in this encyclopedic genealogy becomes even more striking when we recall that the eighteenth-century encyclopedia's three thousand plates of diagrams, sketches, and illustrations were part of an effort to make knowledge available to the greatest number and that its treatment not only of the arts and sciences but also of trades (*métiers*) was meant to challenge the typical hierarchy privileging the liberal arts over the mechanical arts, also known as *manual* arts.

To situate Varda's film in the encyclopedic tradition is not to praise it extravagantly. The film's gesture toward encyclopedic sweep, particularly with respect to the questions of reading and literacy, poses problems. Its attention to seemingly insignificant detail, its throwing into question the relationship between center and periphery and its implicit exhortation that we all look to the margins for what has been overlooked, point in the direction of what could become, if unchecked, a dangerous mode of reading in which everything is of consequence and nothing unimportant.

This caveat has a historical dimension. As we saw in the preceding chapter, Emile Durkheim described a tension between the "encyclopedic spirit" and "literary formalism" running through intellectual history from the Renaissance to the present and that manifested itself in the nineteenth century in terms of an opposition between science and naturalism on the one hand and elite literary culture on the other. Rabelais, according to Durkheim, was the leading figure of encyclopedism, which, in sum, was defined by the spirit of endless inquiry and an insatiable search for knowledge. Erasmus, whom the social scientist Durkheim compares unfavorably to Rabelais, represents literary formalism, which was less concerned with a broad acquisition of knowledge than with the skills of stylistic and oratorical excellence to be obtained by studying the best examples of a select group of Latin masters. In this admittedly schematic opposition there is an opposition between scientific empiricism and aesthetic restraint and judgment.

At the same time that Durkheim was writing and lecturing, this very conflict between scientific encyclopedism and literary formalism became the battleground between Sorbonne professors practicing the new "scientific" literary history and defenders of the traditional classical humanities curriculum.[26] The latter were mercilessly critical of the encyclopedic, scientific tradition that had become the reigning method of literary study in the university. Henri Massis and Alfred Tarde, writing under the pseudonym Agathon, denounced the influence of scientism in literary studies and the scientific pretensions of "lansonism," or literary history, which, they complained, sacrificed questions of form and interpretation for the sake of meticulous philological and historical details. They argued that the prevailing "disdain for form" at the Sorbonne not only confused students under heaps of historical detail but also hindered students' ability to judge the quality of texts and prioritize significance. Today one hears the survival of Agathon's criticism in certain critiques of New Historicism, namely in the complaint that New Historicist readings, by pursuing the significance of minor aspects of a text, can obscure a literary work's main point.[27]

One might argue that my own reading of the film enacts this very historicist menace, that I have developed a sweeping historical contextualization based on what is only a brief mention or glimpse of the *Nouveau Larousse illustré*. This arguably insignificant detail, the criticism would go, becomes a pretext for constructing a reading of the film that shifts our focus away from what may well be the film's more urgent social commentary regarding practices of consumption and waste in contemporary society.

My view acknowledges this paradox in Varda's own message. Her relentless concern for, and collection of, the overlooked detail or neglected object promotes a reading of her film that overlooks or neglects her primary concern. Her game of associations and cross-references leads in directions that move away from what the film's title suggests is its essence. In other words, the encyclopedic impulse — which may be another kind of intellectual gleaning — can lead us away from interpreting, making judgments, getting to the point, making sense. The attempt to waste nothing and include everything in our reading can become a form of overconsumption in and of itself.

Though Varda's film does indeed exhibit this encyclopedic impulse, it also cautions us against it. Gleaning is not about collecting any and every leftover; it is about a selection process. Though her camera may seem bulimic, her editing process is abstemious. She offsets what sometimes seems like aimless wandering, or cinematic vagabondage, with structure, symmetry, and balance. It is as if she were seeking an equilibrium between two opposing tendencies: encyclopedism and historicism on the one hand and formalism and classicism on the other. More important than this opposition itself is the way the film draws our attention to it, makes us look at it, makes us see it — and even experience it — as an integral part of the act of reading.

FRAMING LITERACY: THE CASE OF ALAIN FONTENEAU

This chapter's final section centers on the penultimate segment of the film, the segment in which Alain Fonteneau, a hawker of street magazines and urban gleaner by day, spends his evenings teaching immigrants to read in a hostel on the outskirts of Paris. It is worth repeating here a point made earlier. By appearing at the end of the film, this scene of reading instruction functions as a companion piece to the Larousse segments at the beginning. It recalls Larousse both ideologically and methodologically. Depicting literary lessons for African immigrants in the Parisian *banlieues* — for people, that is, with otherwise limited access to learning in present-day France — the scene illustrates the commitment to universal education of which Larousse was an avatar. Moreover, Varda insists on showing us that games of word-image association reminiscent of Larousse's lexicological gymnastics play an important role in Fonteneau's lessons. Together these scenes — Larousse at the beginning and Alain Fonteneau at the end — constitute a framing device that highlights not only the fact that a question of reading encompasses Varda's entire project but also that a history of reading instruction survives in the way we read today.

In the basement classroom Varda's camera pans slowly across an assortment of sundry drawings, charts, and posters that Fonteneau has assembled in makeshift fashion to serve as instructional materials for his lessons. Fonteneau has used newspaper clippings, photos from magazines, and out-of-date textbooks — anything he can get his hands on — in order to build his arsenal of teaching resources. He gleans his materials from that which others have discarded. The products of his labor are thus comparable to the works of the bricolage artists encountered earlier in the film. Fonteneau's classroom walls recall the art studio of Louis Pons. The analogy is no accident. It reinforces the idea suggested earlier: Varda's art film is a pedagogical tool, a reading lesson, and, allowing for the wordplay developed above, a literacy manual. Varda, like Fonteneau, is a teacher of reading.

Varda's pedagogical purpose appears most strikingly when we attend to the details of one image in particular — an image that requires a meticulously close reading and that constitutes, in and of itself, a reflection on close reading. The image in question appears only briefly on the screen. The viewer has little time to make out any more than a figure of a woman pointing to a chart or table of letters. With the Larousse leitmotif in mind, we naturally interpret this image as a scene of reading instruction. It appears to be a picture of someone teaching the alphabet. We have before us a representation of an elementary encounter with reading instruction just as we did at the very start of the film.

The reminder of the film's beginning becomes even more pronounced when we note that the female figure in the center of the frame evokes Varda herself. The simple drawing, after all, is of a woman pointing to the letter *G*. The gesture recalls the first words of the film: "G is for gleaning." Varda has serendipitously found a likeness of herself in one of Fonteneau's reading exercises. This image, gleaned by chance, reinforces the idea I suggested at the outset. Varda sees herself and her film as belonging to a tradition of reading instruction. And reading for Varda includes reading visual images. She is a teacher of visual literacy.

FIG. 4. Close-up of instructional materials found in Alain Fonteneau's makeshift classroom. Agnès Varda, *Les glaneurs et la glaneuse.*

A second look at the image underscores just how intertwined reading and viewing really are. Closer inspection reveals that the primary depiction here is not that of a reading lesson after all. It is a picture of an eye exam. The words below and to the right of the woman pointing — "He has good vision" (*Il a une bonne vue*) — help us identify that curious splotch below the letter chart as a person having his vision tested. (We are looking at him as if from behind; he has his right hand over his right eye.) The table of letters, the viewer now understands, is not an alphabet chart at all but rather a Snellen eye chart, a chart used to measure the strength of one's vision. We now identify the figure wearing a dress as an optometrist or vision specialist.

Which is it then, a reading lesson or an eye exam? In the context of this film that opens with a woman's voice indicating the letter *G* on the spine of the Larousse dictionary — an *illustrated* Larousse dictionary no less — it is both. Reading and visualizing (seeing) coexist. The film keeps them both in play as if in an oscillating relationship of foreground and background. Reading is likened to seeing, and looking becomes a mode of reading. What is more, Varda has found here the visual equivalent to Larousse's lexicological exercise in which the student must make distinctions between primary and secondary meanings of words.

Wordsmith that she is, Varda never abandons the lexical for the visual. Consider, for example, the features in this image — namely, words — that assist us in bringing its primary reference, the eye exam, into focus. The written sentence, "He has good vision" (*Il a une bonne vue*), helps us recognize the image for what it really is and what it tells us: it is reading, the reading of words, that enables us to see. In this single drawing tucked away among the various instructional materials that Fonteneau uses to teach literacy in the basement of a hostel on the outskirts of Paris, Varda has found the ultimate image for communicating all of the strands that her film weaves together. It would be hard to imagine another image that could so effectively capture the symbiotic relationship between seeing and reading that Varda promotes throughout the film.

But Varda, again, does not merely *show* us reading; she *teaches* us to read. She manipulates the images she presents so as to compel her viewer to play an active role in selecting, choosing, prioritizing — all of which are components of gleaning. And gleaning for Varda is tantamount to reading. We see this pedagogical strategy in the way Varda frames the eye chart/reading lesson figure. In order to direct our attention to the central figure of the woman and the letter chart, Varda could have cropped the frame more closely. She could have exercised more control over what her viewer sees (and does not see). She has chosen, however, to include the fragments of words and sentences that surround the central figure. It is as if she wants us to negotiate, or pick our way through, this semiotic clutter or bric-a-brac. Her organization of the frame, or lack thereof, passes interpretive responsibilities to her reader/viewer. We see this, for example, as our eye moves across the frame. As we read the image from top to bottom and left to right, it is not immediately apparent what the relationship is between the uppermost sentence — "She washes the glasses" (*Elle lave les verres*) — and the central figure with which it borders. It is only when we read the sentence below the letter chart — "He has good vision" (*Il a une bonne vue*) — that we understand that the sentence above has, in fact, no immediate semantic relationship with the woman pointing at the letters.

There is one more element here that reinforces the idea that Varda has cropped or composed this image in such a way that reveals the tensions and tasks involved in any act of looking, reading, and gleaning. Knowing what we do about Varda's predilection for wordplay, we cannot overlook the pun in this frame on *verres* as "drinking glasses" and *verres* as "looking glasses." Though we may understand "drinking glasses" as the primary meaning of the word *verres*, a Francophone viewer might well notice the rather simple pun. Doing so reintegrates the upper sentence into the semantic logic of the eye exam/reading lesson.[28] Such wordplay, recalling the concern for "relationships of meaning" that we saw in Larousse's lexicology, pulls our attention back toward the uppermost sentence, challenging the more obvious, more convincing relationship between the picture and the sentence underneath it: "He has good vision."

To read and get the pun is to put into play a decision-making process, an activity of organizing, selecting, prioritizing, determining which relationships are legitimate and which are "stretching" it. It raises a tension between indiscriminate, all-inclusive, or encyclopedic reading and a more judicious act of interpretation that involves selecting, privileging, and discarding. Varda composes the frame such that the reader/viewer must take responsibility for doing part of the framing. She places the editing process, so to speak, in our own hands. As with the playful montage, voiceover, and manipulation of the handheld DV camera that we observed earlier, Varda's art here again doubles as a kind of manual — an instructional work intended to train her own viewer in the act of viewing/reading. And it is in such maneuvers, given the Laroussian context we have developed up to now, that we see a pedagogical gesture that is decidedly republican. It aims to teach everyone to read.

My own reader might object that Varda could not possibly expect any ordinary viewer to read this one image as closely as I have done. It is necessary to stop the film and isolate this frame in order to study it in such detail. No ordinary moviegoer can do this. But it is something we *can* do on our DVD players or personal computers. In other words, modern digital technology enables us to study the film meticulously. It permits us to glean (read) its most minute details. This is an obvious point about technology and might ordinarily go without saying. But, in *Les glaneurs et la glaneuse*, by repeatedly showing us her handheld DV camera and all that it allows her to do, Varda makes this point with particular vehemence. Modern technology, such as new electronic media, is *manual* technology insofar as it enables us to *manipulate* and read the film in new ways, in ways that put control into the hands of the individual user, viewer, and reader.

Varda, I suspect, would disagree with this last point about modern digital technology. She would say that this technology enables us to read the film precisely in old ways because it enables us to read the film much as we would read a book. The ability to start, stop, go back, and zoom in on a particular passage is in some ways more like reading a book than what has traditionally been the twentieth-century experience of watching film or television. Here again, we encounter Varda's concern with historical continuity and change. The past, she would argue, is still with us. Just as she documents the legacy of gleaning, the way an old practice survives today in altered form, and just as the artistic portrayal of gleaning so famously exemplified by Jean-François Millet survives in the example of her own filmic art, so, too, does a republican idea of reading and the spread of literacy survive in the possibilities afforded by our modern digital technology. Varda salvages a republican tradition of reading instruction and recycles it for the digital age.

3

Teaching Suspicion

Erik Orsenna's *La grammaire est une chanson douce*
as a Modern *Tour de la France par deux enfants*

"Beware of me!" (*Méfiez-vous de moi!*)[1]

So reads the first line of Erik Orsenna's best-selling tale, *La grammaire est une chanson douce* (*Grammar Is a Gentle, Sweet Song*).[2] Spoken by the narrator, a sassy ten-year-old girl named Jeanne, the opening words are intended to grab our attention, to put us on alert. They give us reason from the start to be suspicious of the character relating the story about to unfold. Indeed, Jeanne goes on to warn us that she is not what she seems. She may appear "mild-mannered, shy, dreamy and small" (11) for her age, but the reader should think twice before attacking her. "I know how to defend myself," she quips before reminding us that she has "the most warlike of given names": "Jeanne as in Jeanne d'Arc, the shepherd girl turned general, scourge of the English" (11, 9). She delivers this menace playfully, of course, as would any smart-alecky kid. Then, suddenly, Jeanne reverses course.

No sooner has she cautioned us not to be fooled by her gentle appearance than she retracts her warning and calms her menacing tone. "That said," she adds, "I am deep down what I appear to be on the surface" (11). Jeanne, in other words, is and is not what she seems.

It is one thing for a narrator to put the reader on guard, to pique his curiosity by warning that things are not as they appear. Much literature, and perhaps art in general, depends on this device to engage its audience. It is another matter, however, to pique the reader's distrust *and* attempt to allay this caution in what amounts to the same breath. The opening of Orsenna's little tale displays a curious attempt to both win and shake the reader's confidence from the start, to make the reader simultaneously suspicious and trustful.

Jeanne's comments about her uncertain reliability as a narrator raise questions as to how we should read her tale. It is the story of a transatlantic voyage she takes with her brother that is cut violently short by a storm at sea. The resulting shipwreck leaves the two schoolchildren unable to speak. They wash ashore on an enchanted island "inhabited" by real, live words and eccentric wordsmiths where they begin the process of reacquiring their lost language. Their reeducation, which is also an intellectual journey through French grammar and parts of speech, begins from scratch. They first discover individual letters and then words and phrases. Later, Jeanne (her brother, Thomas, turns his attention to music) will begin to form sentences and paragraphs on her own. By the end of the story, when Jeanne regains the ability to speak, she also begins to invent a story of her own: she becomes a budding creative writer. She also chances upon, in the fictional flesh, three of France's literary giants: Antoine de Saint-Exupéry, Marcel Proust, and, most importantly, Jean de la Fontaine. Her reacquisition of language thus culminates in a communion with France's literary patrimony. In sum, the story traces a direct line from the acquisition of language to literary invention, a trajectory, moreover, that describes a renewal of ties with a national literary tradition.

But, again, what are we to make of the mixed message in Jeanne's opening remarks? Of her ambiguous warning — or reassurance — that the reader must be both suspicious and trusting of what she has to say? Should we take her story at face value, as just a charming and fanciful children's tale? Or is something more cunning lurking in its pages? Like Jeanne herself, is it or is it not what it seems?

It is of course both. Jeanne's two-facedness corresponds to two different levels on which the story operates. It is, on the one hand, a children's story, a story for and about children. It is also, however, a subtle and sophisticated reflection on a tradition of language and literary education in France. Like Jean de la Fontaine's *Fables* or Saint-Exupéry's *Little*

Prince, illustrious works in the moralist tradition in which Orsenna's story seeks a place (so much so that these writers have a place in his story), *La grammaire est une chanson douce* speaks to children and adults at the same time. It addresses young, innocent readers and those who read between the lines. Needless to say, it is this second type of reading that we pursue in the following pages.

The present chapter argues that the language of trust and distrust in Jeanne's opening words refers to more than just this story alone. The opposition points to a longstanding tension with respect to literary studies in republican education, one that is hotly debated today but that has its roots in the pedagogical doctrines of the Third Republic. The language of trust and distrust is but a simplified manner of designating competing positions regarding literature and literary education; it crystallizes conflicting attitudes about the status and practice of reading. As our discussion of *La grammaire est une chanson douce* shows, this opposition can be reformulated in several different ways. It is a contest between, on the one hand, a sentimental, trusting admiration of the literary work and, on the other, an investigative, critical approach to the literary "text" that treats it first and foremost as an object of dispassionate study. The first attitude understands the work as an object of beauty, a source of moral guidance and a means of personal edification. The second treats it like (almost) any other object of scientific observation: a thing to be dissected, analyzed, and exposed, the concealed inner workings of which can only be explicated by a trained reader. What emerges in this cursory unpacking of the trust-distrust opposition is that it contains within it the classic struggle between a traditional appreciation of literature and a modern, scientific analysis of literature — a binary that can be reformulated yet again and even more generally in terms of a feud between humanistic and scientific learning, between tradition and progress, past and present, and, of course, ancients and moderns.

My reading of *La grammaire est une chanson douce* shows how Orsenna, using the vehicle of the children's tale, navigates his way through the competing imperatives of literary appreciation and scientific analysis. To see this we need to consider the double logic of the text. It attacks the encroachment of science on literary studies, and yet it uses the very principles of active, inductive learning and object lesson pedagogy — emblems of the republican commitment to elementary scientific methods in all areas of study — to stimulate the characters' and readers' direct encounter with language. Like the other works examined in *The Pedagogical Imagination*, *La grammaire est une chanson douce* displays an explicit debt to a longstanding tradition of experiential, "realist" (Durkheim) learning; it turns reading into an unmediated encounter with verbal and visual facts and literary objects. At the same time, however, Orsenna's text cautions us against the excesses of scientism in the literary domain.

The first chapter, set in a literature classroom before the adventure proper begins, sets up the Manichean lens (trust versus distrust; literature versus science; magic versus reason) through which the rest of the story will be read. It is here that Orsenna delivers a polemic against the nefarious influence of scientistic (mainly structuralist) approaches to literature in the secondary school curriculum. The story seems to side with defenders of traditional, humanistic literary studies who claim that the overly technical, jargon-filled literary education promoted by the Ministry of Education in recent years fosters a disenchantment with literature and a disregard for the study of the language from which such literature is produced. The opening chapter, a structuring device for the rest of the story, unequivocally takes up the cause of this traditionalist position.

Once the journey is underway, however, the children's reeducation bears the mark of the legacy of republican scientific learning. They explore the French language in all of its constituent parts. Their gradual rediscovery of letters, words, and phrases as the raw material of literary production simulates an extended exercise of hands-on, experiential learning. Their voyage starts from the most simple, concrete elements of language and arrives at an abstract concept of French literary patrimony: it is, in other words, a literary object lesson. What is more, Orsenna's story bears a remarkable resemblance to one of the most famous literary monuments to republican education, which also happens to be a famous children's travel narrative, *Le tour de la France par deux enfants*, G. Bruno's best-selling school manual published in 1877.[3]

By reading Orsenna's story against the backdrop of this consecrated site of republican memory (*"un lieu de mémoire"*), a dialogue emerges between past and present.[4] The striking similarities between the two tales suggest that Orsenna is working within a republican pedagogical tradition of which *Le tour de la France par deux enfants* is the quintessential monument. But these similarities also throw into relief key differences, the most significant of which concerns the status of literature and French literary patrimony. Reading these works together brings into the open a neglected or muted theme in Bruno's republican paean: the underside of the manual's enthusiasm for scientific knowledge and education harbors an understated yet sustained distrust of fictional literature. In the end Orsenna's story may display a debt to republican scientific pedagogy, but it also constitutes a corrective to what could be described as latent republican mythophobia, the fear and distrust of stories.

A MANICHEAN CLASSROOM

Before turning to the adventure story proper, we must look more closely at the opening chapter because it establishes the framework through which the rest of the narrative will be viewed. The narrator, Jeanne, just after introducing herself to the reader and before she describes the ocean journey, recounts a scene that takes place in her French class prior to Easter break. She describes a confrontation between her French teacher, Mademoiselle Laurencin, and an inspector from the Ministry of Education, Madame Jargonos, who has come to observe the quality of Laurencin's teaching. It is clear from the conflict between these two characters, both educators, that they are meant to allegorize conflicting views toward the teaching of language and literature.

The characters' names indicate the nature of their opposition. The innocent and youthful Mademoiselle Laurencin's name calls to mind the laurel crown worn by victorious athletes, warriors, and, of course, poets; it is a symbol associated with Apollo, the youthful god of truth, music, poetry, and the arts. That Laurencin's name should bring to mind Apollonian attributes is reinforced by its evocation of Marie Laurencin, the cubist painter and one-time lover of Guillaume Apollinaire. The young French teacher thus symbolically celebrates not only the literary arts but all arts and the relationships between them.

Laurencin's opponent, Madame Jargonos, is an irascible older woman whose job is to ensure that teachers adhere to the official state curriculum for teaching French language and literature. As her name suggests, Jargonos personifies an entirely different relationship to language, literature, and the arts. Literary studies for her and the ministry she represents consists of using pseudoscientific, technical terminology in order to analyze texts dispassionately. The literary jargon that she embodies is at best utilitarian and at worst artless and dull. And, indeed, she quite literally embodies it: she is pure skin and bones, so wizened and skeletal that for a moment Jeanne cannot tell if she is a man or a woman. If Mademoiselle Laurencin is youthful and full of life, Jargonos is her cadaverous opposite. The allegorical logic is plain to see: literature, represented by Laurencin, is a world of lively and innocent enchantment; the science of literature is its mortal enemy.

The inspector's visit coincides with a unit devoted to Jean de la Fontaine's *Fables*. Mademoiselle Laurencin is passionate about the seventeenth-century moralist and guides her students from fable to fable as if strolling "through the brightest and most mysterious of gardens" (12, 10). She emphasizes how the poet's careful word choice makes his subjects — the frogs, foxes, and rabbits that inhabit his fables — come alive. "Words," she reminds her students, "are real magicians. They have the power to make things spring up before our very eyes, things that we aren't actually seeing" (10, 13). In her discussion of one particular fable, "The Wolf and the Lamb," Mademoiselle Laurencin draws her students' attention to La Fontaine's surprising manipulation of verb forms. The poet unexpectedly shifts from the past to the present tense, the teacher explains, in order to make the wolf's arrival seem all the more sudden and thus frightening for the reader.

At the very moment Mademoiselle Laurencin pronounces these words, Madame Jargonos, as if she were the wolf herself, interrupts the peaceful lesson and chastises the younger teacher for her "unorthodox" pedagogy: "Yes, yes," snaps the Inspector,

I can see the approach you're using. Approximation, lack of precision . . . Paraphrase, when your assigned task is to make the students aware of narrative structure: What is it that provides for textual continuity? What type of thematic progression are we dealing with here? What are the component elements of the enunciative situation? Are we dealing with narrative or discourse? Those are the basic elements that must be taught! [. . .] Mademoiselle, you do not know how to teach. You are not following any of the directives of the [Ministry of Education]. Complete lack of theoretical discipline, complete absence of scientific method, complete failure to distinguish between narration, description, and argument. (16–17, 14–15)

When Mademoiselle Laurencin diffidently protests that her students are only in sixth grade, Madame Jargonos retorts, "What of it? Are French youngsters not entitled to sound scientific principles?" (17, 15). The inspector thereupon sends the young teacher off for retraining, or "pedagogy treatments" (*soins pédagogiques*), at what is ominously referred to as the "institute" (17, 16).

It is worth underscoring Madame Jargonos's insistence on rigor, precision, and *scientificité*. One might be inclined to see this overblown language as only a sendup of the pseudoscientific jargon of recent literary studies and their institutionalization. We should not, however, let this obvious fact dull our perception of a larger historical comment. Madame Jargonos's wording recalls a longstanding association between scientific learning and republican ideology, the very association that one finds crystallized in object lesson pedagogy and its pivotal place ("*à la base de tout*") in republican education reform. When Jargonos asserts that French children should have a right to the exact sciences ("*Les petits Français n'ont pas droit à de la science exacte?*"), she uses a language of justice and democratic equality hitched to scientific learning that would have easily rolled off the tongue of a republican educator in the 1880s. In other words, Jargonos's position suggests a continuum running from an older republican enthusiasm for scientific education and a more recent scientification of literary studies.

Madame Jargonos's display of absolute power over the gentle and defenseless Laurencin, moreover, identifies these two characters with La Fontaine's wolf and lamb. Orsenna has adapted the seventeenth-century allegory of strength versus weakness, or brutish force versus cultured civility, to address the contemporary power struggle in French literary education. It is particularly fitting that a fable of La Fontaine should provide the lens through which to examine the question of literary education in today's republican school, for, as Ralph Albanese reminds us, the seventeenth-century fabulist was one of if not *the* most studied French poets in the schools of the Third Republic; like Victor Hugo, he is "the poet par excellence of republican France."[5] Orsenna's story is, in other words, layered with multiple evocations of La Fontaine. To consider today's school question through such a filter is not only to bring a neoclassical, humanist sensibility to bear on the present but also an earlier republican tradition as well. We return to this question of the republican tradition when we consider the extent to which the scientific republicanism of G. Bruno's *Le tour de la France par deux enfants* can be shown to provide an alternative and partially competing paradigm through which to read Orsenna's story. For the moment we must turn our attention to the contemporary debate that Orsenna's characters allegorize.

THE DISCOURSE OF SUSPICION

Any reader following French education debates in recent decades would probably recognize the unspecified institute where Madame Jargonos sends Mademoiselle Laurencin for retraining as an allusion to the *Instituts universitaires de formation des maîtres* or IUFMs, as they are commonly called. Created by Lionel Jospin's government in 1989, these teacher training institutes were meant to consolidate and modernize the training of future primary and secondary school teachers. Since 2000, however, they have come under frequent and often scathing attack. Critics denounce them as bastions of a spurious science of education and purveyors of feckless pedagogical fashions. They are accused by some of bearing the responsibility for the recent decline in the quality and rigor of French education.[6]

More important than the allusion to the IUFMs is the evocation of recent debates regarding the permeation of secondary school French class by what some regard as arcane literary theories and needlessly complex — and deleterious — practices of literary analysis. For Madame Jargonos insists on the importance of scientific rigor in literary education in a language (or "jargon," according to detractors) that brings to mind the vocabulary of structuralist theory and its kindred theories, narratology and discourse analysis. She uses the words (*discourse, text, structure, enunciative situation*, etc.) that aficionados of literary studies readily recognize as the terms of literary analysis bequeathed to us by critics and theorists such as Gérard Genette, Tzvetan Todorov, and, above all, Roland Barthes.

It is not necessary to review the details or various permutations of structuralist literary theory or, for that matter, its influence on advanced literary studies. It should suffice to recall that, in its heyday of the 1960s, theorists and practitioners of structuralism sought to bring a new scientific rigor to literary studies based on methods of analysis borrowed from structural linguistics. As its name suggests, literary structuralism ("structuralist poetics") may be summarized as, above all, the study of the way literary texts are structured or assembled. It follows from this that structuralist analysis, as it is often said, shifts attention away from *what* a literary work means to the analysis of *how* that meaning is produced by the text — in other words, how such meaning is "constructed."[7] Gérard Genette succinctly captures the would-be scientific and objective nature of this approach to literature when he writes: "Literary structures are at the heart of the work of course but like its hidden framework, like a principle of objective intelligibility [that is] only accessible, by means of analysis and communication, to a type of geometric mind that is distinct from conscience."[8] This is no doubt why Madame Jargonos resembles a skeleton. All skin and bones, the "skeleton-lady," as she is called by Jeanne, quite literally embodies the idea of hidden, underlying structure exposed.

According to critics of the excessive influence of structuralist theory in the classroom, the methods of literary analysis personified by Madame

Jargonos breed a harmful distrust of literature among students. The "science of literature" promotes a suspicion of literature that in the end tolls the death knell for literary studies in general since it quashes the development of a sentimental, personal relationship with the literary work of art. We find an example of this complaint leveled against "official" literary studies in an article by two teachers, Mireille Grange and Michael Leroux, appearing in a 2005 special issue of *le débat* devoted to reform of the French curriculum. Grange and Leroux reserve their strongest criticism for the emphasis in government directives (*"instructions"*) on the teaching of discourse analysis, the systematic study of the mechanisms of language with which texts are constructed. Such analysis, lament Grange and Leroux, privileges questions of form and method over questions of content. It is more concerned with how meaning is produced than with what works actually mean. Grange and Leroux also criticize the way the curriculum treats every kind of text as an example of "discourse" and, consequently, subject to the same kind of critical analysis. This approach, they complain, minimizes the distinction between literary works and other "textual objects" composed of linguistic signs (e.g., newspaper articles, song lyrics, political speeches).

Of the different types of discourse studied, the argumentative discourse (*"argumentation"*), according to Grange and Leroux, causes the greatest concern because it is viewed as ubiquitous: every text is a potential argument and can be analyzed as such. To illustrate the prevalence of this viewpoint among leading French education officials, the authors cite the following observation made by Alain Boissinot, a high-ranking administrator in the Ministry of Education: "There is no impermeable wall separating different kinds of discourse, and often, that which is perceived as the most eminently literary, the metaphor, or the aesthetic display of description, belongs to the discourse of argumentation."[9] Recognizing a certain value in this idea, Grange and Leroux argue, however, that it has been carried too far. When it goes unchecked, it promotes an act of reading that amounts to little more than trying to "outsmart a Voltaire or a Hugo" (*déjouer les manigances d'un Voltaire ou d'un Victor Hugo*).[10] Reading, in other words, becomes an act of distrust, of suspecting the author of trickery, and structuralist analysis provides the tools needed for exposing, dismantling, or deconstructing the supposed stratagem.

This culture of suspicion, note the critics, spreads beyond the secondary school classroom. The writer and literature professor Danièle Sallenave hears it expressed in the way university students talk about literature. In oral exams, for example, she has observed that students habitually preface their comments with "the author claims that ..." (*l'auteur prétend que...*). Sallenave interprets these words as the expression of "[a] distance with respect to the author, the desire not to be trapped or tricked by him or quite simply influenced by his thought."[11] Sallenave, like almost every teacher, recognizes the importance of teaching students to read critically, a sine qua non of the school's (and university's) mission to educate freethinking individuals. But the excessive emphasis on treating all texts as if they were argumentative discourses produces a dangerous kind of double standard. It teaches a distrust of what the other — any other — has to say and fosters an uncritical faith only in the student's own point of view, in what "I" have to say. The program that teaches this culture of suspicion turns students away from the time-honored idea that one finds oneself through great works of literature. It dismisses the (Arnoldian) idea that one is educated with the help and guidance of those who have come before. "On the contrary," write Mireille Grange and Michel Leroux, "the study of argumentative discourse aims to construct the 'self' not with the help or beneficial influence of the other but rather with a preset refusal to consider the discourse of any authority. Without appearing so, the introduction in French class of the study and practice of the 'argumentative discourse' is the total reversal of the foundation of all teaching, the destruction of what makes teaching possible."[12]

The concerns expressed by Grange and Leroux and by Sallenave are not limited to France. A similar complaint can be heard in discussions of literature programs in the American university. In a 2002 essay appearing in the *PMLA*, David A. Bell, then chair of the Department of Romance Studies at Duke University, laid a certain responsibility for undergraduate disaffection for literature at the feet of their professors trained in the era of "high theory" of the 1970s and 1980s. Inspired by what Bell calls "watered-down Derridianism" or the Foucauldian idea that the literary text is a discursive field like any other in which power and ruse are played out, they teach their students to view every literary text as "somehow a lie and a subterfuge."[13] In language redolent of the charges that Grange, Leroux, and Sallenave direct against France's literature curriculum inspired by structuralist theory, Bell observes that "[h]igh theory in the 1970s and 1980s supposedly taught us how to manipulate literary texts without being manipulated by them."[14] He concludes by saying that in order to stimulate undergraduate interest in literary studies, "university literary critics will have to abandon easy exercises in undermining the credibility of the literary text, which means they must overcome suspicion and once again give a modicum of respect to what the literary texts have to offer."[15]

Whether or not one subscribes to the foregoing assessments of the impact of the literary "sciences" on students' disaffection with — their distrust or suspicion of — literature, it is clear that laments of this sort have increased in recent years on both sides of the Atlantic and in both secondary and postsecondary education. Consider, for example, the recent book by Anthony T. Kronman, *Education's End: Why Our Colleges and Universities Have Given Up on the Meaning of Life*. Kronman, former dean of Yale Law School, paints in broad brush strokes the way disciplinary specialization and the research ideal among university faculty depreciates the kind of communion with great literature that was the hallmark of traditional humanistic studies. The research ideal, writes Kronman,

> devalues the communion with past writers and artists to which secular humanism attached such importance. The immediacy of one's engagement with the great works of the past; the sense of being in the present company of their creators; the experience of contemporaneity that is implied by the idea of the great conversation which the tradition of arts and letters sustains: all of these ideas become suspect, or worse, from the standpoint of the ethic of supersession. The notion of a timeless conversation in which the great voices of the past still speak with undiminished authority, that never concludes and never

changes, where all the generations are present at once, is to those who judge things from the standpoint of this ethic not an impractical ideal but a bad one that denies the possibility of that very progress in understanding that is the scholar's deepest reward.[16]

Kronman does not explicitly mention any of the particular variants of structuralist or poststructuralist theory. And yet these have been the mainstays of literary research and scholarship since the 1970s and thus the driving intellectual force behind the research ideal that Kronman describes. Indeed, it is commonly argued that part of the appeal of high theory and the "science of literature" among literary scholars is that they lend a methodological rigor to the study of literature, thereby according it greater disciplinary respect next to the more "solid" social and natural sciences.[17] Most striking in the above passage is the way Kronman uses the language of distrust and suspicion ("all ideas become suspect") to describe the forces undermining the tradition of secular humanism. The idea of the "timeless conversation" with the "authoritative voices" of past writers is precisely the sort of communion that Danièle Sallenave, Mireille Grange, Michel Leroux, and others hope to restore. It is, moreover, this kind of "immediate engagement" discussed by Kronman that Jeanne's teacher, Mademoiselle Laurencin, aims to produce between her students and La Fontaine. In fact, at the very end of the story, Jeanne even meets in person Jean de la Fontaine, Antoine de Saint-Exupéry, and Marcel Proust and speaks with these immortal "voices of the past." Orsenna's story, in other words, gives creative expression to the humanistic credo expressed by Kronman and others concerned with what they see as the disappearance of the humanistic literary tradition.

I have traced a line connecting French secondary schools to literary studies in American colleges and universities to Anthony Kronman's sweeping discussion of the shortcomings of liberal studies in order to show the reach and ramifications of the questions raised in Orsenna's book. Here is yet another way in which Orsenna's book is not what it seems at first blush. A children's story that doubles as a polemic against recent trends in literary education is also a meditation on longstanding questions about the health and survival of the humanities. *La grammaire est une chanson douce* asks its reader to consider what kind of relationship we should have with literary works and to reflect on the role language and literary studies should play in cultivating that relationship.

TOUR OF FRANCE OR TOUR OF FRENCH?

The classroom scene discussed above establishes a value system that governs the remainder of the story. It provides an ideological lens identifying the good literature teachers and the bad literature teachers, the purpose of which is to color our reading of the events to follow, the adventures of Jeanne and Thomas on the island of language. In other words, we already know how we are meant to understand what comes next: the encounter with language is meant to be a heart-warming, enchanted experience. After all, grammar, the title informs us, should not be viewed as a system of abstract rules. It should be experienced as one would "a sweet, gentle song."[18]

And yet, what is most interesting about the fantastical voyage is that while it certainly does in many respects reinforce the ideological oppositions established in the first chapter, it also requires that we develop a more nuanced understanding of that opposition. It shows that the contrast between gentle literature and cruel science is not nearly as stark as the opening pages would have it. Again, this is so because the way the students will rediscover language in its component parts and as so many concrete, tangible objects evokes the emblematic republican pedagogical method: the object lesson.[19] The children's adventure, however, does more than just give narrative form to intuitive, active learning. Its contours resemble those of the genre that the historian Patrick Cabanel has identified as the "children's tour of the nation" (*tour de la nation par des enfants*)."[20] *La grammaire est une chanson douce* begs comparison with the quintessential children's adventure story of the Third Republic, G. Bruno's best-selling school manual, *Le tour de la France par deux enfants*.

The late nineteenth-century school manual tells the story of André and Julien Volden, two schoolchildren who, following the Franco-Prussian War (1870–71), leave their home in German-occupied Lorraine in order to regain France. In addition to serving as a textbook for reading instruction (a "*livre de lecture*," or "reader"), the manual taught generations of schoolchildren about the nation's history, customs, geography, industries, and products. It also instilled in them a sense of civic duty and devotion to republican ideology grounded in Enlightenment rationalism and the celebration of scientific progress. It is a coming-of-age travel narrative intended to inspire its young readership with patriotic pride and an awareness of a common French national identity.

The number of basic similarities between Bruno's manual and Orsenna's work is striking. Each relates the story of two school-aged, parentless children who undertake an arduous journey to reestablish bonds with extended family and the larger community of the nation, defined in Bruno's story as the geographic entity, France, and in Orsenna's as the linguistic entity, French. Though they are without parents, both sets of children benefit from the guidance of kindly compatriots they meet along their way, characters who act as surrogate parents and teachers.[21]

A catastrophic event marks the beginning of each adventure. The humiliating defeat in 1870 and the annexation of Alsace-Lorraine are the historic calamities that prompt Bruno's heroes to set out on their expedition. In Orsenna's fictional world a storm at sea capsizes the heroes' vessel, which results in their loss of language and fortuitous landing on what we might call "language island." However improbable the shipwreck scenario, it can easily be read as an allegory for what many consider to be the disastrous predicament of the French language today. One need only think of the familiar complaints regarding the steady infiltration of French by English or the perennial grousing about the disregard among French youth for proper usage of their native (or adoptive) tongue. It is no coincidence that aboard the ship carrying Jeanne and her brother there is also a group of champion Scrabble players. The shipwreck sends these masters of the French language to the bottom of the ocean and transforms their plastic game pieces and ripped-up dictionaries — letters and words — into flotsam and jetsam. (That the title of the board game, Scrabble, should be in English playfully suggests already a degree of foreign encroachment on French linguistic purity.) Just like the military rout and ensuing civil war of the Paris Commune that loom in the background of Bruno's story, this linguistic wreckage is a symbol of that which threatens the integrity of France and Frenchness at the beginning of the twenty-first century.

In his study of the educational uses of the "child's tour of the nation" genre, of which Bruno's manual is the centerpiece, Patrick Cabanel observes that such stories belong to a tradition (dating back, in the West, to ancient Athens) whereby societies sent their male youth on a journey to the outer limits of their territory. Only upon completion of this rite of passage, which both tests the youth's mettle and prepares him for subsequent military and civic duties, could he be granted full citizenship and participate in the political life of the community.[22] This is indeed the trajectory followed by Bruno's young heroes: André and Julien begin their journey in the annexed province (i.e., in foreign territory) and follow by land and sea the periphery of the Hexagon until they finally arrive in Paris, the cultural, political, and intellectual center and microcosm of all of France. Amid the myriad topics covered in the manual, knowledge of France's topography is paramount. Geography provides the organizing principle for the entire story, as evidenced by the numerous departmental and regional maps that adorn the manual's pages. "At every moment of their journey," observe Jacques and Mona Ozouf, "André and Julien ask themselves: 'Where are we exactly?' and so, too, does their fellow traveler, the French schoolchild."[23]

When we turn from Bruno to Orsenna, linguistics replaces geography as the unifying discipline. Whereas Bruno's protagonists discover industries, products, and landforms, Orsenna's discover words, parts of speech, and verb tenses. In short, if André and Julien explore *France*, Jeanne and Thomas explore *French*. Language learning is of course important in *Le tour de la France par deux enfants*, which is, again, as its subtitle reminds us, a "reader" — a book intended to foster the student's mastery of the French language. As Jacques and Mona Ozouf remind us, one of the manual's purposes was to promote the spread of a unifying national language that would replace the many regional patois.[24] Thus, a number of episodes in the story underscore the importance of reading and writing in French — essential skills enabling the individual to participate in the economic, cultural and political life of the national community and thus fulfill one of the key obligations of the dutiful citizen. What is more, during much of their journey Julien reads from an illustrated history book about France's national heroes. He is an exemplary reader and, as we shall see, serves as a model for Bruno's own, budding republican reader. Nevertheless, despite the role of language acquisition in Bruno's manual, it does not have the kind of singular prominence that it enjoys in Orsenna's tale.

La grammaire est une chanson douce gives literary expression to Fernand Braudel's famous remark that "France is the French language" (*La France, c'est la langue française*).[25] Indeed, Mademoiselle Laurencin says exactly this during one of her lessons: "Be grateful, children, that you were born in one of the most beautiful languages on Earth. French is your country. Learn it, invent it. It will be your dearest friend for your entire life" (14). The teacher's comment, in part an encapsulation of the book's overall message, does not only underscore, in relation to Bruno's story, the shift from France to French. It insists that France *is* French and that, inversely, French *is* France. According to this logic, one can inhabit a language as one might a physical space or geographical territory. Through her own manipulation of the conventions of combination and selection of words — by placing the noun *French* in the sentence "French is your country" where one would more readily expect the noun *France* — Mademoiselle Laurencin achieves a feat of ontological transformation in the mind of her student (as does Orsenna in the mind of his reader). Her play of language — that is, her poetic speech — gives concrete, physical properties and spatial dimension to the idea of one's spoken tongue.

Mademoiselle Laurencin's comment also announces the adventure story about to unfold: the children will indeed travel to a fantastical island of language inhabited by living, breathing words — a place where words are not only signs referring to other things but are first and foremost "palpable" objects or real things in and of themselves.[26] There, they will learn, as if from scratch, how to create phrases, sentences, paragraphs, and other works of linguistic beauty from the raw materials of language.

Laurencin's words, however, also signal *La grammaire est une chanson douce*'s curious relationship to Bruno's *Le tour de la France*. In her very depiction of language as a concrete thing to discover, as one might discover the nation topographically, she uses the language of object lesson pedagogy that inspires the nineteenth-century republican instructional manual. In other words, language is a thing.

Le tour de la France par deux enfants is committed to the idea of learning through real, lived experience and direct contact with the object of study. While this is hard to achieve through a book, the manual nevertheless simulates this pedagogy by presenting its reader with numerous maps and engravings. It also extols the value of experiential learning through the actions of its exemplary heroes. Little Julien will never forget the engineering achievements of Vauban, about whom he has read a description in his book of France's Great Men, because he has seen with his own eyes the fortified walls of Phalsbourg and Besançon that Vauban designed (105). Similarly, he will never forget the Cantal, he exclaims, because he has climbed it with his own legs (124). Examples of such learning abound in the story. Indeed, the manual's preface presents the entire enterprise as an implementation of the principles of object lesson learning. It is because the *patrie* is such an abstract notion and difficult for the schoolchild to grasp that it is necessary to give it concrete shape in the form of a story: "Our teachers," reads the preface,

> know how hard it is to give the child a clear idea of the fatherland (*patrie*), or even, quite simply, of its territory or its resources. The fatherland only represents for the schoolchild an abstract thing, which, more often than one might think, can remain foreign to him for much of his life. In order to impress this on him, it is necessary to make the fatherland visible, to make it come alive. For this reason, we have tried to take advantage of children's interest in travel stories. By telling them the story of two young Lorrains' adventure through all of France, we have attempted to have them, so to speak, see and touch it.[27]

By simply replacing the word *fatherland* (*patrie*) with *language* (*langue*), Bruno's preface could serve to introduce Orsenna's story. After all, *La grammaire est une chanson douce* is a travel narrative intended to transform the abstract concept of the French language into something concrete, to render it "living and visible," to have the reader-student "see and touch" it. Our own discussion requires that we *see* this for ourselves. We must, therefore, turn our attention to specific examples of the way Orsenna transposes the principles of object lesson pedagogy to the story of language study.

Our reading follows two related but separate strands: on the one hand we examine how the story renders French language tangible and concrete just as Bruno does *la patrie*. On the other hand we want to insist on those moments where Orsenna's story departs from the Bruno model and pursues different — and singularly literary — goals. This divergence becomes apparent when we compare Jeanne's evolution as a writer — a creative writer — with Julien's evolution as a critical (republican) reader whose faith in science, technology, and all things practical occasionally manifests itself in terms of a distrust of fictional literature or works of pure imagination. We use this comparison to throw into relief *La grammaire est une chanson douce*'s ambivalent relationship to the republican pedagogical tradition, a tradition that it employs in order to correct the excesses of republican scientism.

REAL, LIVE SIGNIFIERS

Jeanne and Thomas's reeducation, we have said, begins as a result of a shipwreck that occurs during a transatlantic voyage the children take to visit their father in America. When the children regain consciousness, having washed ashore on a tropical island, they first notice many small, strange objects floating in the water that attract the attention of seagulls who mistake them for food. Gradually, Jeanne recognizes the floating objects as plastic pieces of the Scrabble game that other passengers were playing aboard the ocean liner. What Jeanne sees, therefore, are individual letters of the alphabet, adrift in the water, detached from the game to which they belonged before the catastrophic event. The metaphorical value of this scene is clear. The popular and eminently familiar game of language, a symbol for all alphabet-based language and in this case the

French language, has been overturned. Apart from whatever it may suggest about the present-day "crisis" of French, within the fictional world of Jeanne and Thomas this disruption occasions a process of starting over, of relearning the elements and rules of language.

The appearance of these drifting letters reinforces the idea that we are meant to see them in isolation from the language system, as discrete, tangible objects in and of themselves. The letters, after all, are not only described by the narrator. They are also rendered pictorially. On the page preceding Jeanne's description of these strange floating objects, we see a watercolor illustration of a small tropical island surrounded by a blue sea dotted with an assortment of white letters. That this same image also adorns the book's cover provides some idea of the importance to the entire work of the concept it conveys.

The text presents a striking manifestation of object lesson pedagogy. It is an exercise in learning by looking (*"l'enseignement par les yeux"*) directed at a concrete familiar object that is rendered unfamiliar by way of this unusual presentation. The reader's perception of this otherwise banal thing — ordinary everyday language — is awakened by what we might describe (following Viktor Shklovsky and others) as "defamiliarizing" visual and verbal techniques. The moment brings together pedagogical discourse and formalist discourse in striking fashion. Experiential learning — the seemingly unmediated encounter with real *things* (or what are meant to be perceived as such) — unites with experimental form.

The floating letters constitute merely the first of many stages along this journey — a child's tour of French — that leads from letters to common and rare words alike, phrases, expressions, parts of speech, verb tenses, sentences, paragraphs, and then finally to literary production and French literary patrimony. Immediately after the letters, Jeanne sees still more strange floating objects, this time individual entries from dictionary pages ripped from their bindings as a result of the storm (37). These, too, Orsenna has the reader experience as distinct and independent entities with a sui generis existence. They appear on the page enclosed within a bordered inset. The meanings of the actual words — *"encombre (sans)*" (without mishap) and *"jugeote"* (gumption) — have no logical connection to the story surrounding them. They are, quite literally, "free-floating" signifiers. And both the fictional characters and Orsenna's reader encounter them as such.

We need not review all of the episodes and techniques Orsenna uses to render language unusual, thereby causing the reader to give it more deliberate consideration than he or she might otherwise. Suffice it to say that guided by their songwriter friend, Monsieur Henri, the children visit a marketplace where words are bought and sold, a city where words move about in almost human fashion, and a hospital where hackneyed expressions such as "I love you" can be rejuvenated. Especially memorable is the call they pay to an old lady who "brings rare words back to life" (51). Jeanne listens intently as the woman pronounces in deliberate fashion a word — *"échaboulure"* (archaic for "pustule" or "blister") — that the young narrator (and presumably the reader) has never heard before. The old woman's slow, exaggerated enunciation of each of the word's syllables — É CHA BOU LU RE — before anyone knows what it means underscores the palpability or materiality of the word. Jeanne hears it as distinct phonemes, and the reader sees its phonetic transcription before attaching to it any semantic content. Then, suddenly, a mysterious pink hand appears out of nowhere and rests on the table before them. A red blister forms on the hand. The children's guide, Monsieur Henri, explains, while reading from a dictionary, that this curious object is an *échaboulure*, "a small read blister that appears on the skin during the heat of the summer" (64). After several minutes of silence during which the children gaze at the blistered hand, it disappears: "But the word remained, its five brilliant syllables flying around in the air like a butterfly" (64).

This fantastical scene intertwines the scientific and the supernatural. The reader observes both modes of understanding at once: the rational and natural realm coexists with the nonrational and paranormal. The separation of the signifier from the signified, the word *échaboulure* from the blistered hand, dramatizes a basic concept of structural linguistics, the modern science of language. But Orsenna overlays this "scientific" treatment of language with enchantment and mystery. What begins as an intuitive, concrete encounter with the materiality of the word becomes a fantastical image of syllables flying about like butterflies.

The coexistence of these two modes is what matters here. It echoes the ambivalence we saw in the narrator's self-presentation at the start of the story. Her vacillation, which provokes the reader's hesitation, between trust and distrust is reproduced here in the fantastical intermingling of the supernatural and the scientific. As we observed, this binary appears in the opposition of Mademoiselle Laurencin and Madame Jargonos, the first representing the idea of literature as a wondrous, magical thing and the latter representing the scientifico-structuralist study of discourse that breeds suspicion. But the *échaboulure* scene places wonderment and structuralism on equal footing. Both languages serve to account for what the reader sees and hears. The scene makes sense and appears to us in terms of phonemes and referents, the raw material of linguistic and literary analysis, and, at the same time, in terms of other worldly magic. The text keeps both paradigms in play. They are both suitable modes of reading. The episode suggests an attenuation of the stark opposition between Madame Jargonos (the science of literature) and Mademoiselle Laurencin (traditional literary humanities), as if a compromise between the two traditions were in order. What would such a compromise look like in terms of literary studies and the republican pedagogical tradition? How does Orsenna's text, in other words, have us imagine this relationship anew? To answer this question, we must follow the story through to the end, to the narrator's rebirth as a budding writer.

THE FABULOUS RETURN OF LITERARY PRODUCTION

As we saw in chapter 1, a signature trait of the modernization of literary studies in France's Third Republic is what scholars have described as a shift (to use Michel Charles's terminology) from a culture of rhetoric to a culture of commentary. Whereas previous generations of students learned to write literature through the imitation of the style (rhetoric, eloquence) of great authors of the past, the modern student in the wake of science-driven reforms mastered a discourse *on* literature; he learned to talk *about* literature rather than create it. In other words, modern literary studies trains readers, not authors. As Barthes would say, it gives "birth" to the former and "kills" the latter.

Jeanne's emergence as a writer at the story's end must be read as a reevaluation of this historical evolution. By identifying writing, especially creative writing, as the crowning achievement of language study, the story's denouement celebrates a tradition of literary production over literary analysis, "poetics" over "criticism." It reads like a paean to a literary education grounded in classical humanities that would later be dethroned by the scientifico-republican literary studies of Lanson and others and then, later still, by structuralists and narratologists. In short, Jeanne's birth as a writer honors the ancients over the moderns, the literary Ancien Régime over the scientific Republic. It promotes, it seems, a trust in literature as opposed to a suspicion of all "discourse" that is stirred up, some say, by scientific analysis.

And yet, as we have seen, the text keeps both traditions alive. It is not (or not only) a nostalgic longing for a return to a bygone era of literary education. It would perhaps be more accurate to describe it as the playing out of a competition between coexisting literary traditions. If Jeanne's emergence as a writer can be read as a corrective to the excesses of scientific reading, her education — and the reader's — takes the form of a linguistic object lesson, a kind of Rousseauist peregrination through the wilds of linguistic and grammatical things. Our discussion of Jeanne's apotheosis as a writer requires, once again, that we read it against the backdrop of, or in dialogue with, the Republic's preeminent "tour of the nation" narrative, G. Bruno's *Le tour de la France par deux enfants*. The juxtaposition of the two brings into relief the kind of combination of educational and literary traditions that Orsenna's text represents.

Guided by Monsieur Henri, Jeanne visits "the most vital factory in the world," the "writing factory" where parts of speech are stored and combined (123). Nouns flap about like butterflies and verbs creep along the ground like worker ants; a machine dispenses definite articles. Prompted by her guides, Jeanne captures two fluttering words — "flower" (*fleur*) and "diplodocus" (*diplodocus*) — and fishes out a verb, "to nibble" (*grignoter*), as well as a couple of articles. She hesitates to set the wriggling words to paper, but Monsieur Henri encourages her: "You can trust the paper, Jeanne. Words like the feel of paper. . . . [T]here's no finer sight than a series of words on a sheet of paper." Following Monsieur Henri's advice, Jeanne releases her words and watches them settle calmly before her. Indeed, she says, "paper [is] the true home of words" (122, 103).

Jeanne marvels at her sentence: "the flower to nibble the diplodocus." Though grammatically imperfect, it is the first she has produced since the shipwreck. The factory manager explains the grammatical relationship of subjects to objects and suggests that Jeanne reorder the words to create the more logical scenario of a dinosaur nibbling at a flower. A "cluster of grandfather clocks" helps Jeanne conjugate her verb. Jeanne spends the entire day in the factory playing with words: "I felt as though someone had given me back the wooden alphabet blocks from my childhood. I combined, added, expanded. Ferreting around in the factory, I had discovered more dispensers" (129, 109).

Jeanne's reacquisition of language is not only about recovering the ability to speak. It is also — and more importantly — about writing. And it is not just any kind of writing; it is creative writing. The terminus of her journey is literary invention, fiction. Literature, according to the logic of the story, represents the apogee of linguistic production. Moreover, that Jeanne's rediscovery of language is likened to a return to her childhood has metaphorical significance that goes beyond the fictional character's experience. There is a historical comment here. Jeanne metaphorically expresses nostalgia for an earlier time when the study of French was truly a literary experience.

The character's very last discovery at the writing factory makes this point exceedingly clear. Wandering into a forbidden area, she meets and briefly chats with three of France's greatest writers: Antoine de Saint-Exupéry, Marcel Proust, and Jean de La Fontaine. This culminating visit lays bare the purpose of the children's journey and the argument underlying Orsenna's moral tale. The trek through the underbrush of the French language, through the phonemes and morphemes and the grammatical rules that assemble them, leads, in the end, not only to literature but also to French literary patrimony. In other words, the study of French not only hones the skills needed for literary production; it also unites the student to a national literary tradition, to the nation's past.

The natural bond between language and literature suggested by the story would be unremarkable if not for the fact that in recent years, as we have seen, the study of literature in the French secondary schools has lost its traditional prestige and been displaced by more comprehensive and variegated language and communication studies that no longer privilege the literary text but rather treat all texts of any kind as equally important objects of study. *La grammaire est une chanson douce* is, among other things, a literary attempt to thwart this trend.

Jeanne's visit to the writing factory curiously recalls — and simultaneously distinguishes itself from — episodes and themes in *Le tour de la France par deux enfants*. Jeanne's literary education turns Bruno's republican message in certain respects on its head. Read against the backdrop of Bruno's manual, Orsenna's story becomes a critique not only of the scientification of literary studies in recent decades but also of the excessive utilitarian spirit and surprising aversion to literature in the quintessential textbook of the Third Republic. The juxtaposition of Orsenna's Tour of French and Bruno's Tour of France points up Orsenna's tale as a critical comment on — and corrective to — a version of republicanism that can be said to be suspicious of literature.[28] To pursue this conversation between Orsenna and Bruno, between the republican present and the republican past, we need first to recall the role of factories and industrial production in Bruno's manual.

Bruno's child-heroes travel to several of France's industrial centers where they learn about the country's major agricultural and manufacturing sectors. They also visit local farms and small-scale artisanal operations to see how items such as shoes, cheese, and knives are made. National strength, the story reminds its reader, is measured by the quality and quantity of goods it produces. A particularly impressionable stop on their journey occurs at the enormous smelting works and ironworks of Le Creusot. The rumbling, hissing, and smoke-spewing chimneys at first inspire fear and awe in André and Julien, but their fears are allayed as they learn how the furnaces and forges work and discover the usefulness of the materials produced there. Like Jeanne's step-by-step rediscovery of language, Bruno's protagonists come to understand industrial manufacturing by examining the individual stages of the production process. This is a recurring theme in *Le tour de la France par deux enfants*: fear and wonderment are the result of ignorance. Learning how things work and where they come from produces a different kind of astonishment. It replaces naive wonderment with admiration for human achievements through the application of scientific knowledge and technological know-how.

Given the importance of setting words to paper in Orsenna's story, it is especially noteworthy that one of the most edifying visits made by André and Julien on their tour of France is to a paper factory in Epinal. If the writing factory is for Jeanne the place where the mystery of language and the magic of literary production are most fully realized, its near counterpart in Bruno's story delivers almost the opposite message. When André tells Julien about his trip to the paper factory, both boys express their amazement at the way the enormous paper rollers apparently turn all by themselves. The inexplicable movement of the machine parts appears to be the work of magic, and the scene reminds André of a tale he has heard about a castle inhabited by fairies in which doors open and close by themselves and music emanates from a mysterious source (47). But Julien, who "knew full well that there are no such thing as fairies," is determined to find a scientific explanation for the rollers' action (48). By the end of the next chapter he learns that the factory is powered hydrodynamically. The experience of the paper factory at Epinal and the discussion that ensues illustrates the next chapter's moralizing epigraph: "The so-called magic wand was less powerful than man's science is today" (48).

The Epinal paper factory episode does more than demonstrate technological progress and celebrate republican rationalist ideology. Its underlying utilitarian spirit, especially when compared with Orsenna's factory, betrays and announces an underlying message in Bruno's story. Writing not based on verifiable fact and whose aim is other than the explanation of natural truths should be distrusted. Bruno's heroes, we learn, are suspicious of made-up stories.

Paper serves strikingly different purposes in Bruno's and Orsenna's tales. In both cases it is a highly esteemed product. For Orsenna it is the essential medium for creative writing. In *Le tour de la France par deux enfants* the setting of words to paper is largely a means of practical communication, a tool for establishing and maintaining social ties and facilitating professional advancement. Julien, for example, writes a letter to Madame Etienne to thank her for her kindness. Mother Gertrude and others, in order to help André find future employment, write letters attesting to his skills and good character. Writing in Bruno's manual, while a prized skill essential to the functioning of republican society, is above all an instrument. It is valued for what it can do or accomplish, not for its inherent worth as an aesthetic object or product of the imagination.

There are a number of indications in Bruno's manual that works of fiction are meant to be distrusted. The moving parts of the paper factory, we recall, remind André of a fairytale, an idea with which Julien dispenses quickly since it provides no guidance for finding a rational, scientific explanation for the mechanical mystery. This aversion to fiction, or "mythophobia," appears again in Julien's comments about his illustrated book of "Great Men" (*Grands Hommes*). At various moments along the journey Julien reads from the book about national heroes who hail from the places he visits. His reading, in other words, is intimately linked to his real lived experience. The value of reading depends on the extent to which it is empirically verifiable. And Julien never misses an opportunity to remind his acquaintances that his book is no mere work of imagination. When a friend (Jean-Joseph) expresses delight that Julien will read to him from his book and thus share with him his "recreation" (*récréation*), Julien bristles at the suggestion that his book is mere amusement, as if this might somehow be opposed to truth: "These stories," he says, "are not at all tales, this really happened" (132). And when another fellow traveller, the skipper of the "Perpignan," asks if Julien is reading Tom Thumb or Little Red Riding Hood, Julien shoots him an astonished look: "Tales? . . . Not at all, Skipper. These are beautiful true histories. And even the pictures in the book are true" (202). Julien's remarks reveal a general anxiety about "made-up stories" or fictional literature. It is an anxiety that is not only about the truth-value of stories but also their use-value. What can one learn about France if one reads stories that are not true? Julien's comments express a commitment to the value of scientific knowledge and scientific truth that runs through Bruno's manual and the entire century of science.[29]

Julien's suspicion of stories must also apply to the book he holds in his own hands containing the "true histories" of France's Great Men. After all, its legitimacy stems in part from the fact that Julien can verify its claims through his own real adventures. The text alone cannot be entirely trusted. In other words, Julien's relationship to reading, reading of any kind it would seem, is marked by an attitude of suspicion. It is a sentiment that finds its boldest expression in the preface to the botanist and republican educator Georg Colomb's elementary science textbook when he tells his young reader: "Listen! You must always conduct yourself as if you suspected the book to relate occasionally lies or to give you false information; you must therefore verify what it says whenever possible."[30]

The distrust of fiction and to some extent all "word learning" (what Marie Pape-Carpantier and republican educators disparaged as "*l'enseignement par les mots*") expressed in *Le tour de la France par deux enfants* is driven by a nineteenth-century positivist imperative. It does not emanate from the same epistemological tradition underlying twentieth-century structuralist theory that many complain has infiltrated (in various guises) literary education and fomented general suspicion of the literary (and any other) text. Despite the philosophical difference, there remains a political, cultural, and intellectual kinship between both of these positions of literary suspicion. Both throw into relief the independent experience of the reader. Needless to say, this idea does not receive the kind of treatment in Bruno's school manual as it would in twentieth-century experiments in literary criticism (*la nouvelle critique*) and production (*le nouveau roman*). Despite the manual's resounding didacticism, however, its model reader and budding republican citizen, little Julien Volden, reminds the real reader that "one must not read without thinking" (213). And Julien's uncle demands that his nephew provide his own account of what he reads rather than merely repeat the words on the page (233). To be sure, this elementary school primer is not a manifesto for the autonomous reader that would a half century later be announced by Roland Barthes and others. Nevertheless, there is an ideological continuity between these two concepts of reading. They both promote an attitude of circumspection on the part of the reader vis-à-vis the written word and its relationship to truth. And they both do this in the name of democratic, egalitarian principles that are supposed to constitute the core of republican ideology.

Julien's distrust of fiction (and book learning more generally) brings us back to the comparison with Jeanne's experience in Orsenna's story. For the writer's — the literary author's — relationship to truth is a culminating theme in Jeanne's adventure. Truth, the fictional La Fontaine tells Jeanne, is the writer's highest goal. This lesson is reinforced by the factory manager moments later who explains that a great writer is "someone who constructs sentences without worrying about fads, only for the purpose of exploring truth" (146). The concept of truth that presides over the conclusion of *La grammaire est une chanson douce* is very different from the scientific, positivist truth sought by Julien. The question of truth in *La grammaire est une chanson douce* is not a matter of epistemology. The discussion aims, rather, at influencing the reader's attitude toward the literary work. It encourages the reader to enter into a more trusting relationship with the text. But, again, this message comes at the end of a work that begins by putting the reader on guard.

Of the many scholars who have taken up the question of literary truth, it is Lionel Gossman's treatment of the matter that is most pertinent to our discussion. Gossman observes that Voltaire regards Virgil's *Aeneid* as true because the materials used by the Roman poet were "part of a widely accepted tradition": they were "familiar," "legendary," and "held to be true." Literary truth, according to this conception, depends on the writer's selection of materials "filtered and shaped by literary tradition and popular imagination."[31] This may well be the kind of truth that Orsenna, through his fictional characters, intends to evoke. After all, if conformity to a "widely accepted tradition" or use of "legendary" and "familiar" materials is the criterion for literary truth, then Orsenna's story is among the most truthful. For the story situates itself in a French moralist tradition of which Antoine Saint-Exupéry's *Le Petit Prince* and, above all, La Fontaine's *Fables* are some of the most well-known examples. Of course, La Fontaine's *Fables*, as modern rewritings of Aesop, are eminently "truthful" in precisely the way Gossman describes. At the same time, however, as so many commentators, including La Fontaine himself, remind us: "The *Fables* are lies [. . .] a trap, a lure, the opposite of what they seem. In order to appreciate them, one must overturn the obvious."[32] They are, paradoxically and simultaneously, both truthful (by their membership in a literary tradition) and deceitful.

But the literary tradition defined by these canonical French writers is not the only one in which Orsenna's text operates. It also recalls, to use Durkheim's term, the "realist" pedagogical tradition and displays a debt to Rousseauist experiential learning promoting the student's direct encounter with real things. If grammar must take corporeal form, it is because Orsenna subscribes to a tradition that places a premium on concrete over abstract learning, direct, personal experience over the passive study of abstract rules. The text is unmistakably shaped by the fabulist tradition of La Fontaine, but it is also a literary enactment of the point made by the republican linguist and educator Michel Bréal: "Nobody speaks deliberately in order to apply a rule of grammar."[33] *La grammaire est une chanson douce* demonstrates that grammar, and language more generally, must be encountered in the flesh, so to speak, through active experience and not as a system of a priori abstract rules.

Just as the young narrator warns the reader at the outset, *La grammaire est une chanson douce* is not what it seems. On the face of it, it is a fantastical children's adventure story. On another level it is a polemic against the scientification of literary studies. It denounces the dispassionate analysis of literature that renders the literary work of art indistinguishable from other types of "texts," training the reader to distrust and dismantle the text's strategies of rhetorical persuasion. But as Jeanne's opening warning also suggests, Orsenna's tale does not entirely dispense with the scientific tradition. If we must "beware" of the story Jeanne tells, it is because it functions on even more levels and within more traditions than it would at first appear. *La grammaire est une chanson douce* is not a simple nostalgic cry for a return to a prescientific, classical humanistic study of literature. It would be more accurate to read it as a corrective to the possible excesses of the science of literature, but a corrective that simultaneously remains indebted to the contributions of the very tradition that it critiques.

4

A Classic Dodge

Republican Conflict and Islamic Solutions
in Abdellatif Kechiche's *L'esquive*

There is no liberal education if one does not place before the mind
differing assertions and opposite opinions, if one does not put it in
the presence of both the 'for' and the 'against' and tell it: Compare
and decide on your own!
— FERDINAND BUISSON, "Discours au congrès radical de 1903"

The view expressed above by the republican educator Ferdinand Buisson
will undoubtedly strike some present-day readers as banal. [1] What could
be more obvious than the idea that the object of liberal education is to
present the student with divergent points of view and require that after
careful evaluation he arrive at some independent judgment on the matter
at hand? Buisson's point, we all know, recalls a teaching philosophy dating back to the ancient Greeks, a Socratic mode of inquiry lying at the
foundation of Western thought. If it sounds unoriginal to our twenty-
first-century ears, it is because this pedagogical objective has become an
article of faith, a tenet of teaching and learning in a democratic society.

For Buisson there was nothing trite about these ideas. As a leading
education reformer under France's Third Republic, he had devoted his
entire career to promoting these principles that remained uncommon
in late nineteenth-century France, where the Catholic Church still held
considerable sway over matters of education. As we have seen, reformers
like Buisson viewed the traditional pedagogy influenced by the church as

authoritarian to a fault, relying excessively on methods of rote learning and unthinking parrotry. They accused it of teaching students to receive knowledge passively rather than training them to seek it out actively on their own. It was catechistic rather than Socratic.[2] Furthermore, Buisson and other progressive educators did not view the kind of liberal education described above as only suitable for advanced students and the learned elites. The development of one's intellectual autonomy, as they saw it, should be the centerpiece of republican education, extended to all citizens at every level of schooling. The intellectual challenge that Buisson describes above is but a reformulation of the concept of active, autonomous learning that lay at the core of republican pedagogy at the turn of the twentieth century. Buisson's comment, in other words, is directly inspired by the principles of intuitive learning and object lesson pedagogy that together had become the (quasi)official pedagogical doctrine of the French Third Republic.

Abdellatif Kechiche's award-winning film, *L'esquive* (2004), reveals a debt to this tradition.[3] It gives cinematic form to the pedagogical imperative that Buisson identified as the sine qua non of liberal education. My argument may come as a surprise to readers already familiar with this film about working-class, minority high school students rehearsing for a school production of a classic French play, Marivaux's *Le jeu de l'amour et du hasard* (*The Game of Love and Chance*). Scholars and critics have often read the film as an indictment of the republican school, specifically of the school's failure to integrate France's multicultural population and of the authoritarian manner in which it imposes high literary culture on students unable to benefit from it.[4] I contend, however, that the film offers a more balanced and nuanced view of republican education.

When we attend to *L'esquive*'s scenic structure, we find that it contains two antithetical attitudes toward traditional literary studies, and it appears to defend the validity of each. At one crucial moment the film exposes as spurious the republican claim that knowledge of French literature facilitates the integration of minorities into mainstream French society. At another moment, it roundly defends the study of great literature as a means of self-realization and self-emancipation. Corresponding to these two views of literary studies are two attitudes toward republicanism. *L'esquive* sets up in dialectical opposition a progressive version of republicanism that seeks to accommodate France's multicultural population and a conservative, universalist version that hews to the orthodox view that great literature is generally valuable regardless of one's cultural origins. The film resists deciding in favor of one view or the other. It passes this task on to the viewer. Already we detect one of the many meanings of the film's title derived from the verb *esquiver*, meaning *to dodge* or *avoid*, for the film avoids choosing between the alternative viewpoints it puts before us. In a manner reminiscent of Buisson, it tells the viewer: "Compare and decide on your own."

The present chapter does more, however, than demonstrate that *L'esquive*'s dialectical structure reproduces a conflict at the heart of republican literary education and ideology. Like the other chapters of *The Pedagogical Imagination*, this one also examines the way republicanism intersects with the question of reading. To put it another way, it explores the way the act of reading enacts — and in so doing interrogates — republican ideology. In the end *L'esquive* shows how rereading literary classics is coterminous with rethinking republicanism.

In order to see how *L'esquive* treats the question of reading, it is important to keep in mind the film's complex relationship to the original Marivaux play. *L'esquive* does not only depict a high school rehearsal and performance of *Le jeu de l'amour et du hasard*. The film itself is a loose adaptation — and therefore a type of reading — of the eighteenth-century dramatic work. An intricate game of disguise and role-playing in which servants dress up as masters and masters as servants constitutes the stage play's central conceit, and much of its comedic effect results from the servants' awkward attempts to affect the language and manners of their cultured superiors. In Kechiche's filmic version of this role reversal, the high school students become the functional equivalents of Marivaux's servants. The difficult language and dramatic demands of the Marivaux text become their disguise. We watch the film to see if these adolescents from working-class, immigrant backgrounds can "pull off" the canonical literary work, an emblem of refined French culture, just as Marivaux's eighteenth-century audience delighted in watching the domestics try to play the part of the elites. Kechiche, in other words, converts the class and caste conflict of Marivaux's time into a twenty-first-century question of the French Republic's ability to integrate its ethnic, religious, and racial minorities.

But the most creative part of Kechiche's reworking of the Marivaux play reveals itself in the filmmaker's inclusion of Farid al-din Attar's *Conference of the Birds* near the end of the film. As we shall see in the final section of this chapter, Kechiche's adaptation of the twelfth-century Islamic poem performs a function in the film that is structurally analogous to a brief but important moment just before *Le jeu de l'amour et du hasard* concludes. When the curtain falls on Marivaux's play, the games of role-playing come to an end, and the traditional class system is reestablished. Just before this return to the status quo, however, a brief exchange between two protagonists, Dorante and Sylvia, hints at the possibility that true social change is at hand. In the penultimate scene of the final act, the nobleman Dorante declares his true love and intent to marry the noblewoman Sylvia, who at that moment is disguised as the servant girl Lisette. In other words, the nobleman, mistakenly thinking his beloved to be low born, is prepared to violate traditional prohibitions against intermarriage in order to follow his heart. Though this violation of social mores does not occur, the scene expresses an alternative vision of society; it is a harbinger of things to come. In *L'esquive* this intimation of future sociocultural change is communicated through the language of Attar's *Conference of the Birds*. The subversive episode in Marivaux's play is replaced by the Islamic poem in the film. Attar's text, performed onstage by elementary schoolchildren, simultaneously pays homage to an age-old Islamic literary tradition and, when examined more closely, expresses a fundamental tenet of republican universalism. Kechiche's use of the Islamic poem points to a means of circumventing the ideological impasse that both underlies the film and besets the present-day Republic. It suggests a compatibility between purportedly irreconcilable ideologies just as Marivaux's text, albeit fleetingly, smooths over seemingly insurmountable class oppositions. In so doing and as a result of its position in the structure of the film, which corresponds precisely to Marivaux's penultimate scene, Attar's *Conference of the Birds* demonstrates a fidelity to the message of emancipation delicately woven into the theatrical work. In sum, Kechiche's insertion of Attar's poem amounts to, among other things, a translation of the eighteenth-century French classic. It constitutes an oblique (and thus "esquive-ing") rereading of the Marivaux text.

READING OBLIQUELY

There is a moment early in *L'esquive* in which a teenager named Rachid rehearses with classmates his part in a school performance of Marivaux's play. Outfitted in the motley costume of his character, Arlequin, Rachid delivers the following line: "*[J]urons-nous de nous aimer toujours en dépit de toutes les fautes d'orthographe que vous aurez faites sur mon compte.*" ([L]et us swear to love each other forever despite any spelling mistakes you will have made on my account.)[5]

In Marivaux's eighteenth-century comedy of manners, Arlequin, Dorante's manservant, addresses these words to another domestic, Lisette. Both Arlequin and Lisette, unbeknownst to the other, are in disguise: the valet pretends to be his master, and the handmaiden her mistress. In other words, Arlequin thinks he declares his love to a woman of high birth, and Lisette believes she is wooed by a nobleman. Both are mistaken. It is, however, the words *fautes d'orthographe* (spelling mistakes) that should hold our attention. Marivaux's spectators, versed in the rhetoric of the commedia dell'arte, would have chuckled upon hearing these words, understanding them not as a reference to orthography but as an allusion to the game of mistaken identity performed before their eyes.[6] They would have heard in these words the playwright's gentle mocking of each character's ignorance of the other's true identity. In short, they would have grasped the dramatic irony, the playful wink the playwright sends in their direction.

Spoken by Rachid, an adolescent of North African origins practicing his part for a school play, Arlequin's line takes on new meaning. In the context of present-day alarm about what some call the crisis of

French — the problem of teaching skills of written and oral communication to today's students — the words *fautes d'orthographe* no longer concern only the question of mistaken identity. They now also refer, quite literally, to spelling mistakes and basic competence in French.[7] To stress this point, the filmmaker has Rachid stumble over his lines just as they come from his mouth.[8] The teenager bungles Marivaux's text at the very moment that the sentence he pronounces asks us to forgive such errors. Kechiche has seized upon this moment of dramatic irony in Marivaux's text, but he has now invested it with a meaning that is more grave than playful.

The crisis of French is not only about language skills per se. As Rachid's botched delivery of a line from a literary classic symbolically reminds us, the problem is also one of literature, literary culture, and literary studies. The crisis of French encompasses a widespread preoccupation with a (perceived or real) decline in the reading and study of literature, long understood as an indispensable component of the acquisition of the language. The fact, of course, that Rachid is a young *beur* presumably from a family of recent immigrants brings a now familiar dimension to widespread concerns about the teaching and learning of French language, literature, and culture.[9] It underscores the changing demographic makeup of France's school-age population and the subsequent question of whether the growing number of students from immigrant families have the cultural background needed to succeed in the traditional French curriculum. Though there is a consensus among educators that language and literary studies must play a vital role in the process of integrating all citizens into French society, the precise definition of this role — the actual methods for achieving these ends — remains an ongoing topic of thorny debate.[10]

The crux of the controversy can be expressed in terms of the following questions: Should the privileged place of literary studies based on solid grounding in the national canon — the classics of French literature — be modified to adapt to today's student body? And if so, how? How exactly should educators, government leaders, and the general public understand the relationship between the school, literary studies, and the fundamental tenets of the French Republic?

Kechiche's *L'esquive* is a cinematic study of these now familiar questions. It treats them, however, in unfamiliar ways. As suggested above, the film uses the very concept of *esquive* — or dodging — to address the topic of literary studies in today's schools. It is a study in the art of indirect and oblique communication, skillful avoidance, and clever circumvention. These notions provide a language for reframing — and thus getting around or sidestepping — the shopworn and stereotyped discussions of republican literary education. The concept of *esquive* even constitutes a technique of reading and thus salvaging literary classics. As a consequence, it points toward a novel way to think about literary studies in the Republic and, arguably, elsewhere.

Before moving on to these questions, we need to recall certain basic features of the film's intricate plot line. In Kechiche's loose (and thus indirect) adaptation of Marivaux's play, which itself, we have seen, is a study in the art of indirection and ruse, the school play becomes a device through which the main character, the shy, introverted and love-struck Abdelkrim, aka Krimo, can spend time with his classmate, the beautiful and vivacious Lydia, without having to expose his romantic feelings for her. The play-within-the-film thus represents a means of indirect communication. It is yet one more form of *esquive*. But Krimo is unable to make good use of it. While his classmates learn their lines and play their Marivaux roles moderately well, Krimo's performance is an utter disaster. His chronic taciturnity and introversion prevent him from succeeding on stage and, as a result, from winning over Lydia. His language challenge seems to be compounded by a literary challenge. According to his ex-girlfriend, Krimo "has never read a book in his life" (38), and he can hardly understand the Marivaux text that he struggles to memorize. He has difficulty delivering his lines or comprehending the demands of theatrical performance. In sum, the evasion or sentimental end run that Krimo hopes to perform through the theater requires language and literary skills that he hopelessly lacks.

Krimo is not the film's only dodger. Lydia, too, is a master of *esquive*, albeit of a different sort. During a private rehearsal in the park, Krimo finally musters the courage to declare himself to Lydia. (He does so quite clumsily, lunging at her in a desperate and almost bestial attempt to steal a kiss. We are once more witness to his language deficiency and his failure to use the subtle art of indirect address.) Confronted with Krimo's request to "go steady," Lydia avoids giving him an answer. Claiming she needs time to reflect, she evades the question entirely.

Lydia is an evader in another sense as well. She lives for the theater and is completely consumed by her part in the school play. It is there that Lydia lives out a fantasy of escaping from her drab and modest life in the working-class suburbs, or *banlieues*. When the film ends, Lydia still has not responded to Krimo's declaration; the terms of their relationship remain unresolved. The denouement, or lack thereof, constitutes yet another way in which the film enacts the very concept of dodging proposed in the title. It evades clear resolution.

PEDAGOGICAL RUSE

In 2004, the same year *L'esquive* was released, Alain Finkielkraut interviewed the teacher and philosopher Philippe Choulet on his weekly radio show *Répliques* to discuss Choulet's recent essays on the school problem in contemporary society.[11] In their conversation Finkielkraut takes Choulet to task for the latter's criticism of the way French language and literature are taught in the French secondary schools. "You describe our country," he says to Choulet, "as being still fettered to its literature. The classical French that school manuals persist in teaching is, according to you, a 'new dead language, comparable to ancient Greek or Latin and, therefore, an instrument of selection, marginalization, and cultural exclusion.'"[12]

Finkielkraut, a longtime defender of humanistic learning and the idea of the republican school as protector and purveyor of this literary tradition, has spent much of his professional life rooting out and denouncing those he views as the enemies of this solid and time-honored education. He has been particularly unforgiving toward those whom he perceives as trying to reform the literary curriculum by reducing its rigor in order to make the study of French more accessible to a greater number of students.[13] In Finkielkraut's characterization of Choulet's position, one detects the drawing of the usual battle lines. On the one hand, there are what have come to be known as the "*Républicains*," the defenders (such as Finkielkraut) of a tradition of literary education firmly rooted in the study of the national literary patrimony, the French classics. On the other hand, there are the "*Pédagogues*," reformers who want to adapt the curriculum in ways that are thought to suit the new demographic and cultural reality of today's student population.

Philippe Choulet, while certainly a proponent of change, resists being characterized as an enemy of literature. Speaking for himself and his coauthor, Philippe Rivière, Choulet declares:

> We do not hate literature and we even feel like its friend. But it is a question of getting at it indirectly. Because the sensory and affective experience of people today has changed — with all of the machines, speed, new media, and images — our starting point in the classroom cannot be the great literary canon, Racine, for example, [. . .]. We must get there — we have no negative attitude in that regard — but we must get there by means of *ruse*. *The art of detour* must be at the heart of the teaching profession. Though we have forgotten this, it seems to me that our own teachers knew this well. Our mistake is to have conceived of the relationship with literature as one of imme-diateness, to have ascribed to our children a natural desire for this literature. (my emphasis)[14]

That Choulet should express his position in terms of hatred or amity vis-à-vis literature illustrates the kind of polarizations that debates over literary studies have produced of late. Most interesting in Choulet's comment is the way he articulates a nuanced relationship to the study of the national literary canon. He does not deny the importance of the classics as an object of study. It is *how* they are taught that must change.

Choulet's paean to the art of detour evokes a long history of pro-gressive pedagogy. The emphasis he places on the nature and learning capacities of the student ("the sensory and affective experience today") as a primary determinant of proper teaching methods recalls a tradition of student-centered learning beginning notably with the Czech educator

Jan Comenius (1592–1670), the "father of the intuitive method."[15] It is precisely this concern for methodology and the student's nature that, in the mind of conservative critics, amounts to a disregard for specific disciplinary knowledge and is a cause of the weakening of academic standards.[16] Consistent with this outlook is Choulet's concept of "the great literary canon." The value or greatness of the literary work can no longer be taken as self-evident, as an a priori truth. The student must arrive at this understanding through a process of discovery — a gradual process, one that does not assume the student has an "immediate" — that is, preestablished, readymade — relationship with literature.

Choulet's insistence on placing ruse, indirection, and the art of detour at the center of literary education echoes the empiricist impulse underlying progressive education. When he notes that "our own teachers knew this well," we might add that several centuries' worth of teachers have placed versions of this idea at the center of their pedagogy. From Comenius and Rousseau to Froebel and Freinet, countless progressive pedagogues have insisted on the importance of play in education, on disguising the work of learning as recreation.[17] We have already seen in an earlier chapter how Agnès Varda, echoing the legacy of Pierre Larousse's lexicology, subscribes to this tradition in her own brand of cinematic wordplay. In *La grammaire est une chanson douce*, the playful transformation of grammar study into a wondrous adventure story (and polemic) shows that Erik Orsenna also adheres to this venerable principle of pedagogy. It recalls, moreover, Rousseau's famous comment that the student teaches himself best when he is oblivious to the fact that he is learning at all.[18] Though Choulet's language may be different, using the terms *ruse* and *detour* instead of *play*, the concepts he advances belong to the same pedagogical heritage. Unwittingly perhaps, he situates himself in a lineage that passes directly through the pedagogical reforms of the Third Republic and its signature method of modern active learning.[19]

Kechiche's film is an art of detour in precisely Choulet's sense of the term. The filmmaker uses ruse to lead us indirectly, in roundabout fashion, to a new reading and thus rediscovery of the Marivaux classic. One of many ways in which Kechiche does this is by drawing a comparison between the colorful language of the banlieues teenagers and the distinctly precious literary style of Marivaux. Numerous scenes in the film seem intended first and foremost to have us listen to the dynamic parlance of the adolescents. Whether lively banter or heated wrangling, their conversations are invariably peppered with slang, terms imported from Arabic, and a solid dose of vulgarity. The piquant dialect seems less to transmit a direct, denotative message than to convey implicit affective information.[20] We are meant to marvel at this shocking language even if — or especially since — it is difficult to grasp its meaning. It is a language, above all, of performance. Kechiche is clearly playing with the analogy between the banlieue idiom and Marivaudage, "a style of writing," Felicia Sturzer observes, "which was difficult to understand, for it seemed to express ideas in an obtuse way." "What appeared to be trivialities," she writes, "were pursued ad infinitum and the ultimate meaning of these 'verbal acrobatics,' maintained the critics, remained elusive and ill-defined."[21] Why should one make the effort to understand him, wrote a contemporary critic of Marivaux, if he seems to write precisely in order not to be understood.[22] It is easy to imagine a similar comment directed against the language of the film's characters. Kechiche's crafty comparison brings a fresh historical perspective both to the vulgar acrobatics of the adolescents and to Marivaux's now canonized style, which, itself, was once deemed scandalous and offensive.[23] The art of detour works two ways: the lens of the banlieues renews our reading of Marivaux, and the Marivaudage casts the language of contemporary youth culture in a new, and perhaps more dignified, light.

Again, as explored at the end of this chapter, Kechiche's masterful, and at times dizzying, deployment of detours takes him outside the European tradition. Marivaux is not his only model. He also locates the art of detour and its pedagogical potential in the Islamic tradition, in Farid al-din Attar's twelfth-century poem *Conference of the Birds* that the filmmaker adapts for insertion at a brief but crucial moment at the end of the film. The most cunning ruse of the entire film lies here. Kechiche turns the Islamic poem into an interpretive device for resolving the standoff between progressive and conservative republicans. He also uses it to suggest an original reading of Marivaux's play. It provides an indirect way to look at the French literary tradition anew. Before arriving at this, the film's supreme and final ruse, we must take a closer look at the conflicting versions of republican literary studies that comprise the center of the film. It is here that we encounter the opposition of "for" and "against" that, for Ferdinand Buisson, was a necessary condition for liberal — and thus for him, republican — education.

ELUSIVE AUTHORITY

By examining the film's treatment of its central authority figure, the teacher, we gain the clearest view of its refusal to present the republican school as solely an authoritarian institution. The teacher's voice is easily recognizable, at least at first, as a voice of authority. It is a voice vested with the power to give assignments. In the very first words we hear from her mouth, she announces to the class an assignment related to their study of Marivaux's play. She asks the students to reflect on the extent to which the playwright in Act I scene 5 privileges the analysis of feelings at the expense of action. This is the scene, she reminds them, that they have just looked at in their class discussion. A student interrupts to ask that she speak more slowly, upon which the teacher restates the assignment, this time in a more deliberate, painstaking manner so that no one will miss a word.

Under ordinary circumstances there would be nothing unusual about the teacher's delivery. Teachers, after all, often slow down and repeat themselves so as to be clearly understood. What is remarkable here, however, is the contrast between the teacher's mode of expression and the breakneck delivery and often incomprehensible lexicon used by the teenagers when speaking among themselves. We recognize her manner of speaking as both instructional and authoritative. It is a manner whose clarity informs us that its aim is to communicate a message. The *how* of her speech draws attention to *what* she is saying, as opposed to the adolescent banter that seems to insist more on the nature of their relationships than on the denotative content of their speech.

But the teacher's authority stems equally from the fact that her voice is also that of the filmmaker. When she slows down to inform the students that in their homework they must discuss the Marivaux scene they have just studied (the scene privileging sentiment over action), we hear in her words an assignment for the film audience as well. The scene immediately preceding the classroom scene, like the Marivaux scene to which the teacher refers, is also an intensely emotional and actionless scene. It is the solemn bedroom scene in which Krimo stares longingly at the watercolor paintings of sailboats that his father has made for him in prison. By means of this double enunciation, when the teacher refers to the play the students are studying, her voice is also that of the filmmaker directing our attention to the previous scene in the film we are watching. This moment (and there are others like it) suggests in powerful terms a conflation of the teacher and the filmmaker, which bears out Kechiche's own comment that he sees the teacher as a kind of *metteur en scène* or director.[24]

Such a doubling of the teacher and the filmmaker adds yet another dimension to the thematics of dodging so prominent in both Marivaux's play and this cinematic adaptation. Now it is the filmmaker who reveals to us that he, too, wears a disguise. Metaphorically speaking, he steps out from behind the camera and dons the modern equivalent of the proverbial black gown and mortarboard. Such role-playing raises fundamental questions regarding authorial intentions and the film's message or lesson. If the teacher is a figure of authority and the filmmaker speaks through this figure, to what extent can it be said that the filmmaker, too, by association, is a representative of the school? At the very least, acknowledgment of this identification must give us pause before concluding, as certain of its critics have done, that the film presents any simple, unambiguous image of the school.[25] It suggests that the school, too, is a cover, a disguise, a language that one can put on and speak through. As we shall see, the teacher does not express a univocal message. She expresses contradictory and competing messages, each of which could be said to express different visions of republican education. Thus, insofar as it can be said that the school represents the voice of republican authority — and part of my argument is that this is not so easy to maintain — it is an authority that encompasses more than one position and plays more than one role.

A particularly important sequence for observing the teacher's authority occurs when she explains to her students the basic lesson of the Marivaux play. This is one of the most straightforwardly didactic moments in the film. The teacher offers — or professes — what sounds like a most authoritative interpretation of the literary text. (Again, I later argue that through the lens of the Islamic poem, Kechiche proposes an alternative reading of Marivaux.) The official explication, or reading, is prompted by a disagreement between two students, Lydia and Frida, concerning the latter's performance in the role of Silvia, Marivaux's bourgeois lady who pretends to be a servant. Lydia complains that Frida maintains her bourgeois demeanor to excess, that she insufficiently affects, as the play requires, the uncultivated manners of a commoner. The students' dispute, the teacher is delighted to observe, invites a discussion of Marivaux's central message regarding social mobility or, more precisely, lack thereof. "What [Marivaux] shows us," the teacher explains, "is that we are completely imprisoned by our social condition and that, [even though] a rich person can always dress up in rags and a poor person can always put on a fancy gown, one doesn't get rid of the language, certain topics of conversation, a certain way of expressing oneself or behaving that indicates where one comes from. [. . .] We are completely conditioned by our social background and we remain among our own kind. We can put on disguises, but we never escape our social origins" (33).

As the teacher pronounces these words, the camera pauses on the faces of individual students representing France's racial and cultural minorities, the groups disproportionately occupying the lower echelons of France's class structure. The extreme close-ups on their faces visually render a sense of confinement, transposing the Marivaudian theme of social imprisonment to the here and now. It is impossible not to hear the double discourse in the teacher's explanation of Marivaux; while she discusses the rigid class system of Marivaux's age, Kechiche's camera requires that we compare it to the lack of social mobility in present-day France. The teacher's reading of Marivaux, in other words, doubles for Kechiche's reading of today's Republic. The double enunciation, however, complicates the identification between teacher and filmmaker.

Kechiche uses the teacher's words, but the visual images inform us that he uses them to different ends. The scene thus establishes an identification between the two authority figures — the classroom authority and the film's author — and simultaneously reveals the gap separating the two. It signals the teacher as a role the filmmaker plays, a mask from behind which he can wink at us, a disguise he can put on or take off. This game of resemblance and dissemblance, this vacillation between identification and difference, both privileges the teacher's words as an expression of authorial intention and lays bare their instability as such. The paradox points up the fundamental ambivalence in the film regarding republican education. The film is simultaneously critical of an institution whose values it nevertheless wants to defend.

Such ambivalence regarding the teacher's authority creates a vantage from which to question the teacher's lessons. It opens up possibilities for interpretation. We might ask, for example, if the teacher's reading of Marivaux is also the filmmaker's? Is it the only reading of Marivaux available to us? Is it an authoritative reading? There is no denying that at the end of Marivaux's play, as the teacher explains to her students, the bourgeois gentleman, Dorante, does indeed marry the bourgeois lady, Silvia, and the manservant, Arlequin, marries the handmaiden, Lisette. Despite their disguises and role-playing the rigid eighteenth-century class structure ultimately remains intact. Marivaux could not have proposed a different outcome given the mores of his time.

This interpretation, however, neglects a crucial moment in Marivaux's play. Before the denouement, there is a moment when Dorante, still believing Silvia to be a humble servant, is prepared to break social codes and marry her out of pure love. The moment is a subtle and perhaps scandalous allusion to the idea of potential change in social structures. To be sure, it is an oblique and fleeting moment in Marivaux's play. The eventuality does not come to pass. But in the context of Kechiche's *L'esquive*, in which sidestepping and dodging are the modus operandi, is not an indirect and evasive message precisely what requires our attention?

The point here is not to determine which reading of Marivaux's play is correct, the teacher's or my own. It is to show, rather, that we need not take the teacher's reading of Marivaux as definitive. This does not necessarily make her less of an authority figure (not yet, at least). It may, however, make her reading of the classic literary work less authoritative. Although the alternative reading of Marivaux that I have just proposed is not expressed by the teacher, it does get recuperated by Kechiche and occupy a place in the film. Kechiche will find a way in the film's conclusion to give full voice to the theme of social change that is only heard sotto voce in Marivaux's play.

THE PROBLEM OF IMITATION

A different challenge to the teacher's reading of Marivaux comes from one of the students. Lydia, who lives for the theater and traipses through the housing projects in full costume, has difficulty accepting the teacher's explanation. She resists the idea, Marivaux's idea according to the teacher, that one is "completely conditioned by one's social origins." Lydia protests by objecting: "Yeah, but still, you can still imitate" (*Oui, mais quand même, on sait imiter quand même*) (34).

Lydia puts her finger on a longstanding and fundamental question regarding the art of acting and, more philosophically, the location and formation of the self. What is the relationship between the actor and her role? To what extent is there an identification between the two? And what is the nature of that identification? The student and the teacher agree that Marivaux's play throws into relief the question of imitation. They disagree, however, as to the value they ascribe to it. It is quite understandable that Lydia should put great store in imitation; it is for her a means of escaping, or dodging, the imprisonment of her modest station. She is committed to the idea that, by means of pretend, she can practically become her character.

The teacher, however, has the last word in this scene: "Sure, there is imitation," she says apologetically, "but it is just imitation. Mere imitation. Do you understand?" (34). As if to underscore the gravity of her comment that deflates Lydia's fantasy, the camera zooms in on the teacher's face. The extreme close-up asks us to weigh her words carefully. They clearly refer to more than Marivaux's play and the inability of his characters to change their social station through disguise. They refer to more than just theatrical performance.

Since discussions of Marivaux's play double as discussions of today's republican school, the teacher's disparagement of imitation hits closer to home than it might at first appear. Behind her words we can detect a profound calling into question of core republican principles and the relationship of literary studies to them. Her dismissal of imitation as "mere" imitation implies a critique of republican integration and universalism. It is an attack on the republican logic captured in the following remark by Alain Viala: "Unlike other countries, like the United States for example, where community membership plays an important role, the republican tradition in France is universalist. Literary studies and the human sciences have, in every respect, a vital role to play in [republican] integration. A culture of integration assumes everyone has equal opportunities to succeed at school. To achieve this goal, there must be a space of common reference of which literature is the crux, a shared language and an awareness of a cultural heritage indispensable for dialogue to take place."[26] It would be hard to find a more concise articulation of the relationship between the study of French language, literature, and culture and the universalist ideal. In essence, Viala says that knowledge of French literature is a necessary condition for being French.

But in the classroom scene above, the teacher's easy dismissal of "mere" imitation suggests that the promise of integration of which Viala speaks is empty talk. In reality, as everyone knows, the Republic does a poor job of integrating its cultural minorities. Regardless of one's achievement in school and mastery of French cultural codes, discrimination in the workplace and other forms of social and cultural exclusion prove false the theory that any individual, regardless of origins, can become a fully integrated member of French society. The teacher's veiled comment says, in sum, that literary studies do not make one French. One can pretend to be French, but one cannot become French. It is always pretend, always imitation. Ultimately, one's identity remains defined by one's cultural, ethnic, racial, and socioeconomic background and particular group membership.

It is significant that this criticism should issue from the mouth of a teacher, in other words, by a member of the very institution that, in theory, is committed to the principles of integration that the teacher implicitly denounces. The very foundation of the mission of the school is being called into question by one of its own. One hears in this self-criticism not an assertion of authority, but on the contrary an abdication of authority. In exposing the inefficacy of literary studies and thereby highlighting a defect in a central disciplinary pillar of national education, the teacher undermines her role as a guardian of that discipline.

At this one particular but crucial moment in the film, the teacher's position resembles that of the progressive educator who has a fundamental distrust of her own authority as a transmitter of knowledge and steward of the institution's traditional mission. She represents an attitude, increasingly widespread since the 1970s among teachers and education scholars that Bruno Robbes calls "evacuated" or "empty authority" (*autorité évacuée*). According to Robbes, because the teacher's disciplinary knowledge no longer garners the respect that it once did, many teachers become generally suspicious of the very institutional foundations that supposedly legitimize their authority to teach. "Many teachers," he explains, "continue to feel uneasy with the evocation of authority, which explains why they do not want to or are unable to maintain their role as guarantors of the law. Experienced negatively, the term 'authority' has pejorative connotations. It is even more strongly spurned by those who attach to it the caricatured image of the 'cop,' an image they reject since it does not correspond to their idea of their profession."[27]

We could push this interpretation even further and hear in the teacher's disparagement of "mere" imitation a resonance of progressive attitudes in education that has a much broader historical sweep. After all, a common feature of education reform for centuries, but especially since the republican watershed of the late nineteenth century, has been an ongoing distrust of pedagogical practices relying on passive rote learning — in other words, imitation — at the expense of active, experiential, Rousseauist learning that emphasizes the student's autonomy. Indeed, one of the paradoxes of republican education is that the leading reformers of the Third Republic's schools advocated the cultivation of the students' intellectual autonomy in terms that appeared implicitly — and sometimes explicitly — to compromise the authority of the very institutions they sought to establish. Although the Catholic Church, with its longtime influence in education matters, was the primary target of the republican critique of authority, republican discourse did not leave untouched other kinds of institutions of authority. Let us consider, for example, the remainder of the passage by Ferdinand Buisson with which the chapter began (and that is discussed in chapter 1): "To make a republican, it is necessary to give every human being, no matter how young or meek, [. . .] the idea that he must think on his own, that he must be faithful or obedient to no one, that it is up to him to seek truth and not receive it ready-made from teacher, guide or leader of any sort, temporal or spiritual."[28]

The progressive, anti-authoritarian discourse within republican education leaves its mark on literary studies in different ways at different historical moments. At the turn of the twentieth century, as observed in chapter 1, a change occurred in literary education that amounted to a shift in emphasis from imitative writing to critical and analytical reading. Gradually, literary studies became less a matter of learning to imitate the rhetorical techniques found in the classic works from antiquity and more a matter of historically informed commentary and explication of texts drawn from a wider selection of historical periods.

I am necessarily simplifying a more complicated story. It is not entirely accurate to portray the imitation of classical rhetorical models as a purely slavish exercise. Such imitation was, in fact, a training stage in the student's development of his own literary voice.[29] It would likewise be an exaggeration to insist that the culture of literary commentary that replaced the culture of rhetoric gave the student total independence. Modern literary studies in France, M. Martin Guiney reminds us, was intended, in part, to promote patriotic pride and forge a sense of national identity. New techniques of literary study could be said to have lent merely a veneer of scientism to what was essentially adulatory criticism.[30] These qualifications notwithstanding, a celebration of student autonomy and distrust of (especially traditional) authority runs through republican discourse on education at the turn of the twentieth century.

I have taken this historical detour through some of the hidden implications of "mere imitation," in order to establish a context we must keep in mind in our discussion below of another classroom scene in which the teacher appears to contradict what she says at this moment. But my detour is also intended to underscore once again the very elusive nature of the topic of republican education. At the very moment that the teacher seems critical of the academic discipline and republican institution that she represents, she steps into a role — that of the progressive, critical reformer — that situates her squarely in the venerable republican tradition of breaking with tradition. It is not only inaccurate to speak of the republican school as a monolithic, authoritarian institution. It is also a misreading of the film's own treatment of the question.

A discussion of the critique of imitation, moreover, would be incomplete without mention of the fact that the teacher's comment appears to be contradicted by the example of Kechiche's film itself. That a low-budget film by a Tunisian-born director using (mostly) unprofessional actors of working-class origins and from ethnically diverse backgrounds should win so many mainstream film awards belies the message of social rigidity in the teacher's interpretation of Marivaux. One might hesitate to say that *L'esquive* has transformed the social reality in France. Nevertheless, we must acknowledge that the film bypasses, and thus weakens, longstanding sociocultural rigidities. In the case of Sabrina Ouazani, who plays the part of Frida, the film has launched her professional career.[31] The film itself, despite what the teacher says, maintains a certain faith in the transformative potential of imitation.

REPUBLICANISM BESIDE ITSELF

The first classroom scene provides only a partial view of the film's treatment of literary studies and republican education. It cannot be treated in isolation. Its full significance only becomes clear when juxtaposed with a later and equally important scene of classroom instruction — the scene in which the teacher explodes with frustration over Krimo's inability to perform the part of Arlequin. Placed side by side, these two classroom scenes enact a debate between opposing positions in education debates of recent decades.

The teacher's criticism of imitation in the scene discussed in the previous section conjures up key aspects of views held by progressive educators. Her comments betray a distrust of the republican promise of integration and, in particular, the role ascribed to literary studies in that process. They suggest, moreover, longtime misgivings among education reformers about pedagogies of imitation. However, in her emotional entreaty to Krimo to get him to come out of his shell, to escape from his linguistic and cultural isolation, she articulates an entirely different view of literary studies, one that invites comparison with the classic discourse of republican universalism. In short, if earlier she disparaged imitation, in a later classroom scene (to which we now turn), she insists on its vital importance. It is not my purpose to catch this character in contradiction with herself or to argue that she undermines her earlier position. What matters here is that we read this juxtaposition of opposing viewpoints as a means of rendering the complexity of the school debate and of capturing the film's own ambivalence with respect to literary studies in the republican school. In a later section of this chapter, we examine how the film attempts to dodge or sidestep this sometimes paralyzed and paralyzing opposition.

In the later classroom scene that now interests us, the students are once again rehearsing Marivaux in front of their classmates. Krimo has replaced Rachid in the role of Arlequin, and we are confronted with the painful experience of watching Krimo struggle to deliver his lines. He utters them with the same monotony and lack of feeling that characterize almost all of his exchanges. The teacher grows increasingly frustrated and impatient with Krimo's inability to play the part. As she struggles to get Krimo to understand his character, the comic valet who imitates his master, we hear a reassessment of the earlier belittling of imitation: "This scene is funny! . . . it's cheerful . . . Arlequin is having fun, he's disguised, he's imitating a master . . . Do you understand what that means? . . . That means someone with power . . . Try to show off . . . try, with some energy"

(59). As the scene continues, her increasingly demonstrative insistence on the need to imitate becomes an urgent corrective to her earlier position: "Try to get outside of yourself in order to go toward a different language (*[Essaie] de sortir de toi pour aller vers un autre langage*) . . . He [Arlequin] is imitating someone else . . . Do you realize the importance of language in this play . . . and in this scene? . . . Arlequin is imitating a master, so, come on, make an effort [. . .] There is pleasure in all of this. There should be some pleasure in getting outside of yourself (*Il doit y avoir du plaisir à sortir un peu de toi*) . . . Get out of yourself! (*Sors de toi!*) . . . Have fun! . . . Change your language, change your manner of speaking, change the way you move your body . . . Have fun!" (60).

At the height of the teacher's fury, she pleads with Krimo: "Free yourself . . . Give of yourself!" (*Libère- toi . . . Donne- toi!*) (60). The teacher's earlier dismissal of mere imitation has been replaced by a plea for more imitation. If imitation was useless (or at least suspect) before as a tool for social mobility, now, on the contrary, it is a vital skill for self-liberation. Before, her words implied that the mastery of the language of high culture does nothing to promote republican integration; now they extol the individual emancipation that comes from the encounter with great works of literature. Before, we detected echoes of a reformist, progressive position in education; now we hear a version of a classic humanistic understanding of imitation, what Lucien Jaume explains as a "process of self-realization in which one finds oneself through an exchange with the classics."[32]

The teacher's position in this scene intersects with some of the most outspoken defenders of traditional literary studies in republican education. It recalls, for example, the remarks of Alain Finkielkraut in the aforementioned interview with Philippe Choulet. Finkielkraut faults the school's excessive commitment to creating a curriculum that valorizes the students' own culture instead of pushing them to discover the unfamiliar cultural universe afforded by the classics. The school, he says, in its obsessive preoccupation to provide a learning environment that is comforting, with which students can identify, fails in its mission to force them out of intellectual, moral, and cultural complacency and conformism. This "demagoguery" (*démagogie*) as Finkielkraut calls it, merely reinforces and valorizes students' "sheep-like subjectivity" (*subjectivité moutonnière*). The school, insists Finkielkraut, should disorient, discomfort, and confront the students with true difference and otherness. It should

> take students off the beaten path, make them unaccustomed to themselves, introduce some "not-I", or even a little superego, in their self-image armored with interjections and certitudes. The only true schooling is subversive (*Il n'y a de véritable école que buissonnière*).[33] You come to high school with a bunch of pre-fabricated, ready-made expressions already in your head. You are suddenly put in contact with new and unfamiliar words. All that seemed clear and obvious begins to waver. You can no longer take your vocabulary for granted. Your familiar expressions begin to quiver. Your subjectivity reveals itself for what it is — conformist. This speaks to you, and what is revealed in this voice is not the uncontrollable desire but the despotism of opinion. (*Vos évidences vacillent. Votre vocabulaire ne va plus de soi. Vos formulations tremblent. Votre subjectivité se découvre pour ce qu'elle est — moutonnière. Ça parle en vous, et ce qui se manifeste dans cette parole, ce n'est pas l'indomptable désir, c'est le despotisme de la doxa*). This experience is disconcerting: another life, more free, can be born from the presence of the dead through their books.[34]

Alain Finkielkraut and Kechiche's teacher are not saying exactly the same thing. Finkielkraut's main purpose is to denounce a general misdirection that has poisoned the quality of education and taken literary studies away from its traditional mission. Finkielkraut's position nevertheless overlaps in remarkable ways with the teacher's desperate plea for Krimo to leave himself and go toward another language. Both posit the encounter with literature as an encounter with alterity, with the language of the Other. In both cases this encounter produces a kind of decentering of the self that is a necessary stage in the autonomous construction of a liberated self. It is worth remarking the similar fervor with which both Finkielkraut and the figure of the teacher express themselves. Anyone having heard Alain Finkielkraut on the radio can hear a familiar pattern in his words above (transcribed from a radio broadcast). There is a repetitive structure in his sentences (*"Vous êtes au lycée... Vos évidences vacillent... Vos formulations tremblent... Vous êtes déconcerté..."*) that builds in incantatory fashion to a near frenzy as he describes the transformative experience that comes through contact with dead writers by way of their books (*"cette présence livresque des morts"*). The teacher's frustration with Krimo also builds to a paroxystic climax: she gesticulates as she yells, "Free yourself... Give of yourself!" She is on the verge of losing control, as if the filmmaker, in order to illustrate the message of self-transcendence or getting outside of oneself, deliberately seeks to show the teacher "beside herself."

What both Finkielkraut and Kechiche's teacher are expressing is the close relationship between language and literary studies and the universalist notion of the autonomous individual — the idea that the true self is only fully realized insofar as it frees itself from particularizing determinants, thereby discovering the universal within. Their respective visions of literary studies adumbrate a method, via the encounter with the literary text, of forming the republican citizen. In other words, they both express a view of literary education that places it at the epicenter of the most fundamental and sacred of republican doctrines. We find one of the most concise and classic formulations of this idea of the autonomous individual in the following passage from Marcel Gauchet's essay, *La religion dans la démocratie: Parcours de la laïcité* (Religion in democratic society: the path of laicity): "The true self is that which one conquers in oneself against all the particularizing associations, against the contingent information that assigns one to a place and a group. It is by distancing myself from the immediacy of myself in order to gain a perspective that has general or universal value that I truly become myself. It is by relativizing the extrinsic determinations that are a fundamental part of me but from which I can free myself. Individuality, subjectivity and humanity all gain, from within, through the liberation from that which determines you."[35] Gauchet's words recall those of Finkielkraut and Kechiche's teacher.

For both of them literary studies — because of the critical distance one gains vis-à-vis oneself that comes from the literary encounter with another voice, language, place, and time — plays a fundamental role in the process of liberation and realization of the self described by Gauchet.

When the teacher cries out, "Leave yourself!" "Free yourself!" "Give of yourself!" there is more than the end-of-the-year school performance that hangs in the balance. The moment is a striking dramatization of the political stakes inherent in literary studies. If Krimo finds himself isolated from his community of peers, it is in no small way due to his inability to go toward another language, to allow himself, as Finkielkraut puts it, to be "disconcerted" and thereby "reborn in the presence of dead writers." In a word, it is due to his inability to imitate. Certainly Krimo's social isolation is not entirely explained by his inability to learn Marivaux's language. Nevertheless, according to the logic of the film, this is a large part of his problem.

The two classroom scenes — "mere imitation" and "more imita-tion" — show more than two conflicting attitudes regarding literary studies. They represent two opposing views of republican education and by extension republicanism *tout court*. In the teacher's disparagement of mere imitation, we hear a critique of the false promise of republi-can integration. It is a reminder that the social reality of youth from immigrant backgrounds is that they regularly face discrimination based solely on ethnic and racial identity.[36] Despite the republican discourse of blindness to the particularities of one's cultural identity, these youth are never perceived in French society free from such sociocultural markers. If imitation can only ever be *mere* imitation for certain minority groups and never lead to *real* social integration, then the concept that literary studies contributes to a liberating transformation of the self and the formation of the French citizen is not a truly universal principle. On the other hand the call for *more* imitation situates the literary experi-ence at the heart of a classic, traditional conception of republicanism. In sum, "mere imitation" is, in the film, shorthand for referring to a particularist political vision: you are and will always be determined by sociocultural origins. "More imitation" expresses the universalist vision of the possibility of individual emancipation.

However contrived the dramatization of the conflict between these two seemingly incompatible positions may appear, it actually captures an aspect of the reality of French school debates for decades. By presenting both of these positions as legitimate and defensible, by making the case for both of them and avoiding the choice between them, the film captures the paralyzed standoff between progressives and conservatives — between "*Pédagogues*" and "*Républicains*" — that has long dominated the French school debate.

It is only fitting that a film entitled *L'esquive* would dramatize this cultural and political standoff without resolving it. For as a film that studies various forms of dodging, sidestepping, evasion, and detour, this avoidance of stating a clear position with respect to literary studies and republican education is yet one more manifestation of its central thematics. Furthermore, recalling the comment of Ferdinand Buisson in this chapter's epigraph, the most republican pedagogical gesture the film can make is in its presentation of a dilemma that it refuses to resolve.

The unresolved conflict between different views of education is reproduced thematically in the unresolved relationships between characters. When the film ends, we still do not know if Lydia will reciprocate Krimo's feelings. Furthermore, the brutal arrest scene near the end expresses deep pessimism regarding the possibility of an improved relationship between the state and its cultural minorities. This scene in which the police use extreme violence — both verbal and physical — to arrest a group of nonresisting teenagers is, as others have observed, a stereotypical feature of the banlieue film.[37] The familiarity of the image of conflict between the police and the banlieue recalls Mathieu Kassovitz's *La haine* (1995), the classic reference for such themes, as well as numerous media portrayals of the situation. Kechiche's inclusion of this stock scene in a film that in so many other respects is *not* a typical banlieue film appears to be a way of insisting on the stasis and irresolution still defining this aspect of contemporary French society. In sum, at the film's end a sense of unsatisfying permanence marks three different domains: the teenage romance, the status of banlieue teenagers in the eyes of the state, and the conflict between competing attitudes toward literary education and the republican school. The film evades, avoids, and dodges a resolution to any of these situations.

ISLAMIC REPUBLICANISM: *THE CONFERENCE OF THE BIRDS*

The avoidance of resolution, however, is not the film's most important *esquive*. I propose in the remaining pages a reading of the film's culminating scene that suggests yet one more form of dodging that circumvents the irresolution and enduring oppositions described above. What is arguably Kechiche's most original, subtle, and unexpected maneuver of the entire film occurs during the end-of-the-year school performance. The event to which I refer, however, is not what one might expect. It is not the much anticipated high school production of Marivaux's play. More significant is the spectacle that immediately precedes it: the elementary schoolers' performance of Farid al-din Attar's *The Conference of the Birds*. It is by turning our attention away from the Marivaux production — from what we assume to be the film's main dramatic event — that we will actually arrive at a more original look at both the French literary classic and the education debates to which it gives rise. In keeping with Philippe Choulet's call for a return to the strategy of detour in literary pedagogy, our reading of the twelfth-century Sufi poem is simply a roundabout — and thereby more pedagogically effective — way of addressing the film's central concerns.

Attar's poem describes a meeting of all the different birds of the world who have assembled to discuss the process of finding a king or leader to bring unity to their nation. The journey they must undertake to find this figure is long and dangerous, and many invent excuses to avoid the quest. When the bravest of the voyagers finally arrive at their destination, they discover that the object of their search from the start has been none other than themselves. In the elementary school stage performance of this poem in *L'esquive*, a little boy delivers the final, edifying line. With help from his teacher, he manages to get out, "We have traveled far and wide to reach ourselves" (*Nous avons fait un long voyage pour parvenir à nous-même*) (86).

The symbolism here is unmistakable. The timid child who utters this line is named Abdelkrim. The character clearly evokes the film's hapless protagonist, Krimo, whose full name, we recall, is also Abdelkrim. Krimo's younger counterpart, however, directs our attention to the future. His mere presence on stage constitutes a message of hope. If today's Krimo is excluded from society, tomorrow's Krimo will find his rightful place. This place is defined, moreover, in terms of education, in terms of the acquisition of cultural codes and linguistic and literary knowledge. If today's Krimo cannot deliver his lines or play his part, tomorrow's Krimo can and will. Allegorically, the young Abdelkrim's performance delivers the hopeful message that the social fractures besetting France today will be reduced in the future and that the school, the setting where such problems are initially staged, will have its part to play in the improved state of affairs. And literary studies will look different in this happier tomorrow. If Kechiche has the elementary schoolchildren perform a classic work from the Islamic tradition, it is no doubt meant to express the hope that tomorrow's school will have a more expansive view of the literary canon and literary patrimony. As such, literary studies will be a less alienating discipline for France's cultural minorities and more representative of its multicultural society.

However heartening, it is not this message that is most interesting here. We must look more closely at the actual words spoken by the younger Abdelkrim: "We have traveled far and wide to reach ourselves." This line conveying the idea that one must leave oneself or one's origins in order to find oneself bears a remarkable resemblance to language we have heard before. It echoes the idea expressed by the French teacher when she pleads with Krimo to leave himself (*"sors de toi!"*) in order to free himself (*"libère- toi"*) from an imprisonment defined in his case by linguistic incompetence. The little boy's line also recalls Alain Finkielkraut's praise for the liberating self-knowledge one gains through a disorienting encounter with the language of great authors of the past. And finally, we can hear in it the vital republican tenet — epitomized in the concept of *laïcité* — that some type of abstraction of the self is a necessary stage in the process of autonomous self-realization. Little Abdelkrim unwittingly gives voice to a fundamental republican principle.

It is clearly significant that Kechiche has located this message in a literary classic from the Islamic tradition. It calls attention to the fact that a basic republican article of faith does not belong to the Republic alone: a comparable (if not identical) idea can be found in a culture far removed both historically and geographically from that of France. The emphasis Kechiche places on Attar's message does not constitute, however, a hostile criticism or scornful rebuke of republican ideology. Surrounded by other young children dressed in their feathery bird costumes, little Abdelkrim diffidently delivers his line before an adoring audience of family and friends representing the gamut of France's racial and ethnic diversity. The scene celebrates social cohesion. And Abdelkrim's words express a spirit of reconciliation.

The message does not only bring together the people in the room. It also resolves the conflicts appearing previously in the film, specifically those taking place in the classroom scenes discussed above and embodied by the conflicting messages articulated by the French teacher. *The Conference of the Birds* communicates a message that speaks to both the progressive pedagogue and the conservative republican. For the former, whose disparagement of imitation exposes the empty republican promise of integration through the compliant study of French literary classics, Attar's poem represents an opening of the canon and a more inclusive idea of literary patrimony. If one of the criticisms often made by progressives is that the French curriculum is alienating and inaccessible to students from non-French backgrounds, then the stage adaptation of the Sufi poem symbolically holds out the promise of a more ecumenical French program for future generations.

The adapted poem also sends an important nod in the direction of republican traditionalists. It insists that opening the curriculum to non-French culture need not be tantamount to an abandonment of the most cherished of republican values. One might even say that Attar's poem makes the case for republican universalism better than any French text ever could, for it situates an argument for the universal value of autonomous political and individual self-realization in a non-French source, thereby corroborating the true universality of the principle. It resolves the self-contradiction apparent in the concept of French universalism: in order for the principle of autonomous self-realization to be truly universal, which is to say, available and applicable to everyone everywhere, then by definition it cannot be particularly French.[38] It cannot belong to any one people, culture, or nation. It is thus eminently logical that Kechiche should locate the universalist doctrine in a work of Islamic origin. The point is not that it is truly an Islamic value, but rather that it belongs to no tradition in particular. And Kechiche achieves this through recourse to an eminently classic, if not French, work of literature. In sum, the conflict between progressive and conservative attitudes vis-à-vis literary studies finds a resolution of sorts in the film's adaptation of Attar's poem. The film, in other words, sidesteps the paralyzed opposition that has defined education debates for decades by outlining a vision for a productive and mutually satisfying coexistence of the conflicting positions. It accomplishes this, moreover, by appearing to step outside the French literary tradition, by locating a solution to France's problem in the cultural tradition of France's most embattled minority population.

The following questions remain: To what extent does this alternative literary classic truly constitute a departure from, or break with, the French stage classic at the core of the film? To what extent does the spectacular placement of *The Conference of the Birds* at the end of *L'esquive* detract from — and thus circumvent — the anticipated high school performance of Marivaux? To what extent is my focus now on the Islamic poem a dodging of the topics I've developed above? Less, I would argue, than it might seem. This apparent detour away from Marivaux actually leads us back to a fresh look at the French literary classic.

Let us recall our earlier discussion of the French teacher's reading of the Marivaux play. The heart of the play for her, its central lesson, is that social mobility is a vain hope. Despite one's efforts to disguise oneself in the cultural trappings of another social class, fundamental class structures persist. In *Le jeu de l'amour et du hasard*, she reminds her students, the rich fall in love with the rich and the poor with the poor despite their games of dissemblance. Although this reading is an entirely accurate description of the social order in place when the final curtain falls, it ignores, as I mentioned, a brief moment just before the play's end when the bourgeois gentleman Dorante prepares to break with tradition and marry a person he believes to be a servant girl. The event does not occur, but its momentary consideration constitutes in shadowy form a radical vision of a changed society.

The Conference of the Birds occupies a similar position in the structure of *L'esquive*. As we observed above, at the very end of the film there is no resolution to the teenage love plot; we still do not know if Lydia and Krimo will form a couple. The unchanging nature of the teenagers' relationship is echoed on a societal level in the brutal arrest scene, a stereotypical reminder of the stagnant conflicts paralyzing French society. In other words, with the exception of the unexpected inclusion of the Islamic poem, there are no surprises at the end of *L'esquive*. Everything remains unaltered and immutable; no change of situation is in sight.

The ongoing, unresolved circumstances at the end of the film might at first strike us as very different from — indeed, the opposite of — the satisfying resolution signaled by the marriages at the end of Marivaux's play. The two endings, however, are more similar than they might at first appear to be. An overriding sense of stasis dominates the end of both works. In both cases the narrative insists on a fundamental permanence in social relations. In Marivaux this is achieved by the maintenance of class structures and hierarchies (elites marry elites, servants marry servants). In Kechiche it is achieved by the all-too-familiar clash between police and youth and, at the very end, the ongoing uncertainty in Krimo and Lydia's relationship. In short, at the end of both play and film, there is a sense that nothing has changed.

Within these overarching structures of changelessness, however, the core message of *The Conference of the Birds* pronounced by little Abdelkrim performs a function similar to that of Dorante's fleeting consideration of taking a commoner as his spouse. It points discreetly, obliquely, and evasively to a possibility of future change. And this change in both cases is marked by getting around and beyond social and cultural rigidities. Both little Abdelkrim's line and Dorante's threat of nonconformity constitute, each in its own way, moments of dodging or sidestepping. They are subtle messages that circumvent the more obvious points of the works as a whole. They are, in sum, moments of *esquive*.

The structural parallel between Attar's poem and this neglected, though potentially radical, moment in Marivaux's play indicates that another artful maneuver is at work here. If the Attar poem performs a role in Kechiche's film analogous to that fulfilled by Dorante's near break with social custom, we can say that the Islamic poem occupies the place in the film corresponding to the scandalous moment in the play. Insofar as Kechiche's adaptation of Marivaux's *Le jeu de l'amour et du hasard* is also a reading of the play, it can be viewed as a corrective to that reading offered by the French teacher. Whereas she fails to mention the potentially unsettling moment in her own reading of Marivaux, the filmmaker recuperates that moment — or, more precisely, the subtle vision of social change contained in that moment — and gives it a place in his film in the form of the Sufi poem. He dresses it up or disguises it, so to speak, as Attar's *Conference of the Birds*.

Kechiche's use of the Attar poem points back to Marivaux's play and thus prompts a rereading that attributes new significance to an otherwise relatively unnoticed passage. In this way it revitalizes our encounter with Marivaux. The dodge or detour through the Islamic poem actually prompts a rediscovery of the French playwright. Such an artful return to the eighteenth-century classic brings to mind the notion of detour that, as we saw earlier, Philippe Choulet invoked in his discussion with Alain Finkielkraut. In today's classroom, explained Choulet, the starting point "cannot be the great literary canon." It is essential to teach such works, but, he adds, "we must get there by means of ruse. The art of detour must be at the heart of the teaching profession." Kechiche's *L'esquive* is a prime example of what such pedagogical detours might look like.

I began this chapter with a brief discussion of Ferdinand Buisson's idea of liberal education expressed a century ago. For this staunch republican pedagogue, such learning entailed confronting the student with competing points of view and requiring that he choose between them. For Buisson, as I explained, this Socratic mode of inquiry, because it cultivated the student's intellectual autonomy by means of active learning, was simply another manifestation of core principles of republican pedagogy. Insofar as *L'esquive* is structured by two conflicting views of literary studies and, by extension, of republicanism, it can be said to enact, or give cinematic form to, Buisson's pedagogical principle. It obliges the viewer to confront this clash of opinions. Buisson demands, however, that a choice or decision be made: "Compare and decide on your own!" he says. It is not enough that one observe the dialectical opposition; the student must arrive at a judgment. The judgment in this case emerges in my explanation of the Sufi poem at the end of the film. The elementary school performance of *The Conference of the Birds* at first appears as an oddity in the film, a somewhat saccharine scene offering a perfunctory message of hope amid an otherwise dismal and static situation. But a careful reading of this moment reveals that it actually occupies a more significant structural role in the film. As we have seen, it gives voice to a neglected theme of social change hidden in the Marivaux play. More importantly, it responds to the dialectic of republicanism that structures the film's center. It symbolizes the fusion of opposing republican attitudes, one progressive and multicultural, the other conservative and universalist. As a symbolic pronouncement on the film's central opposition, *The Conference of the Birds* — or at least my reading of it — fulfills Buisson's command that one choose. While it may not represent a clear choice in favor of one view or the other, the poem does point to a resolution of the deadlock. It thus satisfies the final condition of Buisson's concept of liberal education. In this sense the Islamic poem is the film's quintessential republican gesture.

5

Writing on Walls

Laïcité and Literary Form in François Bégaudeau's *Entre les murs*

Of all of the works under consideration here, François Bégaudeau's *Entre les murs* may seem the most critical of republican education. But this best-selling, award-winning chronicle of life in a troubled Paris middle school is in fact steeped in the very tradition that it appears to critique. Moreover, it enacts republican pedagogical method — however old-fashioned that might sound — as a solution to, or at least a means of engagement with, the current school crisis. One of the most talked about French titles at the start of the twenty-first century, *Entre les murs* has also, in adapted form, become a stage play and an internationally acclaimed cinematic success.[1] If *Entre les murs* has become so popular, it is undoubtedly because its subject matter speaks to everyone.

Through vignettes taken from his own experience as a teacher, Bégaudeau records the signs of the school system's ills: students fail to grasp the basic skills of oral and written expression; they ignore even the most rudimentary notions of general French culture; incidents of disobedience and violence abound; and there is a pronounced divide between the republican institution and the diverse racial, religious, and ethnic make-up of the student body. The question of whether the republican, secular school can integrate or at least find a modus vivendi with this multicultural population produces a discomforting tension throughout the text.

This is not, however, the only picture that Bégaudeau paints. He offsets images of ill health with others more heartening: we encounter a student,

Sandra, who reads Plato's *Republic* in her spare time. There is Alyssa's thoughtful and elegantly written argument against the reestablishment of traditional disciplinary practices. And Bégaudeau counterbalances the many hostile exchanges between students and teachers with displays of mutual respect. In sum, Bégaudeau neither whitewashes nor overstates the crisis. He seems intent on showing the good with the bad, in order that we, its readers, might judge for ourselves.

The book could not be more topical, a point evidenced by the promotional blurbs on the back cover of its English-language (and "movie tie-in") edition.[2] There we read that *Entre les murs*, or *The Class*, as it is known to Anglophone audiences, "explores timely issues of race, class, identity, colonial history, immigration, and education." It "suspend[s] judgment and liberat[es] the raw words of kids in a deconsecrated classroom." Directly below this appears the *New Yorker* film critic David Denby's observation (as if the film and the book were identical — which they are not[3]) that "*The Class* is a prime document of French post-colonial blues, though its relevance to American urban education could not be any greater if it had been made in the Bronx or Trenton or South Los Angeles." "Timely," "raw," and "relevant," *Entre les murs* appears to have a privileged relationship with the here and now.

Readers, reviewers, and critics treat it as an objective report on the reality of the schools. Writing in the pages of *Le Monde*, J.-L. Douin declares that *Entre les murs* is "a work of astounding authenticity."[4] Bégaudeau himself describes it as a "chronicle" of his actual experience in the classroom.[5] It does indeed read like a chronicle. Episodes follow one another according to the school year calendar. There is thus no organized plot in the Aristotelian sense of a purposeful progression uniting beginning, middle, and end in a "complete and unified action." In other words, the chronicle as a formal device reduces the sense of authorial interference and increases the reader's impression that the book is an impartial presentation of fact.

Not everyone, however, commends the book for its truthfulness. Bégaudeau's former colleagues, teachers at Françoise-Dolto middle school, are angered by the work, denouncing it as an inaccurate depiction of themselves and their students.[6] But even these critics who doubt *Entre les murs*'s faithful portrayal of reality express their reservations in terms of the same criteria of truth and falsehood used by everyone else. With few exceptions the first response to *Entre les murs* concerns its verisimilitude, its referential fidelity, its mimetic precision — in short, its accurate representation of the real school.

This focus on accuracy, however, ignores a larger, literary "reality." I do not dispute *Entre les murs*'s relevance or intend to belittle its mimetic qualities. It is indeed a valuable testimonial to the school crisis at the turn of the twenty-first century. But the overwhelming preoccupation with the work's relationship to reality is accompanied by a neglect of its literary qualities. Most of the book's audience, critics and admirers alike, ignore its form. They look past the book itself and focus almost exclusively on what it seems to say about the reality beyond its pages. *Entre les murs*'s obvious engagement with topics of present-day relevance — "race, class, identity, postcolonialism, immigration, education" — eclipse its more timeless literary interest.

The present chapter argues that *Entre les murs*'s deeper political engagement resides in its poetic features. Its themes are indeed of inestimable contemporary importance. But of even greater urgency is the need to look at them in new and fresh ways that only the work of art — because of its formal devices and what they demand of the reader — can achieve. In the case of *Entre les murs*, a neglect of its artistic properties is particularly ironic because the text persistently calls attention to its form. Through its own formal innovations — its metaphorical system, dialectical structure, disjointed composition, and disorienting interpolation of authentic realia — *Entre les murs* reminds the reader that it is much more than a report on the state of the schools. When we attend to its form, we find that it contains a sustained reflection on the relationship between fiction and fact, the literary and the real.

The present chapter's focus on form in *Entre les murs* does not, however, amount to a disregard for the question of schooling. On the contrary. These pages demonstrate that *Entre les murs* turns formal considerations into a meditation on education. Discussions of its form *are* discussions of the school: analysis of the one constitutes an examination of the other. *Entre les murs* projects the subjects of schooling and pedagogy onto the surface of the text; we encounter them in the act of reading itself. As with all of the works discussed in *The Pedagogical Imagination*, reading thus becomes a location for enacting republican pedagogical practice. What is more, the challenge of reading *Entre les murs* — the difficulty of navigating its formal textual complexities — becomes an occasion for working through the epicentral republican topics of *laïcité* and universalism. In other words, *Entre les murs* identifies reading as an activity through which one grapples with the thorniest questions at the heart of republican ideology. To see how *Entre les murs* accomplishes this, we must first consider the way it conflates the space of reading and the space of learning.

WALLS AND THE SPACE OF READING

A language of space and spatial demarcation is everywhere in *Entre les murs*. As is evidenced in its title, which we must translate as "within the walls," the text is concerned throughout with the problem of boundaries, limits, and borders. It constantly plays with the slippery relationship between inside and outside. This binary manifests itself, of course, in the complicated relationship between fact and fiction, between the referential outside world and the fictive environment "inside" the book, defined largely by the work's inherent or intrinsic properties.

The dichotomy of inside and outside applies equally to matters of schooling.[7] The language of walls evokes a classic question: How should the space of learning be defined or delimited? What are its proper boundaries? The entire history of pedagogical thought is in some sense an attempt to address these questions. The evolution of modern, progressive pedagogy from the Renaissance to the pedagogical revolutions of the Third Republic and its twentieth-century iterations (culminating in the present-day vogue of distance learning) resembles one long and gradual extension of the boundaries of the space of instruction. Rousseau remains the emblematic figure in this regard. His legendary insistence on the student's unfettered exploration of nature and the out-of-doors has come to symbolize all kinds of pedagogy promoting the transgression of traditional constraints and boundaries.

In France today the problem of delimiting the space of learning raises a different though related set of issues. It sparks controversies about the need to protect the republican classroom from external, sociocultural forces. The basic question is whether the school should be conceived as a "sanctuary," an enclosed space impervious to the vicissitudes of society at large, an impenetrable "inside" sheltered from the "outside." How one treats this question typically depends on one's ideological alignments. Conservative or orthodox republicans defend the idea of the school as an inviolable institution whose first obligation is to transmit cultural and scientific knowledge and the related skills of intellectual inquiry. Progressive republicans tend to emphasize a more "open" flexible school that places the individual student, whose particular needs are determined by circumstances external to the school, at the center of its mission. These positions correspond to different responses to the democratization of the schools and the changing demographics of the student body. An increasingly diverse student population, both culturally and socioeconomically, has meant that growing numbers of students come to school without the French language skills and cultural background that in earlier generations students acquired at home (or so it was assumed). The question arises whether the school should adjust its objectives and methods to accommodate today's diverse student population. Should the integrity of disciplinary knowledge and methodologies be modified (conservative republicans would say "compromised") in order to address the more immediate needs, abilities, and prior preparation, or lack thereof, of the actual student? In a word, to what extent should the school be exposed to — or protected from — the outside world? *Entre les murs* addresses these questions through a metaphorics of walls.

References to walls pervade *Entre les murs*. The concept occupies the center of a rich semantic field. In the opening pages, the space of the school is clearly marked off from the world beyond its walls. The heavy doors separating the school yard from the street, coupled with the narrator's dread at the return to school after the summer holiday, suggest something almost foreboding about entering this other realm. Once inside, the text is peppered with what in other circumstances would be unremarkable uses of the word *walls*. Walls "shift" when an angry student arrives late for class (26). A teacher trying to strike up conversation with a reticent colleague seeks a "crack in [his] wall," an attempt to penetrate the other's taciturnity (79). The narrator, at one moment, has the sensation that the classroom walls "are drawing together and will crush them all" (251).

Walls, divisions, and barriers exist even when the word is not explicitly used. They emerge, for example, in a student's aggressive disdain for a writing assignment. Asked to compose a self-portrait, the student, Dico, scribbles only these few words: "My name is Dico and I have nothing to say about myself because nobody knows me but me" (22). With this statement, Dico closes himself off or "walls" himself in. Walls often come in the form of a language barrier separating adults from adolescents. Students have difficulty understanding the terms, expressions, and vocabulary used by teachers and school counselors. Walls appear metaphorically in the form of ethnic, racial, and cultural divisions. Students named Souleymane, Khoumba, Mezut, and Ming are taught by teachers with names like Gilles, François, Jean-Philippe, and Sylvie. The students complain that the characters in their grammar lessons are named Bill and Véronique. Why, they ask, is there never a Rachid or a Fatimah? As they see it, even within the classroom the institution walls them off.

Despite these ubiquitous separations and divisions, the text also insists on the permeability of walls. They are at the same time both porous and impenetrable. The paradox emerges early in a brief but suggestive conversation at the very beginning of the book. A teacher identified only as a woman in her thirties discusses with a colleague her recent reassignment to her present teaching position in this particular middle school within the Paris city limits:

'Anyway, I knew that by coming back within the walls, I was laying myself open to that.'

To which another thirty-something added.

'Within the walls . . . gotta say it fast . . . it can go either way.' (12)

(*De toute façon, je savais qu'en rentrant intra-muros, je m'exposais à ça.*
Une autre trente ans passés a renchéri.
Intra-muros . . . faut le dire vite . . . ça se joue à rien.)

The word *intra-muros*, a term referring to an urban center within a city's limits or walls, here specifically denotes the division between Paris proper and its surrounding suburbs. In the context of school debates, it evokes the difference between the supposedly higher achieving schools within the city and the so-called struggling schools in the working-class immigrant neighborhoods of the Paris *banlieues*. The second teacher's "gotta say it fast . . . could go either way" suggests, however, that the ingrained opposition between the flourishing center and the troubled periphery — between inside and outside — does not always hold. The comment has us understand that, in reality, the schools within the city walls are no better than those on its outskirts. The discussion raises the possibility that the distinction between *intra-muros* and *extra-muros* is not hard and fast.

This brief exchange takes on new meaning when it appears in the opening pages of a work called *Entre les murs*. The term *intra-muros* is clearly a direct Latin translation of the book's title. The thirty-something's comment is thus a wink to the reader, a signal that the character's remarks also refer to the book we hold in our hands. The moment presents a striking illustration of the text's dual function by which discussions of schooling double as discussions of reading, as discussions of the act of reading performed in the present by Bégaudeau's own reader. The expression "it can go either way," following as it does the latinization of the book's title, refers not only to the false or exaggerated dichotomy between Paris and the suburbs. It also calls attention to the literary problem — the complex relationship between the fictive and the referential world — I have mentioned from the start. The text reveals a self-conscious reflection on its own relationship to the real. Which is it, fact or fiction? Can it go either way? And, if so, what does that mean for our broader understanding of the work as a whole?

The play on *intra-muros* and the questions that it poses are reinforced throughout the text through narrative structure and other formal devices. They repeatedly move the reader's attention back and forth between the referential world and the page, between the outside reality and an imaginary space created in the act of reading. Again, as we have seen, *Entre les murs* presents itself, in part, as an objective report on the real world of the school. It thus assumes the form of a chronicle. The arbitrary structure gives the impression that the author has had only minimal influence on the overall shape of the work. But herein lies the paradox. While these seemingly unmotivated juxtapositions minimize authorial presence, they also diminish authorial guidance. They leave the reader unsupervised, thereby prompting him to assume a more active, autonomous role in the production of meaning. In other words, at the very moment — and by means of the same formal devices — that the text appears to offer an objective look at the natural world, it draws attention to the act of reading and the reader's negotiation with the medium of the text. Like the word *intra-muros* as it applies to the difference between schools in Paris and those in the suburbs, a simple distinction between inside and outside the text becomes hard to maintain.

This playful destabilization of the inside-outside binary becomes a lens for examining republican universalism and its kindred concept, *laïcité*. According to the logic of *Entre les murs* these ideological pillars of French republicanism must be conceived as questions of space. They raise the intractable problem of distinguishing the private sphere from the public sphere and the aforementioned question of the extent to which social realities should affect the academic endeavor within the school walls. Bégaudeau's great achievement in *Entre les murs* is to have recast these questions in literary terms. Rather than present them in the ordinary ways of so many essays, articles, and books on these topics, *Entre les murs* has the reader work through them in the very act of reading itself.

INSIDE *LAÏCITÉ*

The meaning of the term *laïcité* has evolved dramatically in recent decades. It can no longer be translated into English simply as "secularism." It has come to connote more than it did at the end of the nineteenth century when it referred to the official French policy of separation of church and state written into law in 1905 and, before that, epitomized in the March 28, 1882, law wresting control of education from the Catholic Church. If the term once conjured up images of the conflict between republicans and the institutions of the Ancien Régime, it now evokes tensions between the Republic and its significant Muslim population. Islam has replaced Catholicism as the perceived threat to republican education. This is evidenced most famously, of course, in the successive "headscarf affairs" (*affaires du foulard*), national debates on whether Muslim girls should be allowed to wear the Islamic headcovering, or veil, in the republican classroom. The 2004 law banning, in the name of *laïcité*, the wearing of conspicuous signs of religious affiliation in school has made clear the state's position (for the time being): the student must check her religious identity, or at least symbolic expressions thereof, at the door of the *école laïque*.[8]

But *laïcité* refers to more than religion alone.[9] It embraces a constellation of ideas related to French national identity and republican values. It has become practically synonymous with that quintessential though controversial republican notion of universalism, a radical egalitarianism in which, on matters of law and policy, the state recognizes only the rational individual. It remains neutral on matters of religion, gender, race, ethnicity, and other distinguishing traits that the individual typically inherits but does not freely choose. Defenders of what we might call orthodox or "classic" republicanism see this universalist, laicist ideal as a core value of the Republic rooted in the Enlightenment tradition of rational inquiry and individual autonomy.[10] The school is the principle institution charged with the preservation of this tradition. Critics of this view denounce it as, at best, inflexible and ill-suited for addressing the real needs of France's multicultural population in the present day. They see it, at its worst, in its most authoritarian manifestation, as discriminatory, assimilationist, and thus a hypocritical betrayal of the very republican principles of liberty, equality, and fraternity that traditional republicans and the most outspoken champions of *laïcité* claim to defend.[11]

The equation of *laïcité* with republican universalism appears in a particularly graphic way in what is arguably the single most important scene in *Entre les murs* — the "graffiti" scene. In addition to illustrating the problem of republican *laïcité* in terms of walls, boundaries, and spatial demarcation, it turns the question into a reflection on the status of the literary work as a site for exploring such matters. In this scene, a group of students are on the brink of revolt because their art teacher has gone back on her word. As an end-of-the-year activity the teacher has invited her students to write on the school wall some token, that is, a graffito, by which they might be remembered after graduation. Upon seeing what they have written, the names of their countries of origin — Mali, Tunisia, Senegal, and so on — the art teacher reverses course and orders that the graffiti be erased, declaring: "The names of countries in a laical institution is simply not possible" (*Des noms de pays dans un établisse-ment laïc, c'est pas possible, c'est tout*) (255). The students protest that the teacher's action is hypocritical: she has imperiously restricted their speech in what was announced as an exercise of "free expression" (256). Moreover, they accuse her of being intolerant of expressions of cultural identity that do not celebrate one's allegiance to France above all else. By forcibly crossing out the names of these other countries, complains one student, the teacher has, in effect, "crossed out students" themselves: she has denied them their identity (255).

This conflict plainly illustrates how *laïcité* has become synonymous with republican universalism and French identity. As represented here, *laïcité* stands in opposition to the expression of particular, non-French cultural identities. Though the art teacher's clumsy invocation of the republican doctrine is excessively authoritarian, so much so as to be cari-catural, her comment does capture the intractable opposition between, on the one hand, collective national identity that the school has tradi-tionally been charged with promoting and, on the other, the reality of

a multicultural society. It succinctly portrays the clash between republicanism and communitarianism, or universalism and particularism.

We will return to this scene at the end of the chapter to see how
Bégaudeau proposes a solution (in a manner recalling Kechiche's *esquive*,
or "dodge") to the deadlock, a solution that can be actualized only through
the act of reading. Once again, as with the allusive term *intra-muros*,
Bégaudeau reflects on his own literary project while simultaneously
depicting a debate of longstanding national importance. After all, this
dramatization of the national controversy manifests itself amid a school
graffiti exercise — an exercise of writing and reading on walls. As such,
the scene becomes a microcosm for Bégaudeau's entire project, which
is none other than a two-hundred page exercise of writing "on" — or
"about" — walls.

Our closer look will underscore the graffiti scene as a culminating
moment for *Entre les murs* as a whole and as a unique vantage point
for assessing the nexus between republican ideology and the activity of
reading and writing. In preparation for this later and final argument,
however, we must first look to the past. As with all of the works examined in *The Pedagogical Imagination*, *Entre les murs* concerns more than
the present moment. The complexity of its themes and the way they are
informed — indeed transformed — through techniques of form can
be grasped only by considering the history that weighs on the present.

INSTRUCTION VERSUS EDUCATION

The question of the republican school's relative openness to the world
beyond its walls was already at the core of debates over national education
at the time of the Revolution. Though treated through the metaphorics of
walls and the inside-outside binary in *Entre les murs*, it has been expressed
historically in terms of *instruction* versus *éducation*, notions signaling
two distinct and often competing conceptions of the space of learning
and its purpose. *Instruction* has typically been thought to concern the
acquisition of knowledge and the use of individual reason; *éducation*,
the training of the individual's character and moral conscience.[12] As
slippery and unstable as any of Bégaudeau's binaries and the source of

much confusion, the words nevertheless continue to structure education debates. And they lie in the background of Bégaudeau's work. We must therefore recall their origins.

The opposition has its roots in the distinction drawn between *instruction publique* and *éducation nationale* in the education debates of the Revolutionary period. It was the Calvinist minister and historian Jean-Paul Rabaut Saint-Étienne who, in his insistence on the importance of *éducation* over *instruction*, expressed the difference most succinctly. Speaking before the Legislative Assembly in 1792, he declared: "[P]ublic instruction enlightens and exercises the mind; national education must train the heart. The former teaches wisdom and knowledge, the latter virtue."[13] If everyone requires national education, only a select few must receive public instruction. Though they are "sisters," he argued, priority must be given to national education, the elder of the two.[14] *Éducation*, for Rabaut Saint-Etienne, gives individuals a sense of belonging to a larger community; it teaches love of nation and duty to one's country and prepares one for responsible participation in society. Its concern is not the development of the autonomous, rational individual, but rather the needs of the state. With the dissolution of the Ancien Régime and the church power, so, too, disappeared those collective practices (catechisms, processions, ceremonies, sermons, hymns, pilgrimages, etc.) serving to reinforce moral order and remind individuals of their ties to a larger social whole.[15] According to Saint-Etienne, it was up to *l'éducation nationale* to fill this void. The distinction between *instruction publique* and *éducation nationale* had a spatial dimension. The former required "secondary schools, institutions of higher learning, learned academies, books, equipment, calculating devices and methods, it is enclosed within walls."[16] *L'éducation nationale*, on the other hand, required outdoor events: circuses, gymnasiums, martial arts, public games, festivals — outdoor activities that put on display the beneficence of fraternity and the intermingling of all ages and sexes.

It is, however, Nicolas de Condorcet's defense of *instruction publique* and distrust of precisely the kind of patriotic enthusiasm advocated by Rabaut Saint-Etienne that has come to represent the philosophical foundation of the republican school. The primary mission of the school, for the mathematician and *philosophe*, must be the cultivation of the individual's use of reason: "Train first the students' reason, teach them to listen to it alone, to defend against the enthusiasm that might lead it astray or obscure it and [teach them] to allow themselves to be guided by those who meet reason's approval; such is the course prescribed by the interest of humanity, and the principle on which public instruction must be conceived. One must of course speak to the child's imagination; for it is good to exercise this faculty like the others. But it would be wrong to try to control it, even on behalf of what deep in our conscience we believe to be the truth."[17]

The purpose of public instruction, according to Condorcet, is not to prepare the individual directly for participation in society; it is to train him or her in the free use of reason. By this means the individual will be able, through reflection and informed judgment, to participate in the choice of appropriate political leadership. It is individual freedom achieved through the "laborious mastery" of one's own reason that is the primary goal of the Condorcetian school.[18] For those who see the republican school as the guardian of the Enlightenment project, Condorcet is the institution's patron saint, "the first theorist of the laical republican school" (*l'école républicaine laïque*).[19]

The opposition between Condorcet's *instruction* and Rabaut Saint-Etienne *éducation* delineates theoretical positions that have informed education debates in France ever since. Writing in 1871, Ernest Renan formulated the distinction in terms similar to those of Condorcet: "Instruction is given in class [. . .]; education at home."[20] The state's responsibility to instruct (*instruire*) its citizens must stop, he explained, at questions of religion and morality, which are more appropriately taught by family members, the true teachers of moral education (*éducation*).

In practice, however, the republican school has never been able, or even attempted, to keep *instruction* and *éducation* apart. The Third Republic's school system, despite its declared commitment to the Enlightenment project and its implementation of modern pedagogical methods inspired by scientific inquiry, was also an institution devoted to the inculcation of republican ideology, secular morality, and patriotic pride. The mythic republican school of Jules Ferry, was, in reality, as devoted to moral *éducation* as it was to *instruction*.[21] As the historian Daniel Halévy explained in 1942, republican leaders of the early Third Republic, torn between the competing interests of the theological right and the ideological left, failed to define a clear role for the state in regulating these two rival forces in education, for one man's *instruction* was often another's *éducation*. The opposition between *instruction* and *éducation*, it seems, was easier to define than to maintain.[22] Despite the problems of preserving the distinction in practice, these competing conceptions remain alive and well.[23]

Orthodox republicans champion *instruction*. As defenders of the Condorcetian school as a place of pure intellectual inquiry and the acquisition of disciplinary knowledge, they denounce what they see as excessive adjustment of the curriculum to the particular needs of the individual student. Progressive, "student-centered" pedagogy, they claim, has undermined the intellectual rigor of the school. As mentioned above, much of the problem is explained in terms of decades of democratization of the schools resulting in an influx of students lacking the necessary cultural background and preliminary training to succeed in the traditional curriculum.[24] Instead of finding ways to help these students meet the challenges of a demanding academic course of study, the program, according to its critics, has accommodated the students' deficiencies by "dumbing down" the curriculum (e.g., with simpler, shorter reading assignments and with writing exercises promoting self-expression instead of rigorous literary analysis). The loss of academic rigor, in their eyes, results from allowing the *outside* — the pressures from advocates for a multicultural populace — to exercise too much influence on what goes on *within* the classroom walls.

In *La fabrique du crétin*, Jean-Paul Brighelli's best-selling diatribe against the failure of the progressive pedagogy that has dominated school policies in recent decades, the author continues to use the opposition of outside versus inside. He singles out the excursion or field trip as an emblem of all that is wrong with today's republican school. The school, says Brighelli sardonically, is no longer the place of learning that it should be. It has become, he says, mocking the mawkish language of progressive pedagogues, "a place of living" (*un lieu de vie*). According to this progressive ideology that disparages the classroom, "the school outing [or field trip] has become a must, the magic watchword, the nec plus ultra, the mantra of education."[25] School must "open up to the outside world," laments Brighelli. What outside world? It matters little, he quips, "since everything has the same value, from Disneyland to the Garnier Opera. What matters for the new pedagogy is to discredit the school as a place of cultural learning and, slowly but surely, to fill their innocent little heads with the idea that one can learn without working."[26]

Traditionalist critics of progressive pedagogy such as Brighelli, defenders of the Condorcetian legacy of unadulterated intellectual *instruction*, insist repeatedly that the school must become — become once again, in their view — a kind of sanctuary, a place of pure and peaceful reflection. In the words of the philosopher Catherine Kintzler, a Condorcet expert and ardent defender of republican *laïcité*, the school should remain "closed to opinion and thus open to reason."[27] It must be "a clearly defined space, sheltered from the blindness and sluggishness of the empirical world where that which is essential and elementary is, at least for once, presented in the simplicity, elegance and power of its abstraction."[28] The school, in this view, is a place removed from the real — a sanctuary.

François Bégaudeau has openly expressed his hostility to the idea of the school as sanctuary: "Education with a capital E that would be some sort of abstract entity does not exist, and the school is not a sanctuary: social class, ethnicity and the body do not stay outside of its walls."[29] Certainly, from a thematic perspective, *Entre les murs* depicts a school permeated by the sociodemographic and cultural reality of contemporary France.

But multiculturalism is not the issue, insist staunch Condorcetian republicans. As defenders of universal education, they celebrate cultural diversity in the classroom. It is the republican egalitarian tradition inherited from Condorcet, they claim, that guarantees an institution open to all. These orthodox republicans protest, however, when cultural particularities of individual students diminish what they consider to be the rigor and quality of instruction. Indeed, a number of scenes in *Entre les murs* indicate that this is precisely what occurs. Lessons are frequently interrupted and hindered because of students' inability to understand the very language the teacher uses to explain the topic at hand, and the teacher frequently adjusts his teaching or lessons to accommodate the students' limitations. The classroom scenes illustrate precisely what the republican, Condorcetian traditionalists lament, and yet, at the same time, these scenes suggest that under the circumstances there is no other way to proceed. Bégaudeau's chronicle does not celebrate this state of affairs; it simply reports it. The idea that the outside may be kept out and that pure *instruction* remain protected *entre les murs* is impracticable. The notion of the school as sanctuary is unsustainable, a fiction.

It is one thing, however, to address these questions thematically; it is another to work through them in terms of experiments with literary form and structure. As I argue, it is not what Bégaudeau says about the school that is most interesting but rather how he says it. Although *instruction* and *éducation*, the inside and the outside, cannot be kept apart in the actual everyday practice of teaching and learning, the formal, fictive space of *Entre les murs* reveals a more ambivalent and complicated view of this question. When we consider the way the work explores the relationship between the fictive inside and the referential outside, we discover a different message with respect to this interpenetration. While recognizing the impossibility of the separation, *Entre les murs* holds out the possibility of a privileged space that remains at a remove from the outside — the space of the reader. It is a realm that comes into being through the reader's engagement with form and textuality. It is a fictive space that is paradoxically "realized" in and through the experience of reading.

THE REPUBLIC: REAL OR IDEAL?

In a comment regarding the "pedagogical revolution" that took place under the Third Republic, the political scientist Yves Déloye writes: "[T]he form and method of teaching are as important as its content."[30] To our twenty-first century ears, so accustomed to this mantra of progressive pedagogy, Déloye's comment sounds platitudinous. At the end of the nineteenth century, however, such ideas were far from established.

Republican educators championed modes of empiricist learning typified by the object lesson and intuitive pedagogy as alternatives to a traditional pedagogy that they characterized as a passive, "catechistic" transmission of abstract knowledge. They aimed, as the zoologist and republican politician Paul Bert put it, to "awaken" and "arouse" intellectual curiosity and to bring out the "thinker" (*la personnalité pensante*) in the child.[31] As described in chapter 1, republican leaders such as Ferdinand Buisson and Henri Marion praised the new pedagogy above all for *how* it taught rather than *what* it taught.

This is also, of course, a staple concept of modern literature and art and its criticism. *Entre les murs* attests to the legacy of both of these traditions. In fact, it keeps them in play simultaneously and reveals them to be intertwined. Bégaudeau repeatedly reminds the reader that to consider such questions — the interaction of form and content, the inside and outside, the *how* and the *what* — is tantamount to reflecting on the core doctrines of republican ideology and the values of the republican school.

A particularly memorable example of Bégaudeau's insight manifests itself in a teacher-student exchange regarding Plato's *Republic* and the figure of Socrates. The discussion occurs between the teacher/narrator and a headstrong student named Sandra. On her way out of class one day, Sandra approaches the teacher and asks if Plato's *Republic*, which she has been reading on her own, would be considered a narrative. Stunned to learn that one of his students is voluntarily reading this weighty philosophical work, he probes a bit in order to ascertain how much of it she actually understands. The conversation turns to whether Socrates truly existed, whether or not he was real:

> "Well," [says the teacher,] "he's an invented character — that is, no one knows exactly, so what we can say is that he's like a character in a story."
> "Did he exist a little?" [asks Sandra].
> "Well yes, but no, anyhow that's not the most important thing. The point is mainly that he talks about all kinds of things with the people he runs into."
> "Yeah, yeah, he never stops, I love it."

"'So Socrates is this guy who comes into the agora — the agora is a kind of public square where they all gather together — and there he listens to people and then he says to them — uhh you what was that you were just saying? Are you sure it's true, what you just said? Stuff like that."

"Yeah yeah, that's what he does I love it."

"And so all right — they have discussions, it's like argumentation." (100–101)

It is clear that this discussion of the 2500-year-old philosophical treatise doubles as a discussion of Bégaudeau's own work. Whether or not Socrates truly existed is an oblique comment on the narrator. To what extent does the teacher in the text correspond to the real teacher who wrote the work? Moreover, Sandra's question regarding genre also applies to *Entre les murs*, a text that ostentatiously defies generic classification. In fact, the original publisher, Verticales, offers no indication of genre on the book's cover or title page, leaving the reader to determine the nature of the work he holds in his hands. Is it a novel, an essay, or some other type of work? Is there a storyline? Is it a narrative? Or is it, like Plato's *Republic*, a series of conversations between teachers and students? Insofar as such categories constitute divisions and boundaries, the question of genre adds another dimension to the metaphorics of walls pervading the entire work. Furthermore, there is something ludicrous about this exchange. The artless, ungrammatical slang seems inappropriate for talking about a cornerstone of Western political philosophy. But it is precisely this awkward disproportion that Bégaudeau wants us to confront. The challenge to our sense of decorum regarding discussion of serious intellectual matters amounts to a kind of transgression. It is yet one more way *Entre les murs* draws attention to the crossing of boundaries and the porousness of walls.

What is most significant in this passage, however, is the teacher's reluctance to say whether Socrates really existed or not. At first he maintains that Socrates is an invented character, "like a character in a story." But when the student asks if he existed "a little," the teacher waffles: "Well yes, but no," before finally insisting on the fact that "that's not the most important thing. The point is mainly that he talks about all kinds of things with the people he runs into." The narrator's hesitation to state clearly whether Socrates was a real historical figure recalls what we have already seen about Bégaudeau's book. *Entre les murs* constantly equivocates with respect to its relationship to real events. It refuses to let us know whether it is presenting real teachers, real students, and the real French school.

Emblematic of this equivocation is the author's own description of *Entre les murs* as a "*docu-roment*," emphasizing the letters *m, e, n*, and *t* (i.e., the root of the verb *mentir*, "to lie").[32] Such insistence does more than remind us that the "document" is, like a novel, part work of imagination. For that, the less arcane term *docu-roman* would have surely sufficed. The author's playful homophony draws special attention to the book's departure from the truth. We are faced with a mixed message. *Entre les murs* is at one and the same time a true account and one that we should not rush to believe. Like the figure of Socrates, what is most important about Bégaudeau's work is not whether its characters really exist and whether its scenes really occurred.

What matters most is the *way* Socrates — real or fictive — conducts himself in the agora. It is *how* he talks to people, the *way* he asks questions, probes, and raises doubts that counts. It is his mode of pedagogy — the method and not the content — that stands out. There is an obvious point of comparison here between the West's most illustrious educator, the "father of all pedagogues,"[33] and *Entre les murs*'s pedagogy. Insofar as Bégaudeau's work aims to teach anything at all, it does so in an evasive, dialectical manner bearing a strong resemblance to the method with which Socrates's name is synonymous. The work eschews heavy-handed didacticism; it presents no obvious thesis or fixed position vis-à-vis the school. It proceeds by juxtaposing situations of conflict, presenting the reader with apparent contradictions and engaging him in a process of dialectical reasoning.

A series of episodes immediately leading up to the Plato discussion further demonstrates this point. A conflict arises between the teacher and students because the teacher has used offensive language to chastise

Sandra for her immature behavior. He has accused Sandra of behaving like a "*pétasse*" (skank or bimbo) (78), a word that she takes to mean "whore" (83) but that the teacher understands as something more mild, like "foolish, giggling girl" (*une fille pas maligne qui ricane bêtement*) (83). The situation highlights, among other things, the teacher's failure to respect the hierarchy (ideally) inherent in the teacher-student relationship. Having allowed himself to address a student as if she were an equal, he has failed to conduct himself in a manner befitting his institutional authority. One could interpret his untoward remark as a sign of the undesirable effects of progressive pedagogy. It illustrates what some decry as the excessive egalitarian spirit in education, which long before the cultural revolution of the 1960s was already emerging, as seen in an earlier chapter, in the Rousseauist discourse of nineteenth-century republican pedagogues such as Jules Simon and Marie Pape-Carpantier.

But the teacher's error is preceded by an incident that offsets this one and complicates (Socratically) our reflection. The countervailing event occurs during an Administrative Council meeting in which the same students, Sandra and Soumaya, burst out in uncontrollable and disruptive giggling, the same immature behavior that days later will prompt the teacher's "*pétasse*" remark. The girls serve on the council as elected student representatives and thus work alongside school administrators, teachers, parents, and staff in drawing up school policy. The assembly is thus a model of democratic decision making. But it is precisely this "democratic context," says the narrator, that prevents the adults from reprimanding the students for their childish behavior (70). In other words, the scenes leading up to the discussion of Plato's *Republic* place in dialectical tension a reflection on competing models of government and their relative suitability to the school environment. To what extent is a democratic model of governance applicable to the school? Is the democratic, egalitarian ideal — an article of faith of progressive pedagogy — impracticable in reality? To what extent do hierarchical relationships need to be maintained? Can a traditional notion of the teacher's authority be reestablished in today's society? Is it possible for these models to coexist in the same institution, and what would such coexistence look like? The point here is not to answer these questions but rather to note how Bégaudeau's dialectical presentation of different models of school governance and the slippery nature of hierarchical relationships dramatizes the very mode of Socratic questioning raised in the discussion of Plato's *Republic*.

The discussion of Plato's *Republic* enacts in its very structure the Socratic method the teacher discusses with Sandra. The text's composition, in other words, reproduces its themes. The content reappears in the form. The act of reading becomes a performance of the questions raised in the text. The reader enters the textual "agora," so to speak, and becomes an active participant in the Socratic lesson. This transposition of theme into form constitutes another crossing of boundaries. Formal devices transport the reader "within the walls" of the text, or, conversely, it extends the classroom walls to include the space of reading.

Bégaudeau executes this literary technique with considerable brio, but the interest of his work lies not in its textual self-referentiality and the resulting *mise en abyme* of the reader. These are standard features of modernist aesthetics. Of greater significance is the way Bégaudeau introduces republicanism into the mix, for Plato's *Republic* surely stands here mutatis mutandis for France's Republic. And the key feature of this earliest treatment of republicanism, according to the narrator, resides in its demonstration of the Socratic method of inquiry; it is a matter of form. Similarly, as one of the latest treatments of republicanism appearing 2500 years after the first, *Entre les murs* suggests that we must also look to its form, that therein lies the real reflection on republicanism.

REALIA AND THE OBJECT LESSON

Entre les murs gives literary form to Socratic inquiry. Its reader enters the textual agora, a space of doubting, reflecting, and questioning. But Bégaudeau unites this ancient method of teaching and learning with modern experiments — both pedagogical and formal — that suggest a genealogy connecting a 2500-year-old republican tradition with a more recent one. We discover such linkages, for example, in *Entre les murs*'s use of realia.

Bégaudeau includes on the pages of the book authentic real-world documents culled from his own teaching experience — actual messages from students, samples of student work, excerpts of lessons, lyrics to rap music, a literary passage (from Musset's *On ne badine pas avec l'amour*), and so forth. These verbatim interpolations contrast with the rest of the text. The documentary objects call attention to the text's construction and, beyond what they may tell the reader about the real classroom experience, alert him to the problem of reading. It is here that the text most explicitly functions as an object lesson, demanding that the reader observe and analyze the most ordinary textual objects in extraordinary ways. They are moments that give pause, activate and prolong the reader's contemplation of the text in a manner recalling the pedagogies of observation championed, as discussed in chapter 1, by republican educators such as Ferdinand Buisson and Henri Marion.

One of the most striking examples of the reader's encounter with realia occurs in conjunction with a classroom scene in which a student, Khoumba, rejects the teacher's request that she read a passage aloud. She refuses to read as asked, she explains, because she quite simply "doesn't feel like it" (54). "Like it or not, you're going to read," snaps the teacher. "You can't make me," replies the student. In a testy confrontation after class, the teacher finally drags an uninspired apology from Khoumba, which she immediately retracts upon reaching the end of the hall: "I don't mean it," she yells (56).

This exchange is unsettling in several ways. The student's lack of motivation, insolence, and disrespect for the teacher's authority are, of course, troubling. The teacher, while justifiably impatient, behaves in a manner that is arguably also unbecoming. At the very least, he demonstrates an inability to manage the situation. Part of today's school crisis, this scene suggests, concerns a problem of civility or lack thereof. This is, in any case, what the discomforting student-teacher confrontation most obviously depicts.

But the scene is about much more. It is also about reading. The teacher's request followed by the student's refusal amounts to an invitation and a resistance to reading. What is required, the scene asks, to motivate one to read? Like so many episodes in *Entre les murs*, the problem of reading represented in the text draws attention to a related problem encountered by *Entre les murs*'s own reader.

To see how this scene of (resisting) reading directly implicates the book's reader, we must consider it in conjunction with what immediately follows. From a literary perspective, the succeeding passage is even more jarring. Bégaudeau's text confronts the reader with a list of twenty-two questions, which include the following: "1. What are the values of the republican school and what measures can be taken so that they will be recognized by society? [. . .] 5. What kinds of knowledge, skills and rules of conduct should students be required to master at the end of each stage of mandatory schooling? 6. How should the school adapt to the diversity of its students? [. . .] 8. How can students be motivated to learn and study effectively? [. . .] 15. What should be done to combat school violence and incivility?" (56–57).

The sudden appearance of these questions on the page is disorienting. They strike a bold contrast with the preceding scene. Their tone, austere and ministerial, could not be more different from the colorful dialogue between Khoumba and the teacher. There is no explicit connection to the episodes that precede and follow and no indication of their origin. Moreover, with no deictic indicators, "shifters," or other explanatory information revealing the source of the questions, they appear to emerge out of nowhere. Who, the reader must ask, is uttering these words that seem to intrude unannounced into the text? What is their relationship to what we have already seen?

Such juxtapositions are typical of *Entre les murs*'s overall form, a kind of farrago of individual vignettes interspersed with authentic, real-life documents. Bégaudeau's persistent use of this classic device of modernist aesthetics puts the onus on the reader to make sense of these otherwise unanalyzed textual relationships.[34] Providing little or no guidance as to how to explain what is found there on the page, the literary device leaves the reader to his own devices. It appeals to his imagination, asking him to provide the interconnections between passages, to fill in the semantic gaps. It asks the reader to perform a task, to make the conceptual link-ages that befit his role as a reader. In short, it asks the reader to read. The reader thus comes to resemble *en abyme* the student in the text. Just as the teacher/narrator (and Bégaudeau's "fictional" counterpart) asks the student to read a passage aloud, the text calls on the reader, through its formal device, to assume an active role — to participate — in the challenge of reading put before him in the pages of *Entre les murs*. Of course, like the teacher, the text cannot "make" the reader perform this task. The reader can choose to ignore the curious juxtapositions or reject any attempt to make sense of them.

But *Entre les murs* indicates that high political stakes reside in such a resistance to reading. This becomes apparent when we consider the source of this particular interpolation. The list of questions is a verbatim reproduction of those proposed by the *Commission du débat national sur l'avenir de l'école* (commission on the national debate regarding the future of the school), known as the Thélot commission (after its president, Claude Thélot) and circulated among more than one million participants in the national debate on education that took place in 2003–2004.[35] In other words, the questions originate in an official government document. They voice the concerns of the state and express in particularly bold terms the role of the school as an instrument for diffusing republican ideology throughout society.

The official status of the Thélot commission's questions changes when they appear here in *Entre les murs*. While they still refer to their original context and the national debate, they signify something more by virtue of their presence in the literary text. They perform a literary function, participating in the formal device that serves as an appeal to the reader to read. The appearance of the Thélot commission questions symboli-cally illustrates the way the school debate — which is also a debate about republican ideology — becomes integrated in the literary text. The juxta-position of the authentic real-world document and Khoumba's resistance to reading points up a striking fusion between republican ideology and literary aesthetics. The formal device aestheticizes the ideological. It is as if the textual moment proposed answers to the very questions posed in the official document ("What measures can be taken so that the values of the Republican school will be recognized by society?" "How can students be motivated?"). The text, by means of the disorienting juxtaposition, addresses the reader. It attempts to "motivate" the reader to read. It identifies itself, to borrow the language of the Thélot commission, as one of those "measures" — that is, means or vehicles — through which the "values of the Republican school" might be recognized.

THE FICTION OF *LAÏCITÉ*

Let us return to the "graffiti" scene mentioned earlier in the chapter. We are now in a better position to read it as a culminating moment for the work as a whole. As with the episodes already discussed, it unites a republican pedagogical imperative with literary form and thereby reveals the act of reading as an enactment of republican ideology. This scene raises the political stakes, however, by placing the problem of *laïcité* at the center of its reflection.

Moderate republicans today insist on the need to "desacralize" *laïcité*. They agree with hard-line republicans on the importance of protecting the rationalist, egalitarian tradition and principles that *laïcité* (in theory) represents. The rigid, authoritarian fashion in which the state often applies the doctrine, however, constitutes a violation of these selfsame principles. To desacralize *laïcité*, then, means to approach the concept itself with a critical eye, in the spirit of critical inquiry that *laïcité* is supposed to foster.

The graffiti scene is true to the republican laical tradition in just this way. It constitutes a critique of the way the state, through the channel of the school, imposes *laïcité*. But *Entre les murs* does not discard *laïcité*. It proposes an alternative manner of conceiving of it, one that salvages its underlying principles regarding the education of the autonomous individual. *Laïcité*, in this scene's rewriting of the concept, cannot be handed down from on high as one might a sacred thing. It must be discovered, enacted, and constructed in the present moment, in the individual student's immediate and unmitigated encounter with the object of study. What this scene does with striking originality is identify the act of reading itself — and explicitly the reading of *Entre les murs* — as the ideal site for this encounter.

We recall in this scene that the art teacher, Rachel, suddenly changes her mind with respect to an exercise of "free expression." Having first invited students to write something on the school wall — a graffito — by which they might be remembered, she abruptly halts the activity. When she sees what the students have written — the names of their countries of family origin, Mali, Tunisia, and so on — she demands that the words be erased. Their graffiti violate, she says, the principle of *laïcité*: "The names of countries in a laical institution is simply not possible" (*Des noms de pays dans un établissement laïc n'est pas possible*) (272). Her action sets off an uproar. The students denounce the teacher's hypocrisy and restriction of their speech. They accuse her of wanting to impose French identity on everyone, of denying students' rights to affirm their own identity.

The scene makes no reference to headscarves or other signs of religious belief. *Laïcité*, it reminds us, embraces broader questions of republican identity and ideology and the role of the school as the institutional guardian of these beliefs and values. The real conflict here is that of republican universalism versus communitarianism. Through the teacher's impetuous invocation of *laïcité*, the scene dramatizes the perceived threat that a multicultural population and the expression of cultural particularism represent for national unity and collective republican values. Though distressing, there is also something commonplace about this teacher-student exchange. We immediately recognize it as an illustration, albeit schematic, of an enduring standoff between the authoritarian state and its so-called immigrant communities.[36] Scenes such as this have become set pieces in contemporary depictions of French society.[37]

If the scene were to end here, it would require little comment. It would be yet another depiction of an all-too-familiar crisis tragically dividing French society for decades. But the scene does not end here. It goes on and, in so doing, goes beyond the caricatural stalemate presented above. A longer look at the graffiti scene — at its structure, logic, and allusive language — unveils an alternate conception of *laïcité*, one that is less categorically authoritarian but that nevertheless aims to retain key aspects of the doctrine.

The scene proposes that we locate this mainspring of republicanism in the experience of critical reading itself. Amid the row over the graffiti exercise, a second teacher, the narrator and Bégaudeau's "fictional" counterpart, passes by. The angry students inform him of what has occurred and try to convince him to take their side in the dispute. "M'sieur," one of them asks, "you agree with us like it's not right to cross students out?" The narrator responds by saying: "I don't know if it's right or not, but couldn't you find anything more original to write than names of countries? If it was me in these circumstances, if somebody asked me to make up something to represent myself, I wouldn't have written France or Vendée, you know?" (*J'sais pas si ça s'fait, mais y'avait pas plus original à peindre que le nom d'un pays? Moi en l'occurrence, si on m'vait demandé de faire un truc qui me représente, j'aurais pas écrit France ou Vendée, vous voyez?*) (255–56).

This evasive answer is revealing. The narrator avoids aligning himself with either the students or his colleague. Rather than take sides, he reframes the debate. In true Socratic fashion, he turns the question back toward the students: "Couldn't you find anything more original to write?" The valorization of originality contrasts with the students' perfunctory recourse to places of family origin as the primary index of their identity. It celebrates the independent construction of the self and disparages the facile, unreflective attachment of one's individual identity to a birthplace or background that one does not choose. In short, it contrasts originality with origins. The narrator's remark suggests that the students have not really *chosen* their words at all, at least not in any active, meaningful way. They have acted mechanically. Their self-expression is not as free as they might think. But the narrator's remark applies to his colleague as well. She also behaves in an unthinking, automatic way. The clumsy manner in which she invokes *laïcité* suggests that she, too, communicates by rote. Neither the art teacher nor the students seems truly adept at the art of free expression.

And yet, while he does not subscribe to the art teacher's rigid interpretation of *laïcité*, the narrator implicitly defends the republican principle. His appeal to originality indicates an abiding commitment to the concepts of individual autonomy and independent thought, pillars of republican *laïcité*. The mention of *La Vendée* as an insignificant, unoriginal indicator of the narrator's own identity brings a historical perspective to the scene. In addition to being Bégaudeau's true birthplace, The Vendée was a royalist stronghold and enemy of the republican cause during the Revolutionary period. The reference to it here reminds the reader of the two-hundred-year-old challenge to integrate the French nation's diverse populations divided by different regional, cultural, and ideological allegiances. It also reminds us, given the immediate context, of the role of the republican school as the primary institution devoted to fashioning a cohesive body politic. The present-day tensions between the Republic and its multicultural population belong to this larger story.

What is most significant in this exchange is that Bégaudeau shifts the discussion from politics to poetics. When the students ask the narrator what he would have written on the wall instead of his birthplace, he proposes, among several possibilities, Rimbaud, explaining to the bewildered and unread students that "he's someone your age" (256). While the students may not recognize the name of Rimbaud, Bégaudeau's reader surely does. The reader grasps the symbolic opposition between, on the one hand, the Vendée, region of royalism, counter-Revolution, and nostalgia for a bygone France, and, on the other, the figure of eternal youth, rebellion, and modernity. Bégaudeau opposes intransigent traditionalism and literary innovation.

Bégaudeau's shift also constructs a new way of conceiving of *laïcité*. The mention of Rimbaud is only the first and most obvious sign of the scene's reformulation of a political question in poetic terms. A more subtle and meaningful move emerges in the way the text returns to the metaphorics of walls and thus redirects the reader's attention to the textual object before his eyes. It is here that *laïcité* takes on a truly literary form.

The narrator must explain to the students that the Vendée is a *département*, a French administrative unit. But he has only mentioned it, he tells them, in order to point out its relative insignificance as a factor in the construction of his self-identity. "What I meant was that I don't really give a damn about it" (257). Still curious about this unknown place called the Vendée, Salimata asks if it is far away. "You see this wall?" the narrator replies, "Well, it's beyond it. Far far beyond it" (257). His answer does more than clarify a point of French geography. It elaborates on his previous remark regarding originality as opposed to origins. The Vendée is analogous to the names of foreign countries invoked by the students. Though the narrator dismisses the *département* as insignificant, the *way* he dispenses with it — the language he uses — *is* significant. He explains it in relation to the school wall. He uses the language of inside and outside. In so doing, he turns the student's attention away from the distant place ("far far beyond") and toward the present location. The foreign geographic entity becomes a meaningless name. It is a mere abstraction in contrast with the actual wall, a real or concrete object that the student can see before her very eyes ("You see this wall?").

The scene pushes the metaphor even further, applying to it a pressure we find nowhere else in the book. Another comment by the narrator emphatically reinforces the significance of "this wall" before their eyes. Once again, a student asks for an explanation of a term: the expression "*en l'occurrence*" (in these circumstances). Frustrated by the students' persistent incomprehension, the narrator replies with surprising vehemence: "In these circumstances means here, in this case, in this situation, now, within these walls, in these circumstances on this one [wall] here." (*En l'occurrence, ça veut dire là, dans ce cas, dans cette situation, maintenant, entre ces murs, en l'occurrence sur celui-là*) (256). The outburst deepens the contrast between inside and outside. It insists on the present circumstances and the experience of the moment as opposed to that which lies beyond and out of reach. The emphasis on the "here and now" ("*là*," "*maintenant*") restates the rebuke of the students' unoriginal appeal to foreign countries and arbitrary places of birth. The narrator celebrates an originality that must arise in the present moment, in the immediate situation in which the students find themselves — "in this case" (*en l'occurrence*) within the walls of the school. The identification of the school as the location for the autonomous construction of identity conveys a most basic — perhaps *the* most basic — republican tenet. It reformulates the view, championed by orthodox republicans and laicists, of the school as a "foundational space" from which the autonomous rational individual and republican citizen emerges.[38] In other words, the narrator's outburst endorses the concept of *laïcité* without using the term.

The most radical recasting of *laïcité* occurs in this scene's explicit self-referentiality. If the narrator's exchange with the students establishes the school as a foundational space for an original construction of the self, the text simultaneously proposes itself as a comparable space. It identifies itself as a site — again, a textual agora — for the performance of *laïcité* in the present. It locates the republican principle in the act of reading itself. In the middle of the narrator's animated explanation of *en l'occurrence*, we come upon the words *entre ces murs* (within these walls). The words, like the term *intra-muros* discussed above, stand out as an allusion to Bégaudeau's own title. What is more, their appearance in a series of near synonyms — "here, in this case, in this situation, now, within these walls, in the circumstances on this one here" — produces an emphatic, almost incantatory, reiteration of the book's name ("within the walls, within the walls, within the walls"). The narrator's remarks to the student thus double as an address to the reader. They exhort the latter to turn his attention also to the "here and now." This means the concrete object before the reader's eyes, the pages of *Entre les murs*. In other words, the text urges the reader to focus on the immediate experience of reading "within the walls." Nor is this moment of textual self-referentiality an isolated occurrence. *Entre les murs* highlights in countless ways the techniques of its own construction. From the metaphorics of walls and interpolated realia to the dialectical structure and seemingly arbitrary juxtapositions, the work constantly redirects the reader's gaze to its own formal properties. It repeatedly reminds the reader that the text is a discourse on literature as much as it is a discourse on the reality beyond its pages.

This particular moment "*en l'occurrence*," however, represents a uniquely powerful integration of literary discourse and the discourse of republican pedagogy and ideology. The emphasis on the "here and now" of the text, the immediacy of the textual object, expresses in literary terms the priority placed on direct observation of concrete things that has long been a central tenet of republican progressive pedagogy of which object lesson and intuitive pedagogy are the quintessential models. The palpability of the text, its own formal constructedness or poeticity, achieves in the artistic realm what a pedagogy based on unmediated encounters with the natural world — on "*les choses*," according to Rousseau, Durkheim, and others — attempts in the progressive classroom. The scene fuses modern formalist reading with modern pedagogy. The literary-pedagogical discourse of the "here and now," moreover, occurs in the context of the narrator's call for originality. He champions the original, autonomous construction of individual identity in the language of active, experiential learning. He expresses, in other words, the paramount feature of *laïcité* in terms that attach it to the republican pedagogical tradition.

What the narrator demands of his students, the text demands of the reader. The appeal to originality simultaneously appeals to the reader's own sense of autonomy. It translates a central tenet of republican *laïcité* into an ethics of reading. It identifies critical reading as a modern-day enactment of what Ferdinand Buisson and other republican educators championed as a mainspring of republican pedagogy. It suggests that the critical reader is a republican reader.

Conclusion

The Strangeness of Republican Culture

In 2002 Flammarion published, under the direction of two of France's leading historians, Christophe Prochasson and Vincent Duclert, the first *Dictionnaire critique de la République* (Critical dictionary of the Republic).[1] With more than two hundred essay-length articles by eminent historians and political theorists, the volume constitutes an editorial tour de force. It is also a sign of the times, a magisterial reminder, among the recent flood of publications on the subject, that the Republic — its identity and values — is in apparent crisis. It is surely no accident that such a compendium of expert analysis should appear at a moment when demographic, geopolitical, and widespread cultural changes are said (yet again) to threaten the survival of French republican traditions. As this publishing enterprise attests, the very meaning of the Republic preoccupies French thought with renewed urgency.[2]

The question of education, moreover, permeates the work. Many of its entries — "Learning," "Condorcet," "School," "Ferry," "Instruction," "Laicity," "Language," "Larousse," "Book" — underscore the indissoluble link between the Republic and its obsession with the school; it is inconceivable to discuss the one without the other. On its face, however, the *Dictionnaire*, hardly concerned with literature or the arts, seems to have only a tangential connection with the central aesthetic concerns of the present study. But a closer look at the editor's presentation suggests that their project is nearer to our own than it would at first appear. In fact, what these concluding pages hope to show is that the stated aims of these historians call for precisely the kind of aesthetic investigations proposed here in *The Pedagogical Imagination*.

The editors insist throughout their preface on the elusive nature of their object of study. Multiform, multifaceted, and ubiquitous, the Republic, they argue, cannot be observed from any one angle. It resides in constitutions and institutions; it provides the conceptual foundation for the construction of French society, the state, and the nation; it preoccupies political philosophers, and it penetrates the collective imagination of the people. For more than two hundred years, they remind us, it has been a source of conflict, tension, and constant questioning. For some, the Republic embodies progress and democracy; for others, it is a frozen object of devotion and an impediment to further democratization. It is a site of paradox where faith in political process meets disenchantment with democracy and its promises. "It would be useless and dangerous," explain Duclert and Prochasson, "to pretend to offer a single vision of the Republic" (11). Their investigation of this multifaceted concept thus requires the dictionary form, a compendium of different perspectives, or, as the editors write, a "plurality of readings."

"Reading" the Republic is not easy, explain the historians. Its very ubiquity makes it hard to see. A constant focus of scholarly study and public debate, the topic itself can seem commonplace and stale. The historian's perception of it, say Duclert and Prochasson, risks growing dull: "A mundane environment (*milieu banal*) in which the contemporary historian finds himself immersed day after day, republican culture must rediscover its strangeness (*la culture républicaine doit retrouver son étrangeté*). Placed at a distance, it will reveal the secrets of its longevity and those of its remarkable plasticity" (12).

The editors are right: "[R]epublican culture must rediscover its strangeness." Historical perspective is essential for seeing republicanism anew. *The Pedagogical Imagination* subscribes to this argument. All of the analyses in the preceding pages have insisted on recovering the historical forces and resonances that bear on contemporary cultural production. Varda's *Les glaneurs et la glaneuse* illustrates the point most boldly. Gleaning, the filmmaker's all-purpose metaphor, refers in part to recuperating the past, to recycling history and integrating it into the frame through which we observe the present. Recalling the legacy of Pierre Larousse and Laroussian pedagogy, Varda unites her own cinematic and instructional project with the nineteenth-century republican lexicographer's promotion of universal education. Orsenna's *La grammaire est une chanson douce* brings together different literary traditions. It reproduces in narrative form the fabulist tradition of La Fontaine, but it also reveals a debt to the "child's tour of the nation" genre of which the republican school manual, *Le tour de la France par deux enfants*, is the prototype. We might say that Orsenna's story continues the republican tradition of fusing traditions, in this case the allegorical tradition of La Fontaine with republican pedagogy.

As an adaptation of Marivaux's *Jeu de l'amour et du hasard*, Kechiche's *L'esquive* obviously harkens back to the eighteenth-century comedy of manners. But its look even further back in time, to Farid al-din Attar's *The Conference of the Birds*, locates a precursor to republican universalist principles in a twelfth-century Islamic poem. Through this transhistorical and multicultural lens, it offers a republican rereading of Marivaux's play. Though François Bégaudeau's *Entre les murs* does not explicitly evoke the past as the other works do (except for its discussion of Plato's *Republic*), it does propose a sustained reflection on the longstanding question of the school as a "sanctuary." As discussed, this topic has deep roots in republican education debates, reaching back to the Revolutionary period and Condorcet's view of *instruction publique* as opposed to Rabaut Saint-Etienne's *éducation nationale*. While different historical lenses apply to each of the specific works, there is one that applies to them all: republican pedagogical discourse forged under the Third Republic.

Les glaneurs et la glaneuse, *La grammaire est une chanson douce*, *L'esquive*, and *Entre les murs* show us many different scenes of formal learning. They are full of classrooms, teachers, and books. But they also place in the foreground their own formal techniques and structural properties. They remind the reader at every moment of their artistic conventions, their own constructedness, their own literary and filmic textuality. This commonplace feature of modernist art takes on new meaning in the context of education, the contemporary crisis of republican schooling, and, more generally, republicanism itself. The formal techniques become themselves sites for interrogating republican ideology, not only that of the present but also that of the past — republican ideology as it has evolved.

The engagement these works demand of their public resonates with a particular pedagogical tradition of active, experiential learning. The reader/viewer's direct encounter with the textual object (its "palpability," as the Russian Formalists would say) stimulates an experience of observation and analysis akin to what was once referred to as object lesson pedagogy and intuitive learning — educational methods that were vehicles for republican ideology. To be sure, these empiricist methods of learning have been widespread throughout the West. They appear in various versions of hands-on, student-centered ("constructivist") learning reminiscent of the theories of Locke and Rousseau. But in the case of France and the founding of the French Republic, these methods became inextricably bound up with republican ideology and national identity. The skills of autonomous rational inquiry acquired in these modern methods were held up as vital to republican democratic values. As the leading republican educator Ferdinand Buisson put it, this progressive pedagogy "succeeds in making the child think because it lets him think on his own instead of obliging him to think as we do, because it has him proceed at his own pace rather than that of his teacher."[3] And Henri Marion insisted that the real value of this education lay in the fact that it "produces free men."[4] For these education reformers and leading intellectuals, pedagogical principles and political ideology were coterminous. By presenting formalist reading as an implementation of this pedagogy, *The Pedagogical Imagination* argues that such reading practices enact republican political ideology. It postulates that critical reading is republican reading.

In chapter 1, by bringing together the insights of Gérard Genette and Roland Barthes, I outlined an intellectual genealogy running from the empirico-positivist mode of inquiry underlying late nineteenth-century education reform to the twentieth-century staple notion of the autonomous reader and the accompanying concept of textuality. Through Genette, we saw how the rise of a scientific study of, and critical discourse on, literature reappears in the autotelic nature of modernist literature, of which Mallarmé, Proust, Valéry, and Blanchot are the representative figures. Literature that reflects on itself — that contains a self-referential critical discourse and thus, by implication, highlights the conditions and materials of its own construction — is, according to Genette, the cultural extension of a mode of literary inquiry begun in the republican classroom. Barthes's concept of textuality has its historical roots in the same transitional moment described by Genette. Modernist innovators like Mallarmé, in conjunction with developments in structural linguistics, give rise, according to Barthes, to a new conception of the literary object. No longer conceived as a "work" produced by a real-life author, the "text" is realized through the practice of reading, through the reader's firsthand exploration of the linguistic and cultural codes of which every text is composed. In other words, Barthes's textuality follows logically from the modernist aesthetic described by Genette that showcases the mechanics of literary production and reception (by representing its own reception) alongside, and perhaps even at the expense of, a work's referential function. In sum, the culture of literary commentary that Genette traces from the classroom to modernist innovation reemerges in the critical reading practice touted by Barthes. The autonomous student of the nineteenth century can be said to herald the autonomous reader of the twentieth.

In strict epistemological terms, of course, this linkage is nonsensical. The nineteenth-century empiricists (and their forerunners) were concerned with observing and knowing the external world or natural reality whereas structuralists, by contrast, shift their interest to semiotic systems and away from the real world to which signs refer. Nevertheless the empiricist language of direct observation is retained in Barthes's discussion of textual analysis. An insistence on the "concrete" object of study — on that which appears immediately before the eyes of the observer (whether researcher, student, or reader) — unites the nineteenth-century empiricist and the twentieth-century structuralist. A freedom from authorial control parallels a freedom from passive submission to the teacher's authority. As we saw in chapter 1, Barthes's wayfaring reader who explores the textual landscape (*"oued"* or "wadi") resembles with remarkable fidelity the ideal student described in Jules Simon's 1872 manifesto for education reform. Simon's student, freed from the routine of slavishly imitating the writings of literary exemplars, is an autonomous reader; his reading experience occasions, as Simon puts it, intellectual "promenades" and "excursions" reminiscent of Rousseau's experiential pedagogy. Barthes's reader, in other words, descends from Émile.

If we return now to Duclert and Prochasson's *Dictionnaire critique de la République*, we discover yet another and even more unexpected way to imagine the nexus between republican pedagogy (with its ideological implications) and modern theories and practices of reading. As we recall, the *Dictionnaire*'s editors assert that *"la culture républicaine doit retrouver son étrangeté"* (republican culture must rediscover its strangeness). Their point, again, is that historical perspective is crucial for gaining a fresh look at this hard-to-see and yet omnipresent thing called republican culture, hard-to-see *because* omnipresent (a *"milieu banal,"* they call it). But their word choice suggests something more. If by the "rediscovery of strangeness" the editors mean a new way of looking at a familiar object, then it is arguably the work of art that is best suited to achieve this goal. As countless theorists, critics, and artists have taught us for almost a century, literature and the arts, because of their formal devices, are particularly adept at making things appear strange. It follows, then, that the skills of critical, formalist reading are as invaluable as those of historical analysis if republican culture — in no small way an emanation of republican pedagogy — is to be seen anew.

Victor Shklovsky's concept of "defamiliarization" or "estrangement" (*ostranenie,* literally in Russian: "the making strange") developed in his seminal essay, "Art as Technique," represents, of course, the most famous exploration of this idea.[5] It also constitutes a primary steppingstone toward — if not an outright cornerstone in — twentieth-century investigations of reader-oriented criticism.[6] By rendering objects in unfamiliar ways — by defamiliarizing them, says Shklovsky — form prompts the reader to rediscover an object so routinely encountered that his perception of it has grown dull. Artistic form, he argues, heightens the reader's or viewer's sensory awareness, shaking him from "habitual," "routinized," or "automatic" perception, which, for Shklovsky, is hardly perception at all. Understood in this way, artistic form becomes precisely what the editors of the *Dictionnaire critique de la République* must consider if they want to achieve their analytical project as they themselves describe it.

It is even possible to read Shklovsky's statement on the estrangement effect of artistic technique in a manner that evokes features of pedagogical doctrine underlying the republican project. By setting Shklovsky's thought side by side with that of republican educator Ferdinand Buisson, we discover a suggestive point of convergence between conceptions of progressive pedagogy and the foundational concepts of twentieth-century literary theory and, in particular, theories of reading. As we saw in chapter 1, Ferdinand Buisson extolled object lesson pedagogy and intuitive learning for their ability to "awaken" and "sharpen" the skills of observation. Use of such methods stimulate the student to search and find knowledge on his or her own (*"on le provoque à chercher, on l'aide à trouver"*) as opposed to the traditional methods relying on rote learning and the passive repetition of ready-made lessons.[7] Buisson and Shklovsky are both concerned with "deroutinized" perception and learning. Moreover, for both the educator and the literary theorist, attaining this sharpness of perception is an exacting task. In order to distinguish his conception of intuitive learning from the German view of intuition (*Anschaung*), understood as an effortless, spontaneous acquisition of knowledge, Buisson, we recall, invoked Descartes's description of intuition as the understanding obtained by the attentive — that is, careful, meticulous, painstaking — mind. In a similar vein Shklovsky disputes the idea, advanced by Herbert Spencer among others, that art should present ideas in an economical fashion making them easily "apprehended with the least possible mental effort" (777). On the contrary, argues Shklovsky, artistic technique should "increase the difficulty and length of perception" (778). The very notion of defamiliarization implies the difficulty involved in the act of observation; when the representation of an object renders it unfamiliar, the reader/observer's efforts of discernment are increased.

One of the most striking points of intersection between Shklovsky's discussion of artistic technique and republican pedagogy is the insistence on the observation of concreteness or concrete things and a related devaluation of abstraction and abstract learning. For Shklovsky, literary language is language that *shows* rather than *tells*. In ordinary, non-artistic uses of language, he observes, we tend to speak in an abbreviated fashion: "[W]e leave phrases unfinished and words half expressed" (778). We communicate without using complete words and only barely perceive the sounds of words uttered by others. Such ordinary communication, says Shklovsky, is a kind of code or shorthand comparable to the symbolic language of algebra; it leaves us with only a vague, imprecise, and abstract comprehension of objects. Literary language restores precision to our perception of things and gives us a concrete sense of them. Art exists, he writes, "to make one feel things, to make the stone *stony*" (778). The heightened perception of the object, in other words, is inseparable from the encounter with the particular, artistic use of language.

The concreteness does not only refer to the object represented; it also resides in the artistic technique itself, in the "palpability" of literary construction.[8] We need only recall from chapter 1 Rousseau's valuation of things over words, Bréal's call for the study of concrete language over abstract rules of grammar, or Durkheim's celebration of pedagogical "realism" — all emblematic expressions of object lesson and intuitive pedagogy — in order to hear echoes of republican pedagogical doctrines in the nature and function of artistic technique as laid out by Shklovsky. The affinity between realist pedagogy and formalist aesthetics becomes more striking still when we recall our discussion (also in chapter 1) of the final lessons of Durkheim's course on the "History of education in France." One of the purposes of concrete, realist learning applied to the humanities, says Durkheim, is that it renders the object of study, Man, unfamiliar. The student discovers the complexity of what the sociologist describes as "the human thing" by treating it not as a timeless model of perfection as one does in the classical humanities but rather as an unknown reality (*"une réalité ignorée"*; 379), and this method of scientifico-humanistic inquiry must necessarily "disorient" the student (*"il faut dépayser l'élève"*).[9] Though Durkheim does not consider the function of artistic technique, he stresses the value of defamiliarization in the humanities in terms that echo the formalist notion of estrangement. To hear such a resonance is to recognize a common imperative shared by republican pedagogy and formalist reading.

It is not enough, however, to observe the methodological and epistemological similarities between formalist theory and experiential pedagogy. Our purpose in these concluding pages is to draw attention to the renewed perception of republican culture that results from the estrangement effect inherent in artistic form and the reading practice that attends to it. To put it another way, our purpose is to show the "strangeness" of republican culture as it is revealed through aesthetic experience, in particular, through the act of reading itself. It is therefore fitting to consider one last reading, a concrete textual example of the confluence of formalist theory and pedagogical doctrine. After all, in both of these systems of "concrete" learning, it is only through a direct encounter with the object itself — aesthetic or otherwise — that the goal of heightened perception can be achieved.

Let us consider, then, a brief scene from François Bégaudeau's *Entre les murs*, one that offers a particularly incisive reflection on the relationship between artistic form and pedagogy. Indeed, the scene relates a class visit to a contemporary art museum in which a group of students find themselves gathered around a bewildering piece of installation art. The sculpture, because of its formal aspects, resembles in miniature Bégaudeau's own literary text, and the student observers become a reflection of Bégaudeau's own reader. Our task now in discussing this episode is to draw out the ways its own formal properties provoke a fresh and unexpected look at republican pedagogy and, by extension, republican ideology. In other words, our task is to see how the work of art "makes strange" and thereby reinvigorates our perception of republican culture.

The scene begins with a museum guide presenting to a group of students a work entitled *L'infini matérialisé* (Infinity materialized); the work is described as "a case built of wood and metal, with mirrored trusses reflecting back and forth endlessly" (201). Attempting to have the students grasp the seemingly illogical combination of concepts that the artwork puts into play, the guide explains in simple terms the basic incompatibility between the material, finite world and the spiritual realm evoked by the infinite. The work is undoubtedly strange and perplexing. Its self-contradictory amalgam of the spiritual and the temporal challenges the mind of the observer, and the docent has difficulty engaging the students in a discussion of it. She eventually draws attention to the inner surfaces or walls (*parois*) of the work and specifically asks the group to identify the artist's materials of construction. A student named Jihad, looking at his own reflection in the work's panels, provides the answer: "Mirrors."

What matters here is that the student sees himself in the act of looking at the very moment that the question of form, structure, and the work's constructedness is raised. In other words, the student/observer's discovery of his own status arises precisely from an attention to the work's form, to the question of *how* it is made as opposed to *what* it represents or means. I have been drawing attention to this point throughout *The Pedagogical Imagination*: in all of the works we have examined we have seen that the reader/viewer's discovery of his or her own active engagement with the work depends on an attention to form. Thus, Jihad's discovery of himself as observer at the moment that he attends to *how* the work is made places *en abyme* the reader of *Entre les murs*. The scene allegorizes the act of formalist reading. The student at the museum is a figure of the reader.

L'infini matérialisé is a complex study in reflection, in both the perceptual and conceptual senses of the word. Just as the inset mirrors produce a seemingly endless game of visual reflection, so, too, do they invite an apparently unlimited number of possibilities for analyzing, attributing significance to — or reading — the work of art. The sculpture puts into play a dialectics of numerous different oppositions: the material and the infinite, the temporal and the spiritual, the real and the imaginary, the particular and the universal. It is, however, the dialectics of opposing spaces, of inside and outside, that is most pertinent for our present purpose. Again, by dint of observing the mirrors, the student/observer standing outside the material boundaries of the work finds himself reflected within. The external world becomes an integral part of the work (a feature of all installation art perhaps). Conversely, the work's subject matter or content — what it is inherently about, that which we expect to find "in" it — is that which lies outside of it. The sculpture brings the outside in and turns the inside out. One could certainly take this dynamic as a universal metaphor for the school itself . . . any and every school: within the classroom walls one finds reflected the outside world or society. This otherwise trite observation is anything but in the case of France's republican school in which, as explored in the previous chapter, so much debate for so long has centered on the extent to which the school, in order to remain true to its supposedly Condorcetian heritage, must remain, like a "sanctuary," protected from the vicissitudes of the outside world. Arguably more than in any other nation, the proper relation between the "inside" and the "outside" of the school is a particularly delicate and complicated question in the history of French schooling.

The dialectics of spatial opposition aestheticized in *L'infini matérialisé* gives form to republican pedagogy in yet another, less obvious way — one that engages more directly the theories and methodologies of object lesson and intuitive learning. These modes of active, experiential learning were (and remain) transgressive in the most literal sense: they promoted in various ways the crossing of traditional boundaries. To see this we need only recall the most rudimentary manifestations of object lesson pedagogy. For example, the shift from "book learning" (*l'enseignement par les mots*) to "learning by looking" (*l'enseignement par les yeux*) entailed a turning of the student's attention away from abstractions (nomenclature, definitions, rules of grammar) to the observation of the natural world, which quite often meant the observation of objects found beyond the classroom walls. A particularly vivid example of such object lesson pedagogy is the *musée scolaire*, a showcase erected in the classroom in which students and teachers displayed plants, minerals, insects, and other sundry objects typically collected in the vicinity of the school, perhaps even on the occasion of a *promenade scolaire*, the precursor to today's "field trip."[10] Of course, most learning activities did not occur literally out of doors. But the idea that the student's attention should be directed away from the teacher's voice or beyond the confines of slavish rote exercises and toward the "real, concrete world outside" — *la chose* — became paradigmatic. Thus, as we have seen, Jules Simon could conceive of reading itself in terms of "*promenades*" and "*excursions*" — in other words, "outings."

If we return now to *L'infini matérialisé*, we see how the dialectics of inside and outside manifested in artistic form brings to the fore fundamental though often overlooked features of republican pedagogy. We must consider, more specifically, the institutional context in which we encounter the sculpture. The students are, after all, on a "field trip" or *sortie scolaire* — literally, a "school outing." They are engaged in a pedagogical activity based on the principle that learning requires excursions, that it occurs beyond the classroom walls. The very exercise that brings them to this direct encounter with the work of art belongs squarely in the tradition of active, experiential learning at the heart of object lesson and intuitive learning. The students are participants in a modern variation on that quintessential exercise that Jules Ferry and others placed at the foundation of republican education reform, "*à la base de tout*."

And yet, to grasp fully the dialectic of spatial opposition at work here, we must note that this excursion or "outing" is also an entry or ingress. The museum setting approximates and thus recalls the classroom itself, the very educational environment from which the organized "outing" is meant to represent an escape. Needless to say, the museum guide, for which the English term *docent* (from Latin, *docere*, 'to teach') seems especially apt, performs the role of the teacher. More importantly, the text specifically draws attention to the resemblance between the museum and the school by means of a curious comment appearing in the middle of the scene. The narrator conspicuously remarks, "Within the contemporary walls (*entre les murs contemporains*) resonated [the docent's] voice" (201–2). The line, containing as it does an unmistakable mention of *Entre les murs*'s title, does more than tell us about the reverberation of sound within the walls of the museum. Given that the words *entre les murs* evoke most immediately, in the context of Bégaudeau's book, the space of a present-day classroom, they serve to remind us that despite the *sortie scolaire* we are still in many respects "within the walls" of an educational environment, which is to say, within the institutional walls of a republican space of learning. To step outside the physical classroom sensu stricto as part of a tradition that makes boundary crossing, "excursions," and "outings," whether literal or figurative, so central to its mission may be no real exit at all. It suggests rather that a dynamics of transgression (in the etymological as opposed to the modish, postmodern sense) is a constitutive feature of the pedagogical doctrine in question. Like the human figures reflected in the sculpture around which the students gather, it remains unclear whether the students are "in" or "out" of school while on their excursion or "outing." They are, in many respects, both at once. My own reader, moreover, will not have missed the connection between the contemporary museum visit in *Entre les murs* and the aforementioned *musée scolaire*, the classroom display case of objects collected from the natural world. This quintessential accessory of nineteenth-century republican schooling and emblem of object lesson pedagogy brings "within the walls" that which naturally lies "beyond the walls." It is a traditional classroom manifestation of the dialectics of inside and outside to which Bégaudeau's work gives contemporary literary form.

Our discussion requires mention of one final boundary crossing, or transgression, that brings us back to the interconnected topics of reading, form, and pedagogy. When the narrator refers to "*entre les murs*" — that is, to the title of the book held in the reader's hands — in the middle of the museum scene, his words send a signal to the reader, a reminder that the latter is in the act of reading a literary text. This direct address to the reader, or double enunciation, disrupts the fictional illusion. It transgresses the boundary separating the space depicted in the text and the space occupied by the actual reader. As we saw in chapter 5, *Entre les murs* plays endlessly with this question. As a work of "documentary fiction" that explicitly draws attention to this double status, *Entre les murs* keeps the reader guessing as to whether, and to what extent, the text depicts the reality of the school or the author's own fanciful invention. Like the mirrored walls of *L'infini matérialisé*, *Entre les murs*'s formal techniques (for example, its extensive use of realia) constantly destabilize the reader's sense of a clear distinction between opposing domains, between the fictional "inside" and the referential world "outside." The double enunciation therefore reinforces the point that careful observation, or study, of the sculpture reproduces within the fictional, imaginary world of the text the real-life experience of the reader.

The reflection of the reader in the figure of the student encapsulates a point made throughout *The Pedagogical Imagination*. In all of the readings in the foregoing chapters I have argued that engagement with the formal devices in the literary and filmic texts in question enacts the pedagogical principles of active experiential learning that, while widespread and in no way the exclusive property of republican France, have been, from a historical point of view, intimately and explicitly bound up with republican ideology and national identity to a degree that is arguably unparalleled elsewhere.

One might ask, of course, to what extent these individual readings tell us anything about critical reading in general? The works of Varda, Orsenna, Kechiche, and Bégaudeau examined here represent, after all, "strong" cases in which the connection between schooling, reading, and artistic form is particularly explicit. To what extent, in other words, do particular cases and particular readings provide evidence of a universal phenomenon? *L'infini matérialisé* addresses this question in a characteristically artful fashion ... by reflecting it back at us. The endless game of reflection that its mirrored walls set in motion require its observer to reflect on the possibility of finding the universal in the particular. *L'infini matérialisé* is a microcosm of *Entre les murs* as a whole in this respect as well. The book generates a similar reflection. It asks us to consider whether a one-year chronicle in a single classroom in Paris's nineteenth arrondissement can say anything about French schooling in general or, for that matter, about education elsewhere in the world. Can this particular case, it asks, represent a universal condition? The international success of *Entre les murs*, both the book and the film, suggests that perhaps it can. By extension, then, and insofar as the book, as we have seen, is also about the experience of reading, it may well be that there is something in this particular reading experience that applies more universally. This is, at any rate, the possibility the work of art asks us to consider.

One might also observe that there could be nothing more obvious than to say that reading practices reenact pedagogical principles and the lessons learned at school. The school, from the elementary grades to the university seminar, is the place where we acquire and hone the skills of reading in the most concerted manner. It could be said, then, that every adult reader, whatever the age, remains in some sense within the imaginary walls of the school. The reader is always a student. It is precisely the obviousness of this point, however, that prevents us from perceiving and thus thinking about it in a deliberate and self-conscious manner. The power of the work of art — in particular, of those examined in *The Pedagogical Imagination* — resides in its ability to defamiliarize this banal and thus overlooked relationship and thereby reawaken our perception of it.

Let us return now to the phrase that launched this close reading of the museum scene and its perplexing sculpture, Prochasson and Duclert's assertion that "republican culture must rediscover its strangeness." *L'infini matérialisé* is a monument to this very concern. It responds to the historians' plea. It does so, however, in an unexpected fashion, by positing aesthetic experience as a means for discovering this strangeness. In the end the most arresting feature of this artwork — and in this respect it stands for all of the works studied in *The Pedagogical Imagination* — lies in the very fact that examination of its form constitutes in and of itself an unusual look at that seedbed of republican culture and ideology, the school. Perhaps the strangest part of the estrangement effect here resides not in the new and uncustomary view of the republican school that the artwork affords but rather in the very identification of works of imagination, in and of themselves, as sites for reflecting on education.

Notes

INTRODUCTION

1. I am referring, of course, to the ongoing debate over whether Muslim girls should be permitted to wear headscarves in France's public schools, which some consider to be a violation of the republican principle of *laïcité* (official state secularism).

2. For an overview of reactions to the story, see Gérard Brault, "Reflexions on Daudet's 'La dernière classe: Récit d'un petit Alsacien,'" *Symposium: A Quarterly Journal in Modern Literatures* 54, no. 2 (2000).

3. Of the literarily countless treatments of this question, see, for example, Jerome J. McGann, *The Textual Condition* (Princeton NJ: Princeton University Press, 1991), 10–12.

4. Pierre Laszlo, "La Leçon de choses, or Lessons from Things," *Sub Stance*, no. 71–72 (1993): 277.

5. Ernest Renan, *La réforme intellectuelle et morale* (Paris: Michel Lévy Frères, 1871), 100–101.

6. Clément Falcucci, *L'humanisme dans l'enseignement secondaire en France au XIXe siècle* (Toulouse: Edward Privat, 1939), 355.

7. For a recent assessment of Bourdieu's influence on subsequent education research, see Annette Lareau and Elliot B. Weininger, "Cultural Capital in Educational Research: A Critical Assessment," in *After Bourdieu*, ed. David L. Swartz and Vera L. Zolberg (Dordrecht: Kluwer Academic, 2004).

8. For an example of a Foucauldian analysis of the republican school with respect to disciplinary practices, hygiene, and the body, see Georges Vigarello, *Le corps redressé: Histoire d'un pouvoir pédagogique.* (Paris: J. P. Delarge, 1978).

9. Christian Nique and Claude Lelièvre, *La République n'éduquera plus: La fin du mythe Ferry.* (Paris: Plon, 1993), 72.

10. Quoted in Nique and Lelièvre, *La République*, 74.

11. M. Martin Guiney, *Teaching the Cult of Literature in the French Third Republic.* (New York: Palgrave Macmillan, 2004), xiv.

12. Guiney, *Teaching the Cult*, 8.

13. Guiney, *Teaching the Cult*, 106.

14. Eric Dubreucq, *Une éducation républicaine-Marion, Buisson, Durkheim* (Paris: Vrin, 2004).

15. Patricia A. Tilburg, *Colette's Republic: Work, Gender, and Popular Culture in France, 1870–1914* (New York: Berghahn Books, 2009).

16. André Chervel, *Histoire de l'enseignement du français du XVIIe au XXe siècle* (Paris: Editions Retz-Nathan, 2006), 530; Violaine Houdart-Mérot, *La culture littéraire au lycée depuis 1880* (Rennes: Presses universitaires de Rennes, 1998), 43–47.

17. See, for example, the entry for *explication de texte* in *Merriam-Webster's Encyclopedia of Literature* (n.p.: Merriam-Webster, 1995), 397–98.

18. For an overview of the various currents that comprise New Formalism, see Marjorie Levinson, "What Is New Formalism?," *PMLA: Publications of the Modern Language Association of America* 122, no. 2 (2007).

19. Levinson, "What Is New Formalism?," 559.

20. What Marjorie Levinson calls "activist" New Formalism is *not* a reaction or backlash against New Historicism. It would be more accurate to describe it as a corrective or readjustment. These New Formalists acknowledge the influence of, and build on, the contributions of New Historicist criticism. They seek, however, to reinvest this critical practice with a renewed sensitivity to form and textuality. The best New Historicist critics, moreover, have always demonstrated an acute sensitivity to formal questions. See, for example, W. J. T. Mitchell's praise of Edward Said: W. J. T. Mitchell, "The Commitment to Form; or, Still Crazy after All These Years," *PMLA: Publications of the Modern Language Association of America* 118, no. 2 (2003): 324.

21. Mark David Rasmussen, "New Formalisms?," in *Renaissance Literature and Its Formal Engagements*, ed. Mark David Rasmussen (New York: Palgrave, 2002), 1.

22. Ellen Rooney, "Form and Contentment," *Modern Language Quarterly* 61, no. 1 (2000): 33.

23. Paul B. Armstrong, *Play and the Politics of Reading: The Social Uses of Modernist Form* (Ithaca NY: Cornell University Press, 2005), x. Though Armstrong does not identify himself as belonging to the movement, his project clearly demonstrates a commitment to it.

24. Rooney, "Form and Contentment," 37.

25. For Durkheim's use of this term, see Émile Durkheim, "La morale laïque," in *L'éducation morale* (Paris: Presses universitaires de France, 1992), 3.

26. Vincent Duclert et al., *Dictionnaire critique de la République*, new ed. (Paris: Flammarion, 2007), 12.

1. A NEW LANGUAGE OF LEARNING

1. Peter Gumbel, *On achève bien les écoliers* (Paris: Grasset, 2010), 12.

2. There exist several excellent historical studies of education reform under the Third Republic. See, in particular, Antoine Prost, *Histoire de l'enseignement en France, 1800–1967* (Paris: Armand Colin, 1968); Françoise Mayeur, *De la Révolution à l'école républicaine*, ed. Louis-Henri Parias, Histoire générale de l'enseignement et de l'éducation (Paris: Perrin, 2004); Theodore Zeldin, *France, 1848–1945: Intellect, Taste and Anxiety*, 2 vols., vol. 2 (Oxford: Clarendon Press, 1977); Eugen Weber, "Civilizing in Earnest: Schools and Schooling," in *Peasants into Frenchmen: The Modernization of Rural France, 1870–1914* (Stanford CA: Stanford University Press, 1976).

3. The historian Ernest Lavisse acknowledges the prevalence of this viewpoint (even while doubting its validity): "It is true that one said: 'It is the Prussian schoolteacher who won the battles of Sadowa and Sedan'; to the schoolteacher, some have added the university professor as well." Ernest Lavisse, "La question du Latin et du Grec d'après M. Raoul Frary et après M. Charles Bigot," *La revue bleue* (1886): 270. See also Célestin Bouglé, *The French Conception of "Culture Générale" and Its Influences upon Instruction* (New York: Bureau of Publications, Teachers College, Columbia University, 1938), 17–18.

4. Renan, *La réforme intellectuelle*, 95.

5. Jacques Ozouf and Mona Ozouf, "Le Tour de la France par deux enfants: The Little Red Book of the Republic," in *Realms of Memory: Rethinking the French Past*, ed. Lawrence D. Kritzman (New York: Columbia University Press, 1996), 136.

6. Louis Liard, *Universités et facultés* (Paris: Armand Colin, 1890), 32.

7. Alfred Croiset, "Les besoins de la démocratie en matière d'éducation," in *L'éducation de la démocratie. Leçons professées à l'École des hautes études sociales par MM. Ernest Lavisse, Alfred Croiset, Ch. Seignobos, P. Malapert, G. Lanson, J. Hadamard* (Paris: F. Alcan, 1907), 43–44.

8. See Prost, *Histoire de l'enseignement*, 501–11.

9. Falcucci, *L'humanisme dans l'enseignement secondaire*.

10. Jo Burr Margadant, *Madame le professeur: Women Educators in the Third Republic* (Princeton NJ: Princeton University Press, 1990).

11. George Weisz, *The Emergence of Modern Universities in France, 1863–1914* (Princeton NJ: Princeton University Press, 1983); Louis M. Greenberg, "Architects of the New Sorbonne: Liard's Purpose and Durkheim's Role," *History of Education Quarterly* 21, no. 1 (1981).

12. Mayeur, *De la Révolution*, 581.

13. Jean-Michel Gaillard, "Éduquer et instruire," in *L'Histoire* (1996), 35.

14. Félix Pécaut, "De l'usage et de l'abus de la pédagogie," in *L'Éducation publique et la vie nationale* (Paris: Hachette et Cie, 1907), 53.

15. Such criticisms of "ed schools" applies to perceptions of teacher training in both the United States and France. For a discussion of the question in the United States, see David F. Labaree, *The Trouble with Ed Schools* (New Haven CT: Yale University Press, 2004). For France, see Jean-Claude Milner, *De l'école* (Paris: Editions du Seuil, 1984); Denis Kambouchner, *Une école contre l'autre* (Paris: Presses universitaires de France, 2000).

16. Falcucci, *L'humanisme dans l'enseignement secondaire*, 355.

17. Pierre Kahn reports in *Leçon de choses* that he has been unable to locate the catchphrase in its original publication.

18. See Jean Hébrard, "L'histoire de l'enseignement des sciences en France," La main à la pâte, http://www.inrp.fr/lamap/?Page_Id=1009.

19. Narcisse Plâtrier, "Leçon de choses," in *Dictionnaire de pédagogie et d'instruction primaire*, ed. Ferdinand Buisson (Paris: Hachette et Cie, 1887), 1534. Plâtrier explains that he is quoting the naturalist and anatomist Georges Pouchet (1833–1894) in these lines.

20. Plâtrier, "Leçon de choses."

21. Élie Pécaut, "Quelques mots au sujet de l'enseignement des sciences physiques et naturelles à l'école normale primaire," *Revue pédagogique* 2, no. 1 (1883): 484. Cited in Pierre Kahn, *La leçon de choses: Naissance de l'enseignement des sciences à l'école primaire* (Villeneuve d'Ascq: Presses universitaires du Septentrion, 2002), 122.

22. Kahn, *La leçon de choses*, 172.

23. Originally published in 1938, the course was republished in 1969: Émile Durkheim, *L'évolution pédagogique en France* (Paris: Presses universitaires de France, 1969). Parenthetical page references in the text are to this later edition. M. Martin Guiney observes that Durkheim's history of modern pedagogical thought relied heavily on Gabriel Compayré's 1879 *Histoire critique des doctrines de l'éducation en France depuis le seizième siècle* (Critical history of doctrines of education in France since the sixteenth century). See Guiney, *Teaching the Cult of Literature*, 83–84.

24. The opposition between these two intellectual traditions (explained in d'Alembert's Preliminary Discourse) is of course less stark than this schema suggests. Baconian/Lockean empiricism is certainly rationalist insofar as it posits that knowledge is established through sense experience informed by reason and not by nonrational (e.g., supernatural) explanations of phenomena. Durkheim expresses this empiricist debt to Cartesian rationalism when he writes: "We must remain Cartesian insofar as we must train rationalists, that is, men committed to [seeing] clear ideas, but rationalists of a new sort; they must know that things, be they human or physical, are of an irreducible complexity and who, nevertheless, know how to look directly and unfailingly at this complexity" (399).

25. Jean-Jacques Rousseau, *Émile, ou de l'éducation* (Paris: Garnier-Flammarion, 1966), 232.

26. In addition to Guiney's aforementioned 2004 study, see Gérard Genette, "Rhétorique et enseignement," in *Figures II* (Paris: Seuil, 1969); Michel Charles, *L'arbre*

et la source (Paris: Editions du Seuil, 1985); Antoine Compagnon, *La Troisième République des lettres, de Flaubert à Proust* (Paris: Seuil, 1983); Martine Jey, *La littérature au lycée: Invention d'une discipline (1880–1925)* (Metz: Centre d'études linguistiques des textes et des discours, Université de Metz, 1998); Violaine Houdart-Mérot, *La culture littéraire au lycée depuis 1880* (Rennes: Presses universitaires de Rennes, 1998); Violaine Houdart-Mérot, "Literary Education in the *Lycée*: Crises, Continuity, and Upheaval since 1880," *Yale French Studies*, no. 113 (2008).

27. Michel Bréal, *De l'enseignement des langues vivantes. Conférences faites aux étudiants en lettres de la Sorbonne*, 2nd ed. (Paris: Hachette, 1900). Cited in Molly Nesbit, *Their Common Sense* (London: Black Dog, 2000), 48.

28. Michel Bréal, *Quelques mots sur l'instruction publique en France* (Paris: Hachette, 1872), 39.

29. The formulation of the opposition in these terms comes from Charles, *L'arbre et la source*.

30. Edgar Morin, "Le trou noir de la laïcité," *le débat*, no. 58 (1990): 38.

31. See Leon Sachs, "Putting History into Practice: Intellectual History as Literary Form in Roger Martin du Gard's *Jean Barois*," *Contemporary French Civilization* 28, no. 1 (2004).

32. For a more detailed discussion of Shklovsky's concept of defamiliarization see the conclusion. For a much longer historical treatment of the concept, see Carlo Ginzburg, "Making Things Strange: The Prehistory of a Literary Device," Representations 56 (1996).

33. Kahn, La leçon de choses, 172.

34. Daniel Hameline, "Les malentendus de la méthode intuitive," in *L'école de la Troisième République en questions: Débats et controverses dans le "Dictionnaire de pédagogie" de Ferdinand Buisson*, ed. Daniel Denis and Pierre Kahn (Berne: Peter Lang, 2006), 82. Hameline, we should note, doubts the influence of Buisson's article on intuition (see note 35).

35. Ferdinand Buisson, "Intuition et méthode intuitive," in *Dictionnaire de pédagogie et d'instruction primaire (partie 1)*, ed. Ferdinand Buisson (Paris: Hachette, 1882–1893). Subsequent page references to this article appear parenthetically in the text.

36. Claude Lelièvre and Christian Nique, *Bâtisseurs d'école: Histoire biographique de l'enseignement en France* (Paris: Nathan pédagogie, 1994), 301.

37. See Pierre Kahn, "Philosophie et pédagogie dans le *Dictionnaire*: La question du sensualisme," in *L'école de la Troisième République en questions: Débats et controverses dans le "Dictionnaire de pédagogie" de Ferdinand Buisson*, ed. Daniel Denis and Pierre Kahn (Berne: Peter Lang, 2006), 98.

38. Rousseau, *Émile, ou de l'éducation*: 219.

39. Kahn, *La leçon de choses*, 48–49.

40. Jules Simon, "Instruction relative à l'institution de réunions périodiques des professeurs dans les lycées et aux réformes que semble réclamer le système d'éducation et

d'enseignement suivi dans les établissements d'instruction secondaire, le 17 septembre 1872," in *Circulaires et instructions officielles relatives à l'instruction publique* (Paris: Delalain Frères, L'Université de France, 1878), 223–24.

41. Cited in Prost, *Histoire de l'enseignement*, 219. See also Yves Gaulupeau, *La France à l'école* (Paris: Gallimard, 1992), 82.

42. Jules Ferry, "Ch. Zevort jugé par M. Jules Ferry," *Revue internationale de l'enseignement* 14 (1887): 644. Cited in Falcucci, *L'humanisme dans l'enseignement secondaire*, 396.

43. Montaigne's remark concerns the qualities of the ideal teacher, but the logic of the essay supports the view that these are also intellectual qualities that should be instilled in the student. Though a cornerstone of Western educational thought harkening back to Socrates and perhaps, historically, more praised than actually practiced, this bias for method over content has come under attack in recent decades. So-called conservatives accuse progressives of excessively emphasizing methods of learning over the transmission of disciplinary knowledge. An overly zealous eagerness to teach students how to teach themselves, they argue, has produced a culture of schooling in which students fail to learn anything at all. Educators imbued with the anti-authoritarian spirit of the 1960s and 1970s are often blamed for this decline in academic rigor defined in terms of the disappearance of substantial content from the curriculum. But long before the cultural watershed of 1968, pedagogical progressivism had taken root in republican educational thought.

44. Henri Marion, *Le mouvement des idées pédagogiques en France depuis 1870* (Paris: Impr. nationale, 1889), 5.

45. Yves Déloye observes in his recent essay on *"Instruction"* in the *Dictionnaire critique de la République* that "form and method of education are as important as its content." Yves Déloye, "L'Instruction," in *Dictionnaire critique de la République*, ed. Vincent Duclert, et al. (Paris: Flammarion, 2007), 186.

46. I am relying here on distinctions proposed by Roman Ingarden in "The General Question of the Essence of Form and Content," *Journal of Philosophy* 57, no. 7 (1960). For a more recent discussion of this question dating back to Aristotle, see Carole Talon-Hugon, *Morales de l'art*, Lignes d'art (Paris: Presses universitaires de France, 2009), 111.

47. Pericles Lewis, *The Cambridge Introduction to Modernism*, Cambridge introductions to literature (Cambridge: Cambridge University Press, 2007), 6.

48. More recently, in *Their Common Sense*, the art historian Molly Nesbit demonstrates how the new scientific education in the Third Republic's schools, and specifically object lesson pedagogy, left its mark on experiments in the visual arts and, in particular, cubism.

49. Genette, "Rhétorique et enseignement," 42–43.

50. Ewa M. Thompson, *Russian Formalism and Anglo-American New Criticism: A Comparative Study* (The Hague: Mouton, 1971), 146; Tzvetan Todorov, "Three Conceptions of Poetic Language," in *Russian Formalism: A Retrospective Glance:*

A Festschrift in Honor or Victor Erlich, ed. Robert Louis Jackson and Stephen Rudy (New Haven CT: Yale Center for International and Area Studies, 1985), 131; Peter Hodgson, "Viktor Shklovsky and the Formalist Legacy: Imitation/ Stylization in Narrative Fiction," in Jackson and Rudy, *Russian Formalism*, 195.

51. Roland Barthes, "La mort de l'auteur," in *Oeuvres* (Paris: Seuil, 2002). References to this edition of the essay, originally published in 1968, appear parenthetically in the text.

52. Roland Barthes, "De l'oeuvre au texte," in *Oeuvres*, 75.

53. Simon, "Instruction relative à l'institution," 221–22.

54. Barthes repeatedly criticizes established academic (positivist) literary criticism (*la critique universitaire*) for being fixated with elements (such as sources) that are external to the text itself; they are abstractions in the sense that they draw attention away from (literally *ab* 'from' + *trahere* 'draw') the text itself: "it is always a matter in [mainstream] university criticism of putting the work under consideration in relation to something *else*, a literary *elsewhere*." Roland Barthes, "Les Deux critiques," *MLN* 78, no. 5 (1963): 449.

2. VISUALIZING LITERACY

1. Released in July 2000, the film has won numerous awards including the Los Angeles Film Critics Association Award for "Best Non-Fiction Film," the European Film Academy Award for "Best Documentary Film," and the Montréal Festival of New Cinema's "People's Choice Award."

2. For other useful discussions of the film, see Ben Tyrer, "Digression and Return: Aesthetics and Politics in Agnès Varda's *Les glaneurs et la glaneuse* (2000)," *Studies in French Cinema* 9, no. 2 (2009); R. Cruickshank, "The Work of Art in the Age of Global Consumption: Agnes Varda's *Les glaneurs et la glaneuse*," *Esprit créateur* 47, no. 3 (2007); Emma Wilson, "*Les glaneurs et la glaneuse*: Salvage and the Art of Forgetting," in *The Art of the Project: Projects and Experiments in Modern French Culture*, ed. Johnnie Gratton and Michael Sheringham (New York: Berghahn, 2005); Maryse Fauvel, "Nostalgia and Digital Technology: *The Gleaners and I* (Varda, 2000) and *The Triplets of Belleville* (Chomet, 2003) as Reflective Genres," *Studies in French Cinema* 5, no. 3 (2005); Agnès Calatayud, *Les glaneurs et la glaneuse*: Agnès Varda's Self-Portrait," *Dalhousie French Studies* 61 (2002); and Mireille Rosello, "Agnès Varda's *Les Glaneurs et la glaneuse*: Portrait of the Artist as an Old Lady," *Studies in French Cinema* 1, no. 1 (2001).

3. See, for example, A. O. Scott, "Film Festival Review; A Reaper of the Castoff, Be It Material or Human," *New York Times*, September 30, 2000, http://movies.nytimes .com/movie/review?res=9C01E0DA173DF933A0575AC0A9669C8B63.

4. Tyrer, "Digression and Return," 162.

5. See Rosello, "Agnès Varda's *Les glaneurs et la glaneuse*."

6. See Pascal Ory, "Le 'Grand Dictionnaire' de Pierre Larousse," in *Les lieux de mémoire*, ed. Pierre Nora (Paris: Gallimard, 1997).

7. See Alain Rey, "Le lexicographe," in *Pierre Larousse et son temps*, ed. Jean-Yves Mollier and Pascal Ory (Paris: Larousse, 1995), 133.

8. André Rétif, *Pierre Larousse et son œuvre, 1817–1875* (Paris: Larousse, 1974), 96.

9. Rétif, *Pierre Larousse*, 72.

10. Rétif, *Pierre Larousse*, 105.

11. Rétif, *Pierre Larousse*, 106–7.

12. Léon Flot, "Lexicologie," in *Nouveau dictionnaire de pédagogie et d'instruction primaire*, ed. Ferdinand Buisson (Paris: Hachette, 1911). Online edition, http://www.inrp.fr/edition-electronique/lodel/dictionnaire-ferdinand-buisson/document.php?id=3052.

13. Michel Bréal, the "father of semantics" and mentor of Ferdinand de Saussure, published his monumental *Essai de sémantique* in 1897.

14. Cited in Rétif, *Pierre Larousse*, 108–9.

15. See Chervel, *Histoire de l'enseignement*.

16. Cited in Rétif, *Pierre Larousse*, 95.

17. Agnès Varda, *Varda par Agnès* (Paris: Cahiers du Cinema, 1994), 6–7.

18. Varda, *Varda par Agnès*, 35.

19. Varda, *Varda par Agnès*, 13.

20. The work of Ségolène Le Men is particularly significant on this matter. See Ségolène Le Men, *Les abécédaires français illustrés du XIXe siècle* (Paris: Promodis, 1984) and "La pédagogie par l'image dans un manuel de la Troisième République: *Le tour de la France par deux enfants*," in *Usages de l'image au XIXe siècle*, ed. Stéphane Michaud, Jean-Yves Mollier, and Nicole Savy (Paris: Editions Créaphis, 1992).

21. Chervel, *Histoire de l'enseignement*, 395.

22. Rétif, *Pierre Larousse*, 124.

23. Pierre Larousse, "Préface," in *Grand dictionnaire universel, français, historique, géographique, mythologique, bibliographique, littéraire, artistique, scientifique, etc.* (Paris: Larousse et Boyer, 1866), lxv.

24. Claude Augé, "Préface," in *Nouveau Larousse illustré; dictionnaire universel encyclopédique*, ed. Pierre Larouse and Claude Augé (Paris: Librairie Larousse, 1898), i.

25. Robert Darnton, *The Great Cat Massacre and Other Episodes in French Cultural History* (New York: Basic Books, 1984), 195.

26. See Sachs, "Putting History into Practice."

27. See Richard Strier, "How Formalism Became a Dirty Word, and Why We Can't Do without It," in *Renaissance Literature and Its Formal Engagements*, ed. Mark David Rasmussen (New York: Palgrave, 2002).

28. There seems to be no end to the number of semantic connections that this frame, like the film itself, invites. The pronoun *elle*, for example, also establishes a relationship between the female figure pointing and the sentence at the top of the frame. In

deference to Varda's own concern for restraint and selectivity in the act of gleaning, I will refrain from offering a reading of Varda's inclusion of the spelling error (*verres* with 3 *r*'s) at the top of the frame.

3. TEACHING SUSPICION

1. Erik Orsenna, *La grammaire est une chanson douce*, Le Livre de Poche ed. (Paris: Stock, 2001), 11. All quotations from *La grammaire est une chanson douce* refer to this edition. Subsequent page references will appear parenthetically in the text. Unless otherwise indicated, English translations are my own. Where I have used Moishe Black's translation, I indicate this parenthetically in the text by a second page number that refers to the following edition: Erik Orsenna, *Grammar Is a Gentle, Sweet Song*, trans. Moishe Black (New York: George Braziller, 2004).

2. Originally published by Stock in 2001, the book had sold, according to Edistat, approximately 280,000 copies by 2009. Writing in 2006, Jean-Benoît Nadeau and Julie Barlow, the authors of *The Story of French*, claim that *La grammaire est une chanson douce* and its sequel, *Les chevaliers du subjonctif* (The Knights of the Subjunctive) had together sold over a million copies. (They are perhaps taking into account sales of translations as well.) See Jean-Benoît Nadeau and Julie Barlow, *The Story of French* (New York: St. Martin's Press, 2006), 381.

3. G. Bruno was the pen name for Madame Augustine Guyau, née Tuillerie, who was the mother of the philosopher Jean-Marie Guyau, author of *L'irréligion de l'avenir*. She later married the writer and philosopher Alfred Fouillée, who played an important role in the publishing of the manual. For details of this history, see Jacques Ozouf and Mona Ozouf, "*Le tour de la France par deux enfants*: Le petit livre rouge de la République," in *Les lieux de mémoire*, ed. Pierre Nora (Paris: Gallimard, 1997).

4. See Ozouf and Ozouf, "*Le tour de la France*."

5. Ralph Albanese, *La Fontaine à l'école républicaine: Du poète universel au classique scolaire*, EMF critiques (Charlottesville: Rookwood Press, 2003), 1.

6. See, for example, Jean-Paul Brighelli, *La fabrique du crétin: La mort programmée de l'école* (Paris: Gawsewitch, 2005) and *A bonne école* (Paris: Gawsewitch, 2006).

7. Roland Barthes provides a classic formulation of this idea when he writes: "We must say farewell to the idea that the science of literature can teach us the meaning that must without fail be attributed to a work. It will not provide nor even rediscover any [single] meaning but will describe the logic by which [many] meanings are engendered in a manner that can be accepted by the symbolic logic of human beings, just as sentences in French are accepted by the "linguistic sense" of French speakers." See Roland Barthes, *Critique et vérité* (Paris: Éditions du Seuil, 1966), 62–63.

8. Gérard Genette, "Structuralisme et critique littéraire," *L'arc* 26 (1969): 39.

9. Mireille Grange and Michel Leroux, "La pédagogie sens dessus dessous: Les programmes de français des collèges," *le débat*, no. 135 (2005): 28.

10. Grange and Leroux, "La pédagogie," 28.

11. Cited in Grange and Leroux, "La pédagogie," 28–29. See Danièle Sallenave, "'L'auteur prétend que . . .' Genèse d'une formule, ravages d'une méthode," in *Propositions pour les enseignements littéraires*, ed. Michel Jarrety (Paris: Presses universitaires de France, 2000).

12. Grange and Leroux, "La pédagogie," 29.

13. David F. Bell, "A Moratorium on Suspicion?," *PMLA: Publications of the Modern Language Association of America* 117, no. 3 (2002): 488.

14. Bell, "Moratorium on Suspicion?," 487.

15. Bell, "Moratorium on Suspicion?," 489.

16. Anthony T. Kronman, *Education's End: Why Our Colleges and Universities Have Given Up on the Meaning of Life* (New Haven CT: Yale University Press, 2007), 123–24.

17. This is an argument that applies also to the New Criticism and to the rise of Literary History, or lansonism.

18. In *L'école de la République sous le choc: Défense et illustration de l'enseignement des lettres* (The Republic's school in a state of shock: defense and illustration of the teaching of literature), the writer and teacher François Aguettaz attacks what he sees as the hypocrisy in Orsenna's disparagement of structuralist literary studies as pure jargon. The literary education that it replaced had its jargon as well. Aguettaz insists that the recent literary education denounced by Orsenna complements (without replacing) the teaching of sentence grammar ("*la grammaire de la phrase*") with another grammar (that of discourse and text) operating on a different, macro level: "grammar of discourse, grammar of the text, these grammars can also be a sweet song" (*grammaire du discours, grammaire du texte, ces grammaires-là aussi peuvent être une chanson douce!*). See François Aguettaz, *L'école de la République sous le choc: Défense et illustration de l'enseignement des lettres* (Paris: Harmattan, 2005), 44–53.

19. See my discussion in chapter 1.

20. Patrick Cabanel, *Le tour de la nation par des enfants: Romans scolaires et espaces nationaux, XIXe–XXe siècles* (Paris: Belin, 2007).

21. Julien and André's mother has already died when the story begins, and their invalid father in Phalsbourg dies in the opening pages, leaving the two boys without biological parents. Their return to France can thus be viewed as an effort to establish the entire French nation as substitute and adoptive family. Orsenna's Jeanne and Thomas, whose parents are divorced, cross the Atlantic on an ocean liner to visit their father during Easter break. While not orphans in the strict sense like Julien and André, they do come from a broken home and are in effect parentless for the duration of their journey.

22. Cabanel, *Le tour de la nation,* 14.

23. Ozouf and Ozouf, "*Le tour de la France*: Le petit livre rouge," 280.

24. See Ozouf and Ozouf, "*Le tour de la France*: Le petit livre rouge," 281–82.

25. Fernand Braudel and Michel Kajman, "L'identité française selon Braudel," *Le Monde,* March 17, 2007.

26. The obvious reference for this concept of the "palpability of signs" is Roman Jakobson's "Closing Statement: Linguistics and Poetics." See also Jakobson, *Six Lectures.*

27. G. Bruno and Jean-Pierre Bardos, *Le tour de la France par deux enfants: Devoir et patrie; Livre de lecture courante* (Paris: E. Belin, 1977), n.p.

28. M. Martin Guiney examines the republican "distrust" of literature throughout his 2004 study, *Teaching the Cult of Literature.*

29. Not only does his comment express an ambivalence toward fictional literature but also, of course, a contradiction. For it is obviously a work of fiction that Bruno's reader holds in his hand. Julien and André are not "real" historical figures.

30. Georges Colomb, *L'enseignement scientifique à l'école; Cours élémentaire* (Paris: A. Colin, 1925), vi.

31. Lionel Gossman, "History and Literature: Reproduction or Signification," in *Between History and Literature* (Cambridge MA: Harvard University Press, 1990), 233–44.

32. Alain-Marie Bassy, "Les *Fables* ou le mensonge avoué," in *Fables* (Paris: Flammarion, 1995), 7.

33. Bréal, *De l'enseignement des langues vivantes,* 51.

4. A CLASSIC DODGE

1. Cited in Prost, *Histoire de l'enseignement,* 219.

2. Kahn, "Philosophie et pédagogie," 98.

3. Released in 2004 in France, the film won César awards (the French Oscar) for Best Director, Best Film, Best Screenplay, and Most Promising Actress. It has also won numerous awards in international film competitions.

4. The film has generated a number of valuable scholarly articles in a relatively short time. For a particularly insightful article, see Ari Blatt, "The Play's the Thing: Marivaux and the *Banlieue* in Abdellatif Kechiche's *L'esquive,*" *French Review* 81, no. 3 (2008). Though my reading of the film differs from theirs, one should also consult the following essays: Vinay Swamy, "Marivaux in the Suburbs: Reframing Language in Kechiche's *L'esquive* (2003)," *Studies in French Cinema* 7, no. 1 (2007), and Carrie Tarr, "Reassessing French Popular Culture: *L'esquive,*" in *France at the Flicks: Trends in Contemporary Popular Cinema,* ed. Darren Waldron and Isabelle Vanderschelden (Newcastle: Cambridge Scholars, 2007).

5. Abdellatif Kechiche, "*L'esquive* (découpage)," in *L'Avant-scène cinéma,* ed. Yves Alion (Paris: L'Avant-scène cinéma, 2005), 26. All subsequent page references to this work will appear parenthetically in the text.

6. Frédéric Deloffre explains that Marivaux's metaphoric use of the term *fautes d'orthographes* to speak of the mistaken identity is evidence that the playwright is drawing on the rhetorical tools of the Italian stage. See Pierre Carlet de Chamblain de Marivaux, Frédéric Deloffre, and Françoise Rubellin, *Théâtre complet* (Paris: Dunod, 1996), 1104.

7. For a good English language introduction to the recent debate, see Ralph Albanese and M. Martin Guiney, eds., *French Education: Fifty Years Later*, Yale French Studies (New Haven CT: Yale University Press, 2008). The number of works in French dealing with this crisis are too numerable to name. A good point of entry into the topic is Alain Bentolila, *Le verbe contre la barbarie: Apprendre à nos enfants à vivre ensemble* (Paris: Jacob, 2007). See also Cécile Ladjali, *Mauvaise langue* (Paris: Seuil, 2007).

8. The historian André Chervel observes that in the past the term *orthographe* referred to what today we would call spelling as well as grammar. See Chervel, *Histoire de l'enseignement*, 204.

9. *Beur* is a French slang term referring to the French-born children of immigrants from the Maghreb countries of Morocco, Tunisia, and Algeria.

10. The debate came to a much publicized head in the spring of 2000. On March 4 of that year, several dozen of France's most distinguished literary scholars joined with other professors and teachers of French to publish an open letter in *Le Monde* denouncing the latest set of reform proposals under consideration by the Ministry of Education. The letter, *"On assassine la littérature rue de Grenelle"* (They're killing literature in Grenelle Street [where the Ministry of Education is located]), has since become a kind of manifesto for an ongoing campaign to defend the nation's literary patrimony, the humanities in general, and the rigorous study of canonical works in secondary schools. In addition to their criticism of specific reform proposals undermining traditional literary studies, the signers of the March 4 article also questioned the logic by which, in their eyes, reformers justified the demotion of literary studies in the name of republican egalitarianism. By decreasing the place of literary studies in the public schools, they warned, the reform measures would ensure that literature "would survive as the privilege and the tool of social superiority among the most wealthy." Only the well-to-do would enjoy the personal benefits of literary knowledge, and only they would learn to write, think, and speak with the "mastery, grace and efficacy" afforded by literary culture. See Jean-Christophe Abramovici, et al., "C'est la littérature qu'on assassine rue de Grenelle," *Le Monde*, March 4, 2000.

Rejoinders to the March 4 manifesto argued that its signers were merely expressing nostalgia for an obsolete curriculum out of step with the needs of today's more socioeconomically and culturally diverse student body. The literary critic Tzvetan Todorov, in an article appearing later that month, accused the traditionalists of having an obsessive preoccupation with defending literature without considering the more fundamental challenges in contemporary education, most notably the problem of teaching basic language competence and communication skills that cannot be acquired solely through the study of great literature. See Tzvetan Todorov, "Education, la mauvaise foi de la contre-réforme," *Le Monde*, March 31, 2000. See also Suzanne Citron, "Cette littérature qui aurait réponse à tout," *Le Monde*, March 9, 2000.

11. Philippe Choulet and Philippe Rivière, *La bonne école I: Penser l'école dans la civilisation industrielle* (Seyssel: Champ Vallon, 2000) and *La bonne école II: Institution scolaire et contenus de savoir dans la civilisation industrielle* (Seyssel: Champ Vallon, 2004).

12. Alain Finkielkraut, "Hier et aujourd'hui. Entretien avec Philippe Choulet et Marc Le Bris," in *La querelle de l'école* (Paris: Stock: Editions du Panama, 2007), 85.

13. See Alain Finkielkraut, "La révolution cuculturelle à l'école," in *Propositions pour les enseignements littéraires*, ed. Michel Jarrety (Paris: Presses universitaires de France, 2000).

14. Alain Finkielkraut, "Hier et aujourd'hui: Entretien avec Philippe Choulet et Marc Le Bris," in *La querelle de l'école* (Paris: Stock; Editions du Panama, 2007), 85.

15. Gabriel Compayré and William Harold Payne, *The History of Pedagogy* (Boston: D. C. Heath, 1899), 124.

16. For a recent, polemical expression of this view, see Brighelli, *La fabrique du crétin*.

17. For a recent historical overview of the specific contributions of these educators, see Georges Minois, *Les grands pédagogues: De Socrate aux cyberprofs* (Paris: Audibert, 2006).

18. Rousseau, *Émile, ou de l'éducation*, 149.

19. That Choulet's progressive pedagogy belongs to a tradition that converges with key tenets of republican pedagogy is evidence of the misleading labels attached to opposing camps in French school debates. The conservative camp identified as *Républicains* are no more the heirs of the republican pedagogical tradition than are the progressive *Pédagogues*.

20. See, for example, Florence Colombani, "Entre les dalles de béton, une parole qui jaillit: *L'esquive* d'Abdellatif Kechiche," *Le Monde*, January 7, 2004.

21. Felicia Sturzer, "'Marivaudage' as Self-Representation," *French Review* 49, no. 2 (1975): 212.

22. "[C]elui qui semble n'écrire que pour n'être pas entendu, ne mérite pas qu'on se fatigue pour l'entendre." Sturzer, "'Marivaudage' as Self-Representation," 212.

23. For a useful discussion of the parallels between Marivaudage and the colorful language of the film's teenagers, see Swamy, "Marivaux in the Suburbs."

24. In an interview published in *Les Inrockuptibles*, Kechiche explains that "the classroom scenes do not intend to reflect a social reality. They aim above all to show the teacher as a metaphor for the director." Jean-Marc Lalanne, "Entretien Abdellatif Kechiche: *L'esquive* — M. Hulot dans le 9-3," *Les Inrockuptibles*, January 4, 2004.

25. See, for example, Swamy, "Marivaux in the Suburbs."

26. Alain Viala, "Questions de programme: Éléments d'histoire et perspectives," in *Propositions pour les enseignements littéraires*, ed. Michel Jarrety (Paris: Presses universitaires de France, 2000), 164.

27. Bruno Robbes, "Les trois conceptions actuelles de l'autorité," *Cahiers pédagogiques*, March 28, 2006, http://www.cahiers-pedagogiques.com/article.php3?id _article=2283. Robbes's article provides a useful introductory discussion of three different types of authority (*authoritarian*, *empty*, and *educative*) currently observable in the schools. For a discussion of the way the school has become increasingly dominated by progressive, anti-authoritarian views of education, see the introduction to Nathalie Bulle, *L'école et son double: Essai sur l'évolution pédagogique en France* (Paris: Hermann Éditeurs, 2009). For a critique of the renunciation by (progressive) teachers of their own authority, which, in turn, ultimately undermines the authority of the institution as a whole, see Hélène Merlin-Kajman, "Combien de mots? 'La maîtrise de la langue française' n'est pas un but en soi" *le débat*, no. 135 (2005): 113–16. See also Danièle Sallenave's essay "'L'auteur prétend que . . .'"

28. Cited in Prost, *Histoire de l'enseignement*, 219.

29. For a recent and concise discussion of the function of imitation in the cultivation of the autonomous individual within the humanistic tradition, see the "avant-propos" in Lucien Jaume, *Qu'est-ce que l'esprit européen?* (Paris: Flammarion, 2010).

30. See Guiney, *Teaching the Cult of Literature*.

31. Since starring in *L'esquive*, Ouazani has had roles in films such as Kechiche's *La Graine et le mulet* [*The Secret of the Grain*] (2007), Cédric Klapisch's *Paris* (2007), and many others.

32. Jaume, *Qu'est-ce que l'esprit européen?*, 19.

33. There is no adequate English equivalent for Finkielkraut's words here. He is playing on the expression *faire l'école buissonnière*, which means to be truant. But the French expression suggests the image, absent in the English, of learning that occurs outside of school, in the wild, in nature, or, quite literally, in the brush or bushes (*buissonnière* is an adjective derived from *buisson*, meaning *bush*). The expression dates back to the Middle Ages and refers to heretical religious groups forced to meet clandestinely, or in the wild. In sum, Alain Finkielkraut's remark conveys the idea there is something inherently and fundamentally transgressive about all true schooling.

34. Alain Finkielkraut, *La querelle de l'école* (Paris: Stock; Editions du Panama, 2007), 89–90.

35. Marcel Gauchet, *La religion dans la démocratie: Parcours de la laïcité* (Paris: Gallimard, 1998), 122–23.

36. Cécile Laborde, *Français, encore un effort pour être républicains!* (Paris: Seuil, 2010), 109.

37. See, for example, Tarr, "Reassessing French Popular Culture," and Swamy, "Marivaux in the Suburbs."

38. For a detailed discussion of the complexities of French universalism, see Naomi Schor, "The Crisis of French Universalism," *Yale French Studies*, no. 100 (2001).

5. WRITING ON WALLS

This chapter substantially revises and deepens arguments initially developed in my 2007 article appearing in *Yale French Studies*, "Finding *l'école républicaine*."

1. Directed by Laurent Cantet and starring François Bégaudeau himself, the film *Entre les murs* won the Palme d'or at the 2008 Cannes Film Festival. The theatrical version of *Entre les murs*, for which preparation began in the fall of 2007 independently of the film, opened at the Théâtre Ouvert in Paris in January 2009. For the script see François Wastiaux, *"Entre les murs": Théâtre-récit d'après le roman de François Bégaudeau* (Paris: Théâtre Ouvert éditions, 2009). Though certain of its claims will apply to the film and stage play, the present chapter's primary concern is with the original "docunovel" published in 2006 by Verticales (now an imprint of Gallimard). Parenthetical page references are to this edition.

2. François Bégaudeau, *The Class*, trans. Linda Asher (New York: Seven Stories Press, 2009).

3. That the film critic's comment (about the film) serves as promotional material for the book is problematic. It overstates the similarity between the two works and suggests that, because of their common subject matter, to speak about the one is to speak about the other. Though understandable given the demands of book publishing and marketing, the publisher's (not Denby's) conflation of book and film in this case is particularly regrettable because the book's deepest reflection on republicanism and education emerges from the act of reading and the direct encounter with the original literary form, features that do not translate easily to the screen. In fact, the film makes almost no attempt to do so. Bégaudeau, Cantet, and their co-scenarist, Robin Campillo, explicitly state that the film is not, strictly speaking, an "adaptation" of the book but rather "an extension of the experience [or experiment] proposed by the book" (*un prolongement de l'expérience proposée par le livre*). François Bégaudeau, Laurent Cantet, and Robin Campillo, *Le scénario du film entre les murs* (Paris: Gallimard, 2008), 7. The book is a point of departure rather than a model for the film. It is precisely the literary *"expérience"* (in both senses of the term) of the book that the present chapter explores.

4. Jean-Luc Douin, "Premier de la classe: Un formidable roman de François Bégaudeau en forme de montage littéraire," *Le Monde*, January 27, 2006.

5. François Bégaudeau and Philippe Meirieu, "Philippe Meirieu dialogue avec François Bégaudeau à l'occasion de son livre, *Entre les murs* (Editions Verticales)," La bibliotheque de l'education: Une émission co-produite par l'IUFM de l'Académie de Lyon et Radio Lyon Première, http://www.meirieu.com/RADIO/radio2.htm; François Bégaudeau, Michel Abescat, and Jacques Morice, "François Bégaudeau, auteur d'*Entre les murs* (le roman): 'L'école n'est pas un sanctuaire,'" Télérama.fr,

May 26, 2008, http://www.telerama.fr/livre/francois-begaudeau-laureat-du-prix
-france-culture-telerama-la-musique-est-l-horizon-ultime-de-l-ecriture,29346.php.

6. Martine Delahaye, "Filmer *Entre les murs*," *Le Monde*, June 15, 2008.

7. *Entre les murs*'s exploration of the inside-outside binary represents the most thorough and sophisticated artistic treatment of this fundamental question of modern, and especially republican, education. There is hardly a work of literature or film about republican schooling from the past one hundred years that does not address it in some fashion. It is a leitmotif in Colette and Willy's *Claudine à l'école* (1900), an autobiographical novel about Colette's experience in a republican school for girls in the 1880s. The eponymous heroine is divided between her attachment to the untamed forest surrounding her village of Montigny and the institution of the school, an unparalleled source of amusement and stimulation. Described as a *sauvageonne* or wild child who is also the brightest student in her class, Claudine embodies the very confusion of these two distinct spaces, the outside and the inside. In a more recent example, Nicolas Philibert's documentary film, *Être et avoir* (2002), also shuttles between scenes of classroom instruction and the out-of-doors, in this case the rustic living environment of grade schoolchildren from farming communities in France's Auvergne region. The opening sequence contrasts the grueling labor of local cowherds and the tranquil setting inside the schoolhouse, a haven from the extreme winter weather beyond its walls. The viewer watches as two small turtles crawl across the classroom floor, a clear symbol of the gradual and painstaking process of learning. The image of the slow-moving reptiles against the backdrop of the contemporary classroom provokes a reflection, moreover, on the coexistence of primeval, slow-changing nature (redolent of Ferdinand Braudel's *longue durée* or geological time) and the more swiftly moving realm of cultural progress.

8. The text of the March 15 law (Loi n°2004–228) is available online at http://www.legifrance.gouv.fr.

9. See John Richard Bowen, *Why the French Don't Like Headscarves: Islam, the State, and Public Space* (Princeton NJ: Princeton University Press, 2007). For a particularly eloquent discussion of the broad significance of *laïcité* in recent years, see Morin, "Le trou noir de la laïcité."

10. Jean Baubérot, "*Laïcité* and the Challenge of 'Republicanism,'" *Modern and Contemporary France* 17, no. 2 (2009): 191. Baubérot does not explicitly mention the Enlightenment tradition of rational inquiry, but he refers to intellectuals such as Jacques Muglioni and Jean-Claude Milner whose own writings on republican education clearly align them with this republican genealogy.

11. For a particularly balanced overview of these opposing positions see Laborde, *Français, encore un effort*. The study published in French in 2010 is a revised version of the English volume: *Critical Republicanism: The Hijab Controversy and Political Philosophy* (Oxford: Oxford University Press, 2008).

12. François Dubet, "La laïcité dans les mutations de l'école," in *Une société fragmentée?: Le multiculturalisme en débat*, ed. Michel Wieviorka (Paris: Editions La Découverte, 1996), 90. See also Déloye, "L'instruction."

13. Cited in Nique and Lelièvre, *La République n'éduquera plus*, 74.

14. Nique and Lelièvre, *La République n'éduquera plus*, 74.

15. Nique and Lelièvre, *La République n'éduquera plus*, 74.

16. Cited in Jean-Antoine-Nicolas de Caritat Condorcet, *Ecrits sur l'instruction publique*, ed. Charles Coutel and Catherine Kintzler (Paris: Edilig, 1989), 13–14.

17. Cited in Nique and Lelièvre, *La République n'éduquera plus*, 74.

18. Condorcet's instruction, writes the philosopher Catherine Kintzler, "consists of laboriously reappropriating [or mastering] the use of reason and it is [thus] a condition for autonomy." See Catherine Kintzler's preface in Condorcet, *Ecrits sur l'instruction publique*: 14.

19. See Catherine Kintzler, *La République en questions* (Paris: Minerve, 1996), 34–46.

20. Renan, *La réforme intellectuelle*, 328.

21. Nique and Lelièvre, *La République n'éduquera plus*.

22. Daniel Halévy, "L'enseignement," in *Trois épreuves: 1814, 1871, 1940* (Paris: Plon, 1942), 70–71.

23. The most famous late twentieth-century formulation of this opposition is in Milner, *De l'école*. For a more recent treatment, see Henri Pena-Ruiz, *Qu'est-ce que l'école* (Paris: Gallimard, 2005).

24. Among the many studies of this topic, see, Philippe Meirieu and Marc Guiraud, *L'école, ou, la guerre civile* (Paris: Plon, 1997).

25. Brighelli, *La fabrique du crétin*, 45.

26. Brighelli, *La fabrique du crétin*, 48.

27. Kintzler, *La République en questions*, 29, 25.

28. Kintzler, *La République en questions*, 29, 25.

29. Bégaudeau, Abescat, and Morice, "François Bégaudeau."

30. Déloye, "L'instruction," 186.

31. Déloye, "L'instruction," 187.

32. Bégaudeau and Meirieu, "Philippe Meirieu dialogue."

33. Alain Vergnioux, *Pédagogie et théorie de la connaissance: Platon contre Piaget?* (Berne: P. Lang, 1991), 15.

34. See, for example, Jonathan Culler's discussion of Cleanth Brooks's "Poetry since the Wasteland" in Jonathan D. Culler, *On Deconstruction: Theory and Criticism after Structuralism*, 25th anniversary ed. (Ithaca NY: Cornell University Press, 2008), 36.

35. See Thélot Commission, *http://www.debatnational.education.fr/index.php*.

36. As Joan Scott observes, many or most of these "immigrants" are full French citizens born on French soil. The use of the word *immigrant* illustrates the extent to which citizens of non-French origin continue to be perceived as outsiders. See Joan Wallach Scott, *The Politics of the Veil* (Princeton NJ: Princeton University Press, 2007), 22.

37. The teacher's imposition of an intransigent idea of *laïcité* is the *Entre les murs* equivalent to the police scenes in Abdel Kechiche's *L'Esquive* or Matthieu Kassowitz's *La Haine*.

38. Catherine Kintzler, *Qu'est-ce que la laïcité* (Paris: Vrin, 2007), 8.

CONCLUSION

1. Duclert et al., *Dictionnaire critique de la République*. The 2007 edition is a slightly revised version of the 2002 volume.

2. The publication in 2011 of an English translation of the *Dictionnaire*, substantially supplemented by essays from scholars working in Anglo-American universities, indicates the extent to which these questions concern an audience outside of France as well. See Edward Berenson, Vincent Duclert, and Christophe Prochasson, eds., *The French Republic: History, Values, Debates* (Ithaca NY: Cornell University Press, 2011).

3. Buisson, "Intuition et méthode intuitive," 1376.

4. Marion, *Le mouvement des idées pédagogiques*, 5.

5. Victor Shklovsky, "Art as Technique," in *The Critical Tradition: Classic Texts and Contemporary Trends*, ed. David H. Richter (Boston: Bedford / St. Martin's, 2007). Subsequent page references to this edition will appear parenthetically in the text.

6. Tzvetan Todorov, among others, has observed a latent "theory of the reader" lurking in Shklovsky's concern with artistic perception, and Jane Tompkins, in her well-known anthology of reader-response criticism, identifies Shklovsky's article, "Art as Technique," as a "classic text." See Todorov, "Three Conceptions," 140; and Jane P. Tompkins, *Reader-Response Criticism: From Formalism to Post-structuralism* (Baltimore: Johns Hopkins University Press, 1980), 260–61.

7. Buisson, "Intuition et méthode intuitive," 1376.

8. Todorov, "Three Conceptions," 131.

9. Durkheim, *L'évolution pédagogique*, 379, 80.

10. See Albert Fatalot, "Musées scolaires," in *Dictionnaire de pédagogie et d'instruction primaire (partie 1)*, ed. Brunetière Ferdinand (Paris: Hachette, 1882–1893).

Bibliography

Abramovici, Jean-Christophe, et al. "C'est la littérature qu'on assassine rue de Grenelle." *Le Monde*, March 4, 2000.

Aguettaz, François. *L'école de la République sous le choc: Défense et illustration de l'enseignement des lettres*. Paris: Harmattan, 2005.

Albanese, Ralph. *La Fontaine à l'école républicaine: Du poète universel au classique scolaire*. EMF critiques. Charlottesville NC: Rookwood Press, 2003.

Albanese, Ralph, and M. Martin Guiney, eds. *French Education: Fifty Years Later*. Yale French Studies. New Haven: Yale University Press, 2008.

Armstrong, Paul B. *Play and the Politics of Reading: The Social Uses of Modernist Form*. Ithaca NY: Cornell University Press, 2005.

Augé, Claude. "Préface." In *Nouveau Larousse illustré: Dictionnaire universel encyclopédique*, edited by Pierre Larouse and Claude Augé, i–ii. Paris: Librairie Larousse, 1898.

Barthes, Roland. *Critique et vérité*. Paris: Seuil, 1966.

———. "De l'oeuvre au texte." In *Oeuvres*, 71–80. Paris: Seuil, 2002.

———. "La mort de l'auteur." In *Oeuvres*, 491–95. Paris: Seuil, 2002.

———. "Les deux critiques." *MLN* 78, no. 5 (1963): 447–52.

Bassy, Alain-Marie. "Les *Fables* ou le mensonge avoué." In *Fables*, 7–34. Paris: Flammarion, 1995.

Baubérot, Jean. "*Laïcité* and the Challenge of 'Republicanism.'" *Modern and Contemporary France* 17, no. 2 (2009): 189–98.

Bégaudeau, François. *Entre les murs*. Paris: Verticales; Éditions Gallimard, 2006.

———. *The Class*. Translated by Linda Asher. 1st English-language ed. New York: Seven Stories Press, 2009.

Bégaudeau, François, Michel Abescat, and Jacques Morice. "François Bégaudeau, auteur d'*Entre les murs* (le roman): 'L'école n'est pas un sanctuaire.'" Télérama.fr, May 26, 2008, http://www.telerama.fr/livre/francois-begaudeau-laureat-du-prix-france -culture-telerama-la-musique-est-l-horizon-ultime-de-l-ecriture,29346.php.

Bégaudeau, François, Laurent Cantet, and Robin Campillo. *Le scénario du film entre les murs*. Paris: Gallimard, 2008.

Bégaudeau, François, and Philippe Meirieu. "Philippe Meirieu dialogue avec François Bégaudeau à l'occasion de son livre, *Entre les murs* (Editions Verticales)." La bibliothèque de l'éducation: Une émission co-produite par l'IUFM de l'Académie de Lyon et Radio Lyon Première, http://www.meirieu.com/RADIO/radio2.htm.

Bell, David F. "A Moratorium on Suspicion?" *PMLA: Publications of the Modern Language Association of America* 117, no. 3 (2002): 487–90.

Bentolila, Alain. *Le verbe contre la barbarie: Apprendre à nos enfants à vivre ensemble.* Paris: Jacob, 2007.

Berenson, Edward, Vincent Duclert, and Christophe Prochasson, eds. *The French Republic: History, Values, Debates*. Ithaca NY: Cornell University Press, 2011.

Blatt, Ari. "The Play's the Thing: Marivaux and the *Banlieue* in Abdellatif Kechiche's *L'esquive*." *French Review* 81, no. 3 (2008): 516–27.

Bouglé, Célestin. *The French Conception of "Culture Générale" and Its Influences upon Instruction*. New York: Bureau of Publications, Teachers College, Columbia University, 1938.

Bourdieu, Pierre, and Jean-Claude Passeron. *Reproduction in Education, Society and Culture*. Translated by Richard Nice. Los Angeles: Sage, 2011.

Bowen, John Richard. *Why the French Don't Like Headscarves: Islam, the State, and Public Space*. Princeton NJ: Princeton University Press, 2007.

Braudel, Fernand, and Michel Kajman. "L'identité française selon Braudel." *Le Monde*, March 17, 2007.

Brault, Gérard. "Reflexions on Daudet's 'La dernière classe: Récit d'un petit Alsacien.'" *Symposium: A Quarterly Journal in Modern Literatures* 54, no. 2 (2000): 67–76.

Bréal, Michel. *De l'enseignement des langues vivantes: Conférences faites aux étudiants en lettres de la Sorbonne*. 2nd ed. Paris: Hachette, 1900.

———. *Quelques mots sur l'instruction publique en France*. Paris: Hachette, 1872.

Brighelli, Jean-Paul. *A bonne école*. Paris: Gawsewitch, 2006.

———. *La fabrique du crétin: La mort programmée de l'école*. Paris: Gawsewitch, 2005.

Bruno, G., and Jean-Pierre Bardos. *Le tour de la France par deux enfants: Devoir et patrie; Livre de lecture courante*. Paris: E. Belin, 1977.

Buisson, Ferdinand. "Intuition et méthode intuitive." In *Dictionnaire de pédagogie et d'instruction primaire (partie 1)*, edited by Ferdinand Buisson, 1374–77. Paris: Hachette, 1882–1893.

Bulle, Nathalie. *L'école et son double: Essai sur l'évolution pédagogique en France*. Paris: Hermann Éditeurs, 2009.

Cabanel, Patrick. *Le tour de la nation par des enfants: Romans scolaires et espaces nationaux, XIXe – XXe siècles.* Paris: Belin, 2007.

Calatayud, Agnès. "*Les glaneurs et la glaneuse*: Agnès Varda's Self-Portrait." *Dalhousie French Studies* 61 (2002): 113–23.

Charles, Michel. *L'arbre et la source.* Paris: Editions du Seuil, 1985.

Chervel, André. *Histoire de l'enseignement du français du XVIIe au XXe siècle.* Paris: Editions Retz-Nathan, 2006.

Choulet, Philippe, and Philippe Rivière. *La bonne école I: Penser l'école dans la civilisation industrielle.* Seyssel: Champ Vallon, 2000.

———. *La bonne école II: Institution scolaire et contenus de savoir dans la civilisation industrielle.* Seyssel: Champ Vallon, 2004.

Citron, Suzanne. "Cette littérature qui aurait réponse à tout." *Le Monde*, March 9, 2000.

Colette and Willy. *Claudine à l'école.* Paris: Albin Michel, 1987.

Colomb, Georges. *L'enseignement scientifique à l'école: Cours élémentaire.* Paris: A. Colin, 1925.

Colombani, Florence. "Entre les dalles de béton, une parole qui jaillit: *L'esquive* d'Abdellatif Kechiche." *Le Monde*, January 7, 2004.

Compagnon, Antoine. *La Troisième République des lettres, de Flaubert à Proust.* Paris: Seuil, 1983.

Compayré, Gabriel, and William Harold Payne. *The History of Pedagogy.* Boston: D. C. Heath, 1899.

Condorcet, Jean-Antoine-Nicolas de Caritat. *Ecrits sur l'instruction publique.* Edited by Charles Coutel and Catherine Kintzler. Les Classiques de la République. Paris: Edilig, 1989.

Croiset, Alfred. "Les besoins de la démocratie en matière d'éducation." In *L'éducation de la démocratie: Leçons professées à l'École des hautes études sociales par MM. Ernest Lavisse, Alfred Croiset, Ch. Seignobos, P. Malapert, G. Lanson, J. Hadamard*, 37–68. Paris: F. Alcan, 1907.

Cruickshank, R. "The Work of Art in the Age of Global Consumption: Agnes Varda's *Les glaneurs et la glaneuse*." *Esprit créateur* 47, no. 3 (2007): 119–32.

Culler, Jonathan D. *On Deconstruction: Theory and Criticism after Structuralism.* 25th anniversary ed. Ithaca NY: Cornell University Press, 2008.

Darnton, Robert. *The Great Cat Massacre and Other Episodes in French Cultural History.* New York: Basic Books, 1984.

Daudet, Alphonse. "La dernière classe: Récit d'un petit Alsacien." In *Oeuvres I*, edited by Roger Ripoll, 581–85. Paris: Gallimard, 1986.

Delahaye, Martine. "Filmer *Entre les murs*." *Le Monde*, June 15, 2008.

Déloye, Yves. *Ecole et citoyenneté: L'individualisme républicain de Jules Ferry à Vichy: controverses.* Paris: Presses de la Fondation nationale des sciences politiques, Université Paris I, 1994.

———. "L'instruction." In *Dictionnaire critique de la République*, edited by Vincent Duclert, Christophe Prochasson, Christian Amalvi, and Perrine Simon-Nahum, 183–88. Paris: Flammarion, 2007.

Douin, Jean-Luc. "Premier de la classe: Un formidable roman de François Bégaudeau en forme de montage littéraire." *Le Monde*, January 27, 2006.

Dubet, François. "La laïcité dans les mutations de l'école." In *Une société fragmentée? Le multiculturalisme en débat*, edited by Michel Wieviorka, 85–112. Paris: Editions La Découverte, 1996.

Dubreucq, Eric. *Une éducation républicaine-Marion, Buisson, Durkheim*. Paris: Vrin, 2004.

Duclert, Vincent, Christophe Prochasson, Christian Amalvi, and Perrine Simon-Nahum. *Dictionnaire critique de la République*. New ed. Paris: Flammarion, 2007.

Durkheim, Émile. *L'évolution pédagogique en France*. Paris: Presses universitaires de France, 1969.

———. "La morale laïque." In *L'éducation morale*, 1–12. Paris: Presses universitaires de France, 1992.

Falcucci, Clément. *L'humanisme dans l'enseignement secondaire en France au XIXe siècle*. Toulouse: Edward Privat, 1939.

Fatalot, Albert. "Musées scolaires." In *Dictionnaire de pédagogie et d'instruction primaire (partie 1)*, edited by Brunetière Ferdinand, 1991–93. Paris: Hachette, 1882–1893.

Fauvel, Maryse. "Nostalgia and Digital Technology: *The Gleaners and I* (Varda, 2000) and *The Triplets of Belleville* (Chomet, 2003) as Reflective Genres." *Studies in French Cinema* 5, no. 3 (2005): 219–29.

Ferry, Jules. "Ch. Zevort jugé par M. Jules Ferry." *Revue internationale de l'enseignement* 14 (1887): 642–45.

Finkielkraut, Alain. "Hier et aujourd'hui: Entretien avec Philippe Choulet et Marc Le Bris." In *La querelle de l'école*, 77–98. Paris: Stock; Editions du Panama, 2007.

———. *La querelle de l'école*. Paris: Stock; Editions du Panama, 2007.

———. "La révolution cuculturelle à l'école." In *Propositions pour les enseignements littéraires*, edited by Michel Jarrety, 91–96. Paris: Presses universitaires de France, 2000.

Flot, Léon. "Lexicologie." Edited by Ferdinand Buisson. *Nouveau dictionnaire de pédagogie et d'instruction primaire*. Hachette, http://www.inrp.fr/edition-electronique/lodel/dictionnaire-ferdinand-buisson/document.php?id=3052.

Foucault, Michel. *Surveiller et punir: Naissance de la prison*. Paris: Gallimard, 1975.

Gaillard, Jean-Michel. "Éduquer et instruire." In *L'histoire*, 30–39, 1996.

Gauchet, Marcel. *La religion dans la démocratie: Parcours de la laïcité*. Paris: Gallimard, 1998.

Gaulupeau, Yves. *La France à l'école*. Paris: Gallimard, 1992.

Genette, Gérard. "Rhétorique et enseignement." In *Figures II*. Paris: Seuil, 1969.

———. "Structuralisme et critique littéraire." *L'arc* 26 (1969): 30–44.

Ginzburg, Carlo. "Making Things Strange: The Prehistory of a Literary Device. " *Representations* 56 (1996): 8–28.

Gossman, Lionel. "History and Literature: Reproduction or Signification." In *Between History and Literature*, 227–56. Cambridge MA: Harvard University Press, 1990.

Grange, Mireille, and Michel Leroux. "La pédagogie sens dessus dessous: Les programmes de français des collèges." *le débat*, no. 135 (2005): 22–36.

Greenberg, Louis M. "Architects of the New Sorbonne: Liard's Purpose and Durkheim's Role." *History of Education Quarterly* 21, no. 1 (1981): 77–94.

Guiney, M. Martin. *Teaching the Cult of Literature in the French Third Republic*. New York: Palgrave Macmillan, 2004.

Gumbel, Peter. *On achève bien les écoliers*. Paris: Grasset, 2010.

Halévy, Daniel. "L'enseignement." In *Trois épreuves: 1814, 1871, 1940*, 68–87. Paris: Plon, 1942.

Hameline, Daniel. "Les malentendus de la méthode intuitive." In *L'école de la Troisième République en questions: Débats et controverses dans le "Dictionnaire de pédagogie" de Ferdinand Buisson*, edited by Daniel Denis and Pierre Kahn, 75–89. Berne: Peter Lang, 2006.

Hébrard, Jean. "L'Histoire de l'enseignement des sciences en France." La main à la pâte, http://www.inrp.fr/lamap/?Page_Id=1009.

Hodgson, Peter. "Viktor Shklovsky and the Formalist Legacy: Imitation/Stylization in Narrative Fiction." In *Russian Formalism: A Retrospective Glance: A Festschrift in Honor of Victor Erlich*, edited by Robert Louis Jackson and Stephen Rudy, 195–212. New Haven CT: Yale Center for International and Area Studies; distributed by Slavica Publishers, 1985.

Houdart-Mérot, Violaine. *La culture littéraire au lycée depuis 1880*. Rennes: Presses universitaires de Rennes, 1998.

———. "Literary Education in the *Lycée*: Crises, Continuity, and Upheaval since 1880." *Yale French Studies*, no. 113 (2008): 29–45.

Ingarden, Roman. "The General Question of the Essence of Form and Content." *Journal of Philosophy* 57, no. 7 (1960): 222–33.

Jakobson, Roman. *Six Lectures on Sound and Meaning*. Translated by John Mepham. Cambridge, Mass.: MIT Press, 1978.

Jarrety, Michel, ed. *Propositions pour les enseignements littéraires*. Paris: Presses universitaires de France, 2000.

Jaume, Lucien. *Qu'est-ce que l'esprit européen?* Paris: Flammarion, 2010.

Jey, Martine. *La littérature au lycée: Invention d'une discipline (1880–1925)*. Metz: Centre d'études linguistiques des textes et des discours, Université de Metz, 1998.

Kahn, Pierre. *La leçon de choses: Naissance de l'enseignement des sciences à l'école primaire*. Villeneuve d'Ascq: Presses universitaires du Septentrion, 2002.

―――. "Philosophie et pédagogie dans le *Dictionnaire*: La question du sensualisme." In *L'école de la Troisième République en questions: Débats et controverses dans le "Dictionnaire de pédagogie" de Ferdinand Buisson*, edited by Daniel Denis and Pierre Kahn, 91–105. Berne: Peter Lang, 2006.

Kambouchner, Denis. *Une école contre l'autre*. Paris: Presses universitaires de France, 2000.

Kechiche, Abdellatif. *L'esquive (Games of Love and Chance)*. DVD. New York: New Yorker Video, 2006.

―――. "*L'esquive* (découpage)." In *L'avant-scène cinéma*, edited by Yves Alion. Paris: L'avant-scène cinéma, 2005.

Kintzler, Catherine. *La République en questions*. Paris: Minerve, 1996.

―――. *Qu'est-ce que la laïcité*. Chemins philosophiques. Paris: Vrin, 2007.

Kronman, Anthony T. *Education's End: Why Our Colleges and Universities Have Given Up on the Meaning of Life*. New Haven CT: Yale University Press, 2007.

Labaree, David F. *The Trouble With Ed Schools*. New Haven CT: Yale University Press, 2004.

Laborde, Cécile. *Critical Republicanism: The Hijab Controversy and Political Philosophy*. Oxford: Oxford University Press, 2008.

―――. *Français, encore un effort pour être républicains!* Paris: Seuil, 2010.

Ladjali, Cécile. *Mauvaise langue*. Paris: Seuil, 2007.

Lalanne, Jean-Marc. "Entretien Abdellatif Kechiche: *L'esquive* — M. Hulot dans le 9–3." *Les Inrockuptibles*, January 4, 2004.

Lareau, Annette, and Elliot B. Weininger. "Cultural Capital in Educational Research: A Critical Assessment." In *After Bourdieu*, edited by David L. Swartz and Vera L. Zolberg, 105–44. Dordrecht, The Netherlands: Kluwer Academic, 2004.

Larousse, Pierre. Préface to *Grand dictionnaire universel, français, historique, géographique, mythologique, bibliographique, littéraire, artistique, scientifique, etc*, v — lxxvi. Paris: Larousse et Boyer, 1866.

Laszlo, Pierre. "La Leçon de choses, or Lessons from Things." *Sub Stance*, no. 71–72 (1993): 274–88.

Lavisse, Ernest. "La question du Latin et du Grec d'après M. Raoul Frary et après M. Charles Bigot." *La revue bleue* (1886).

Le Men, Ségolène. "La pédagogie par l'image dans un manuel de la Troisième République: *Le tour de la France par deux enfants*." In *Usages de l'image au XIXe siècle*, edited by Stéphane Michaud, Jean-Yves Mollier, and Nicole Savy, 119–31. Paris: Editions Créaphis, 1992.

―――. *Les abécédaires français illustrés du XIXe siècle*. Paris: Promodis, 1984.

Lelièvre, Claude, and Christian Nique. *Bâtisseurs d'école: Histoire biographique de l'enseignement en France*. Paris: Nathan pédagogie, 1994.

Levinson, Marjorie. "What Is New Formalism?" *PMLA: Publications of the Modern Language Association of America* 122, no. 2 (2007): 558–69.

Lewis, Pericles. *The Cambridge Introduction to Modernism*. Cambridge: Cambridge University Press, 2007.

Liard, Louis. *Universités et facultés*. Paris: Armand Colin, 1890.

Margadant, Jo Burr. *Madame le professeur: Women Educators in the Third Republic*. Princeton NJ: Princeton University Press, 1990.

Marion, Henri. *Le mouvement des idées pédagogiques en France depuis 1870*. Paris: Impr. nationale, 1889.

Marivaux, Pierre Carlet de Chamblain de, Frédéric Deloffre, and Françoise Rubellin. *Théâtre complet*. Paris: Dunod, 1996.

Mayeur, Françoise. *De la Révolution à l'école républicaine*. Edited by Louis-Henri Parias. Histoire générale de l'enseignement et de l'éducation. Paris: Perrin, 2004.

McGann, Jerome J. *The Textual Condition*. Princeton NJ: Princeton University Press, 1991.

Meirieu, Philippe, and Marc Guiraud. *L'école, ou, la guerre civile*. Paris: Plon, 1997.

Merlin-Kajman, Hélène. "Combien de mots? 'La maîtrise de la langue française' n'est pas un but en soi." *le débat*, no. 135 (2005): 106–22.

Milner, Jean-Claude. *De l'école*. Paris: Editions du Seuil, 1984.

Minois, Georges. *Les grands pédagogues: De Socrate aux cyberprofs*. Paris: Audibert, 2006.

Mitchell, W. J. T. "The Commitment to Form; or, Still Crazy after All These Years." *PMLA: Publications of the Modern Language Association of America* 118, no. 2 (2003): 321–25.

Morin, Edgar. "Le trou noir de la laïcité." *le débat*, no. 58 (1990): 38–41.

Nadeau, Jean-Benoît, and Julie Barlow. *The Story of French*. New York: St. Martin's Press, 2006.

Nesbit, Molly. *Their Common Sense*. London: Black Dog, 2000.

Nique, Christian, and Claude Lelièvre. *La République n'éduquera plus: La fin du mythe Ferry*. Paris: Plon, 1993.

Orsenna, Erik. *Grammar Is a Gentle, Sweet Song*. Translated by Moishe Black. New York: George Braziller, 2004.

———. *La grammaire est une chanson douce*. Le Livre de Poche ed. Paris: Stock, 2001.

Ory, Pascal. "Le *Grand Dictionnaire* de Pierre Larousse." In *Les lieux de mémoire*, edited by Pierre Nora, 227–38. Paris: Gallimard, 1997.

Ozouf, Jacques, and Mona Ozouf. "*Le tour de la France par deux enfants*: Le petit livre rouge de la République." In *Les lieux de mémoire*, edited by Pierre Nora, 277–301. Paris: Gallimard, 1997.

———. "*Le tour de la France par deux enfants*: The Little Red Book of the Republic." In *Realms of Memory: Rethinking the French Past*, edited by Lawrence D. Kritzman. New York: Columbia University Press, 1996.

Pécaut, Élie. "Quelques mots au sujet de l'enseignement des sciences physiques et naturelles à l'école normale primaire." *Revue pédagogique* 2, no. 1 (1883): 481–96.

Pécaut, Félix. "De l'usage et de l'abus de la pédagogie." In *L'Éducation publique et la vie nationale*, 53–68. Paris: Hachette et Cie, 1907.

Pena-Ruiz, Henri. *Qu'est-ce que l'école.* Folio actuel. Paris: Gallimard, 2005.

Philibert, Nicolas. *Etre et avoir.* DVD. United Kingdom: Artificial Eye, 2002.

Plâtrier, Narcisse. "Leçon de choses." In *Dictionnaire de pédagogie et d'instruction primaire,* edited by Ferdinand Buisson, 1528–34. Paris: Hachette et Cie, 1887.

Prost, Antoine. *Histoire de l'enseignement en France, 1800–1967.* Paris: Armand Colin, 1968.

Rasmussen, Mark David. "New Formalisms?" In *Renaissance Literature and Its Formal Engagements,* edited by Mark David Rasmussen, 1–14. New York: Palgrave, 2002.

Renan, Ernest. *La réforme intellectuelle et morale.* Paris: Michel Lévy Frères, 1871.

Rétif, André. *Pierre Larousse et son œuvre, 1817–1875.* Paris: Larousse, 1974.

Rey, Alain. "Le Lexicographe." In *Pierre Larousse et son temps,* edited by Jean-Yves Mollier and Pascal Ory. Paris: Larousse, 1995.

Robbes, Bruno. "Les trois conceptions actuelles de l'autorité." Cahiers pédagogiques, March 28, 2006. http://www.cahiers-pedagogiques.com/article.php3?id_article=2283.

Rooney, E. "Form and Contentment." *Modern Language Quarterly* 61, no. 1 (2000): 17–40.

Rosello, Mireille. "Agnès Varda's *Les glaneurs et la glaneuse*: Portrait of the Artist as an Old Lady." *Studies in French Cinema* 1, no. 1 (2001): 29–36.

Rousseau, Jean-Jacques. *Émile, ou de l'éducation.* Paris: Garnier-Flammarion, 1966.

Sachs, Leon. "Finding *l'école républicaine* in the Damnedest of Places: François Bégaudeau's *Entre les murs.*" *Yale French Studies* no. 111 (May 2007): 73–88.

———. "Putting History into Practice: Intellectual History as Literary Form in Roger Martin du Gard's *Jean Barois.*" *Contemporary French Civilization* 28, no. 1 (2004): 71–89.

Sallenave, Danièle. "'L'auteur prétend que . . . ;' Genèse d'une formule, ravages d'une méthode." In *Propositions pour les enseignements littéraires,* edited by Michel Jarrety, 77–90. Paris: Presses universitaires de France, 2000.

Schor, Naomi. "The Crisis of French Universalism." *Yale French Studies,* no. 100 (2001): 43–64.

Scott, A. O. "Film Festival Review: A Reaper of the Castoff, Be It Material or Human." *New York Times,* September 30, 2000. http://movies.nytimes.com/movie/review?res=9C01E0DA173DF933A0575AC0A9669C8B63.

Scott, Joan Wallach. *The Politics of the Veil.* Princeton NJ: Princeton University Press, 2007.

Shklovsky, Victor. "Art as Technique." In *The Critical Tradition: Classic Texts and Contemporary Trends,* edited by David H. Richter, 774–84. Boston: Bedford / St. Martin's, 2007.

Simon, Jules. "Instruction relative à l'institution de réunions périodiques des professeurs dans les lycées et aux réformes que semble réclamer le système d'éducation et d'enseignement suivi dans les établissements d'instruction secondaire, le 17 septembre 1872." In *Circulaires et instructions officielles relatives à l'instruction publique,* 207–31. Paris: Delalain Frères. L'Université de France, 1878.

Strier, Richard. "How Formalism Became a Dirty Word, and Why We Can't Do without It." In *Renaissance Literature and Its Formal Engagements*, edited by Mark David Rasmussen, 207–15. New York: Palgrave, 2002.

Sturzer, Felicia. ""Marivaudage" as Self-Representation." *French Review* 49, no. 2 (1975): 212–21.

Swamy, Vinay. "Marivaux in the Suburbs: Reframing Language in Kechiche's *L'esquive* (2003)." *Studies in French Cinema* 7, no. 1 (2007): 57–68.

Talon-Hugon, Carole. *Morales de l'art*, Lignes d'art. Paris: Presses universitaires de France, 2009.

Tarr, Carrie. "Reassessing French Popular Culture: *L'esquive*." In *France at the Flicks: Trends in Contemporary Popular Cinema*, edited by Darren Waldron and Isabelle Vanderschelden, 130–41. Newcastle: Cambridge Scholars Publishing, 2007.

Thompson, Ewa M. *Russian Formalism and Anglo-American New Criticism: A Comparative Study*. The Hague: Mouton, 1971.

Tilburg, Patricia A. *Colette's Republic: Work, Gender, and Popular Culture in France, 1870–1914*. New York: Berghahn Books, 2009.

Todorov, Tzvetan. "Education, la mauvaise foi de la contre-réforme." *Le Monde*, March 31, 2000.

———. "Three Conceptions of Poetic Language." In *Russian Formalism: A Retrospective Glance: A Festschrift in Honor of Victor Erlich*, edited by Robert Louis Jackson and Stephen Rudy, 130–47. New Haven CT: Yale Center for International and Area Studies, distributed by Slavica Publishers, 1985.

Tompkins, Jane P. *Reader-Response Criticism: From Formalism to Post-structuralism*. Baltimore: Johns Hopkins University Press, 1980.

Tyrer, Ben. "Digression and Return: Aesthetics and Politics in Agnès Varda's *Les Glaneurs et la glaneuse* (2000)." *Studies in French Cinema* 9, no. 2 (2009): 161–76.

Varda, Agnès. *Les glaneurs et la glaneuse* (*The Gleaners and I*). DVD. New York: Zeitgeist Video, 2002.

———. *Varda par Agnès*. Paris: Cahiers du Cinema, 1994.

Vergnioux, Alain. *Pédagogie et théorie de la connaissance: Platon contre Piaget?* Berne: P. Lang, 1991.

Viala, Alain. "Questions de programme: Éléments d'histoire et perspectives." In *Propositions pour les enseignements littéraires*, edited by Michel Jarrety, 163–77. Paris: Presses universitaires de France, 2000.

Vigarello, Georges. *Le corps redressé: Histoire d'un pouvoir pédagogique*. Paris: J. P. Delarge, 1978.

Vincent, Guy. *L'école primaire française: Étude sociologique*. Lyon: Presses universitaires de Lyon, 1980.

Wastiaux, François. *"Entre les murs": Théâtre-récit d'après le roman de François Bégaudeau*. Paris: Théâtre Ouvert éditions, 2009.

Weber, Eugen. "Civilizing in Earnest: Schools and Schooling." In *Peasants into Frenchmen: The Modernization of Rural France, 1870–1914*. Stanford CA: Stanford University Press, 1976.

Weisz, George. *The Emergence of Modern Universities in France, 1863–1914*. Princeton NJ: Princeton University Press, 1983.

Wilson, Emma. "*Les glaneurs et la glaneuse*: Salvage and the Art of Forgetting." In *The Art of the Project: Projects and Experiments in Modern French Culture*, edited by Johnnie Gratton and Michael Sheringham, 96–110. New York: Berghahn, 2005.

Zeldin, Theodore. *France, 1848–1945: Intellect, Taste and Anxiety*. 2 vols. Vol. 2. Oxford: Clarendon Press, 1977.

Index